Kona Kai Farms

GUIDE TO THE KONA COAST

A COFFEE LOVER'S GUIDE TO THE
VACATION PLEASURES OF THE KONA COAST
AND THE BIG ISLAND
WITH SPECIAL SECTIONS ON OTHER ISLANDS

BY BOB REGLI
WITH CHRIS & EVELYN COOK

FOR TRAVELERS WHO SEEK BEAUTY AND ADVENTURE IN ALL THINGS

© 1995 by Kona Kai Farms.
All rights reserved.
No Part of this book may be reproduced in any form
without written permission from the publisher.
Printed by Offset Paperback Manufacturers, Inc.
Dallas, Pennsylvania, U.S.A.

ISBN 0-9646128-0-1

Cover Design: Ken Salvo, Salvo Design, Walnut Creek, California
Cover Art: Mary Lovein, Holualoa, Hawaii, "Mr. Coffee."
Book Design: Chris Cook
Special Thanks to the Kona Historical Society
Distributed by Island Heritage Publishing,
Honolulu, Hawaii

Full Cup Press
Post Office Box C
Kealakekua, Hawaii 96750

CONTENTS

Introduction 3

Kona Kai Farms 4

KONA AND BIG ISLAND

Geography 7

Weather 10

How to Get Here 12

Places to Stay 15

Places to Go 33

Kona Coffee Country Tour... 33

Historic Kailua-Kona Tour 40

Ka'u/Volcanoes Tour 43

Waimea/Mauna Kea Observatories Tour 44

Hamakua Coast/Waipio Valley Tour 50

Kohala Coast Tour 53

North Kohala Tour 54

Hilo Tour 56

Around the Island Drive 60

Puna Tour 60

The "New Tourism" 61

Activities 63

Sports 68

Golf 84

Tennis 88
Other Sports 93
Massage, Fitness, Well Being 94
Beaches 96
Dining 103
Entertainment 124
Shopping 126
Arts, Crafts, and Cultural Events 128
Real Estate 134
Agriculture and Horticulture 135
Kona On-Line 146
Big Island History–What You Can See Today ... 147
Hawaiian Language 155
Hawaiian Politics 158
Movies Filmed on the Big Island 160

OAHU AND THE NEIGHBOR ISLANDS

Waikiki and Honolulu 164
Oahu (Beyond Waikiki and Honolulu) 168
Maui, Molokai and Lanai 173
Kauai and Niʻihau 185

KONA & COFFEE

Kona Coffee Cultural Festival 194
Kona Coffee History 200
Kona Kai Farms' Guide to Making Good Coffee ... 210

Kona Kai Farms

INTRODUCTION

The author on the Kona Kai loading dock.

INTRODUCTION

This travelers' guide is a collection of the advice we've been giving to our friends and customers over the past several years. The book started out as a list of restaurants and hotels only a few pages long. Over the years it has gradually become a more complete tour guide. Because of the increasing travel to Kona of people connected to the coffee industry, especially for the Kona Coffee Festival, we needed an organized way of suggesting the best things to do on the island. Most vacationers are only here a short time and can only do so much. Choices have to be made, and advice sought out.

Our guide is written from the perspective of someone particularly interested in the Kona coffee industry. We suggest that you read other guide books to get added perspectives, and we hope you find ours helpful. One major difference: ours has no advertising to influence our recommendations! We are always looking for ways to improve the guide, and if you have any suggestions, please feel free to contact us.

KONA KAI FARMS

Kona Kai Farms was established in 1979 on a 16.5-acre overgrown coffee and papaya farm overlooking Kealakekua Bay in the heart of the Kona coffee district. At that time, Kona coffee was the exclusive property of the two coffee co-operatives and their sole customer, Superior Coffee of Chicago. Acreage in coffee had declined from over 6,000 acres in 1959 to less than 2,000, and the industry was in decline. However, by 1983 several new processing companies had come to Kona, and we had begun buying and processing coffee from neighboring farms to add to the coffee we were harvesting on our original five acres and the eight new acres we had planted.

Kona coffee became available in the specialty market, and new customers began to come for vacations mixed with coffee business. By 1988, Kona Kai Farms had become the largest Kona processing company, but there were at least a dozen other processors, and many farms were producing estate coffee which they sold to roasters or to consumers in Kona.

Our original farm has increased to thirty acres of organically grown coffee, macadamia nuts and papayas. Coffee is processed in a modern facility which still uses the old techniques of wet processing, fermentation, and sun drying. We purchase coffee from about 200 other farms, averaging two to three acres in size, usually family-run, part-time operations. There are three Kona Kai retail stores in Kona and our mainland sales office in Berkeley, California, also operates a world famous market garden in Berkeley's "gourmet ghetto" restaurant district.

Kona Kai Farms

KONA AND THE BIG ISLAND

"Kona Coffee Jeep." Watercolor by Alexis Wilson

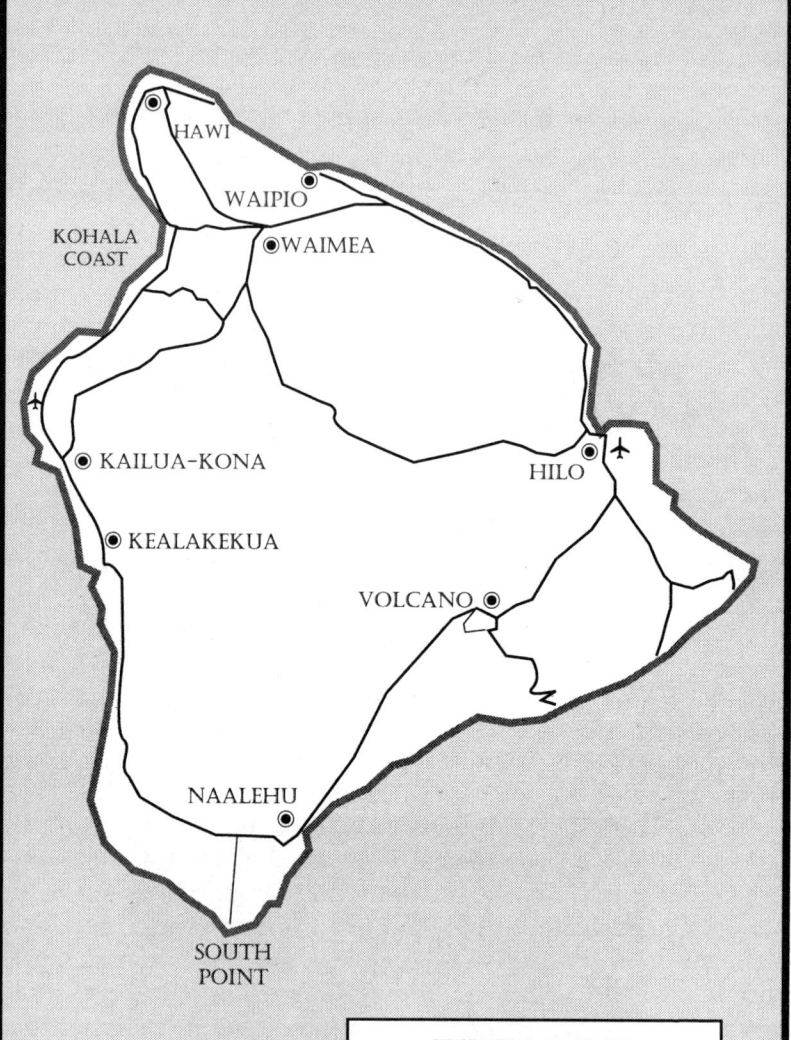

Geography

The Big Island, at over 4,000 square miles, is the largest and newest island in the Hawaiian chain. In fact, it is still growing by hundreds of acres per year as lava flowing from Kilauea volcano continues to add land mass on an almost daily basis. The island, which comprises nearly 63 percent of the state's total land mass and is just about double the size of all the other islands combined, stretches approximately 95 miles from north to south and 80 miles from east to west, and possesses more than 250 miles of coastline. Cape Kumukahi is the easternmost point in the state of Hawaii, and Ka Lae (South Point) is the most southern point in the United States.

There are five distinct volcanic mountains on the island: Hualalai, just east of Kailua-Kona (8,271 feet), Mauna Kea (13,796) and Mauna Loa (13,677) in the center of the island, Kilauea (4,093) in the southern part, and Kohala Mountain (5,260) in the north. Mauna Kea and Mount Kohala are classified as "inactive," and Hualalai is considered "dormant" since its last eruption was in 1801. Mauna Loa last erupted in 1984, and Kilauea's eruption, which began in 1983, was still underway when this book was written in 1995.

Mauna Kea (White Mountain), which has been extinct for over 4,000 years, is so named because its summit is often covered with snow. Sports enthusiasts have been known to ski Mauna Kea in the morning, then make it down to the beach for a late afternoon surf session. Anyone venturing up the mountain should be aware that its high elevation makes altitude sickness a possibility. Local outfitters recommend taking aspirin a half hour before ascending to reduce adverse effects. Those who have experienced it say that altitude sickness is similar to motion sickness, and can occasionally be fatal if combined with too much alcohol or serious health problems.

The skiing isn't all that great because the snow freezes and thaws repeatedly until it's what is called "corn" snow, very slow and mushy. It's more fun is to go bobsledding or boogie boarding down the slopes, or you can ride down on a trash can lid, a flattened cardboard box, or anything that will slide. A four-wheel-drive vehicle (available from many car rental companies) is a necessity for reaching the snow and returning safely.

If measured from its base 18,000 feet beneath the surface of the sea, Mauna Kea is the tallest mountain in the world; at 31,796 feet it is 2,768 feet taller than Mt. Everest!

Mount Hualalai, which forms the dramatic backdrop to Kailua village, was once thought to be extinct, because it hadn't erupted since 1801. Recently, however, volcanologists have discovered that Hualalai could erupt again, at any time, and their findings have led the U.S. Geological Service to list the mountain as one of the potentially most dangerous volcanoes in the United States, since its steep slopes could cause lava to flow with great speed towards heavily populated areas.

Mauna Loa, or Long Mountain, is only 120 feet shy of being as tall as Mauna Kea, and it too sometimes wears a dusting of snow. It is aptly named, as it stretches in one long, uninterrupted slope for almost 60 miles, making it one of the island's most distinctive landmarks.

Kilauea, which means "The Spewing," is the most active volcano in the world. For the past 100 years, it has erupted an average of once every eleven months. As of this writing, the current eruption (which began in 1983) was still underway, and visitors were able to get within picture-taking distance of where glowing red magma was oozing into the sea, hissing and spitting, sending up great plumes of steam. The U.S. Park Service monitors the flows and sets up roadblocks to prevent the public from going too close to the lava, as it can be dangerous. Lava that has recently cooled can look perfectly firm, yet give way unexpectedly beneath your feet. Some people disregard the Park Service's warnings for a closer look, and most of them don't run into any trouble, but some have actually lost their lives or were seriously injured when unstable lava collapsed beneath them.

The drive to the spot where you can see the lava flowing into the ocean is a fifty-mile round trip from the Hawaii Volcanoes National Park visitor's center, and there is nothing when you get there but endless fields of barren lava, a couple of porta-potties, and miles of beautiful but inaccessible black sand beaches.

It's a good idea to bring a flashlight and rubber soled shoes, something to eat and drink, and since it can get chilly in the evening, you might want to bring along a sweater or sweatshirt. A good plan is to walk in right after sunset. The lava shows up best at night, so plan on a long day. Rainfall can be heavy at times, and there are days when it will prevent you from seeing anything. For the most up-to-date eruption info, call the National Park Service's recorded message at 967-7977, or if you want to talk to a live person, you can call the park headquarters at 967-7311.

The Big Island has three main population centers: Kailua-Kona (population 25,000) in West Hawaii, Hilo (population 50,000) in East Hawaii, and Waimea (population 5,000) half way in between. The island's total population is estimated at 120,000. The northwest end of the island is called the Kohala district, and the southern districts are called Ka'u and Puna.

There is almost every type of geography and climate on the Big Island, from lush tropical rain forests around Hilo, to the arid Ka'u desert in the south, and from the rolling green pastures of Waimea and Kohala to the frigid summit of Mauna Kea. It is astonishing how quickly you can drive from one micro-climate to another vastly different one. For example, it can be a sizzling hot sunny day amidst the treeless lava fields outside Kailua, while twenty minutes by car up Mount Hualalai it can be fifteen degrees cooler and pouring rain in a jungle of treeferns and wild orchids.

One of the things that most impresses visitors is the diversity of the terrain and vegetation that can be seen during a five-hour drive around the island. Consider taking the Saddle Road between Hilo and Waimea instead of the main highway – it's not as good a road and there are lots of curves, but it's much less traveled and very picturesque.

Kona coffee blossoms.

WEATHER

Kona's weather is one of the best things about the region. There is no "bad" time to come, as the sun shines most of the time and temperatures remain fairly constant, but there are some slight seasonal differences, mainly between rainy season and dry season.

During rainy season (generally March through October) there are afternoon showers at higher elevations almost every day. Mornings are usually sunny, and it rarely rains at the beach or in Kailua town. Kailua is often referred to as "Kailua-Kona" to differentiate it from Kailua, Oahu, just as the official name of the Waimea post office is "Kamuela" to avoid confusion with Waimea, Oahu. During dry season (November through February) the afternoon showers will be much less frequent, although there will be two or three storms during the winter months when it may rain for three or four days without stopping.

Kona gets an average of 25 inches of rain per year, which is considerably less than what the east side gets – an average of 136 inches annually. Mauka coffee growing areas average about 65 inches.

It is the combination of morning sun with afternoon cloud cover and rainfall that makes Kona an ideal place for growing coffee. Between an elevation of 800 to 2,000 feet along a 20-mile "coffee belt," the rich, well drained volcanic soil combines with the mild breezes and gentle rains to create greenhouse-like growing conditions.

Kona's summer temperatures are generally about five degrees warmer during the day than in winter, and about ten degrees at night. The average summer highs in Kailua are in the 75 to 85 degree range. Nights are balmy in town or on the beach, but often chilly at elevations over 1,000 feet, with a strong wind that blows off the mountain. The annual average high is 82.6 degrees, while the average low is 66.7.

The worst aspect of Kona's weather is the "vog," a smog-like haze caused by ten years of volcanic activity about 100 miles south of Kailua. It has given the coast an almost permanent haze, which disappears only after it rains, and has given rise to studies which seek to determine any adverse effects on humans and/or plants. Some individuals can be sensitive to the vog, and may experience symptoms similar to those of hay fever.

Expect frequent strong winds on the Kohala coast and in Waimea, especially in the afternoon. Hilo, located on the east side, is one of the rainiest cities in the U.S., averaging more than ten inches of rainfall each month. The weather on that side of the island is highly unpredictable.

There are no snakes in paradise but there are mosquitoes, especially in the rainy areas where coffee is grown. If you are going to visit higher elevations, it's a good idea to bring mosquito repellent, a long-sleeved shirt, and long pants.

Sunset is the most special time of the day in Kona. Maybe you will be lucky enough to see the "green flash" at the exact moment the sun disappears. Something else to know about the Kona sun: it burns with a passion, so be prepared with sunscreen, especially between 10 a.m. and 2 p.m.

How To Get Here

Air Line Carriers: United used to be the only airline with direct flights to Kona, which we strongly recommend. Right now they have one flight per day from both San Francisco and Los Angeles, plus good connections from Chicago and New York. Otherwise, you must fly into Honolulu and spend an hour or two in the Honolulu airport waiting for an inter-island flight to Kona. Now there are direct flights on Hawaiian Air from Portland and Vancouver; check with your travel agent. Fiesta West, a Canadian tour packager, also offers direct flights from Vancouver, Calgary and Edmonton (800-99FIESTA). There are three main inter-island carriers: Aloha, Hawaiian and Mahalo Air (United also has a few inter-island flights). At this time, the new Mahalo Air (800/277-8333) offers the best rates but has fewer flights than Aloha and Hawaiian. Aloha consistently rate high in passenger satisfaction surveys. The new inter-island terminal in Honolulu is a ten-minute walk from the main airport, but it takes forever to get there on the tram from the United terminal.

If you do get stuck at the airport, there are a number of fast food stands and an interesting bar in the inter-island terminal. The main terminal features restaurants, an aviation museum, and a quiet Japanese garden (downstairs) if you are on a long stopover. Sometimes your flight may arrive late, after the last flight to Kona for the day has departed. An alternative to staying in Waikiki is a mini-hotel in the main terminal and the nearby Shower Tree mini-hotel, which will pick you up in a van. The rooms are tiny, but relatively inexpensive, clean, and they will awaken you in plenty of time for late-night or early-morning flights. If you have a lot of time and want to explore Oahu while waiting for a plane, luggage lockers are available on the lower level of the main terminal parking building for $1 per day for a suitcase-size locker.

Frequently when you change planes your bags do not make it to Kona with you. Don't worry, they always seem to come on the next flight, and the airlines will deliver them to your door, usually the same day. The Keahole Airport at Kona is expanding and crowded when the United flights arrive. Still, it is much more friendly and not as tense as a big city airports. Hawaiian is at the south end of the airport and Aloha and United are together at the north end. Keahole Airport is the last major airport in Hawaii where passengers deplane to the tarmac rather than through jetways; it's a nice touch that adds to the Neighbor Island feel. It's overbuilt for the traffic (for now, at least), but still small, and easy to find your way around.

The large structure in the center of the airport is the Ellison Onizuka Memorial, which houses a display of the life of Kona's astronaut who grew up on a coffee farm and died in the Challenger Space Shuttle explosion.

Tour Packages and Travel Agents: There are all kinds of deals on air fare, rooms, and car rentals. Prices for Hawaii vacations have come down a bit since the '80s due to stiff competition from Mexico, the Caribbean, and other tropical spots closer to the mainland U.S. Checking the Sunday travel sections for prices before you see a travel agent will give you a good handle on package pricing. For those using the InterNet and on-line services like Prodigy or CompuServe, look for Hawaii specials to be more visible in the travel sections in the near future as the major resorts and visitor bureaus are catching on to this kind of advertising.

Kathleen Powers at Kona Coast Travel is our travel agent (329-2441 or 800/835-6581).

The Islands of Aloha, a glossy advertising-supported magazine produced by the Hawaii Visitors Bureau is a good general reference for planning a Hawaii vacation. It has toll-free 800 numbers for all major resorts and hotels, and a current calendar of events, plus a number of feature stories on Hawaii's history and other topics of interest. You can get a copy by writing or calling a Hawaii Visitors Bureau office. In New York call (212/947-0717) or write to HVB, Empire State Building Suite 808, 350 Fifth Avenue, New York, NY 10118; in San Francisco call (415/392-8173) or write to HVB, 50 California Street, Suite 450, San Francisco, CA 94111.

Hawaii has its high and low seasons, and, like any resort area, prices for rooms fluctuate. From December 21 through Easter is considered the busy season in Hawaii, with summertime, from when school lets out to Labor Day, the next busiest time. From about April 15 to June 15, and between Labor Day and Christmas, there are a lot less people and more deals available. Our suggestion is to try and find the right place to stay, then see if they have a rental car package.

If you are staying with family or friends but want to rent a car, do some shopping before you travel; check with your airline, or the inter-island airline you are flying on, as they sometimes have low-priced specials you can book with your ticket. We think it's worth considering a convertible for your stay; they normally go for $10-$20 per day more than standard cars. A Big Island favorite is a four wheel drive Jeep or Suzuki. Driving a Jeep allows you to go off-road to Waipio Valley, the Mauna Kea observatories, or down the back roads to isolated beaches. At the airport, we use Budget (935-7293) or Alamo (329-8896).

There are often special tour packages offered by coffee industry groups, such as the Specialty Coffee Association of America, during Coffee Festival week – we'll be glad to send you the information.

Ground transportation: Public transportation is minimal in Kona, with only one regularly scheduled bus, the Hele On, making the circle-island route. There is no public transportation from the airport, although many of the hotels have shuttle vans. The Ali'i Shuttle goes between the Kona Surf Resort and the King Kamehameha Hotel until early evening. Other than that, taxicabs are about $15 between the airport and Kailua town, and *SpeediShuttle* (329-5433) provides door-to-door airport service. Hitchhiking is always a hit or miss proposition.

Places to Stay

Hotels – Expensive ($115 to $250 and up): Developers are building luxury hotels and "destination resorts" on the Kohala coast at an astounding rate. The one big disadvantage of staying in Kohala is that you are at least one hour's drive from coffee country, and are isolated from the people who live on the island. Kohala does have the best beaches, though, and if you want to maximize your beach time you should think about staying there. Our recommendations for luxury hotels are as follows. (Rates shown are for double occupancy and will vary somewhat, depending upon season, and whether room is garden or ocean view. Kamaaina rates are generally available to anyone possessing a valid Hawaii driver's license.)

Mauna Lani Bay Hotel and Bungalows (808/885-6622, 800/367-2323) ($275-$750). Built in 1984 by the Japanese owner of the Seibu Railway Group, it features great interior design, refined atmosphere, and exceptional hotel restaurants. If money is not a consideration, you'd be hard pressed to find a reason to stay elsewhere. The $3,000 to $3,500 per night bungalows come with butler, limo, and private pool, and are a favorite of sports celebrities and others in the entertainment industry. The only drawback is the lack of a great beach – theirs is man-made, on a bay. Three restaurants, The Bay Terrace, the Canoe House, and The Gallery on the golf course offer a variety of cuisines including Continental, Pacific Rim, and Hawaii Regional, in the $35-$50 price range. The Beach Club is on a private beach with its own grille. The Mauna Lani has hosted some of the premier events in Kona, such as the Davis Cup matches against Argentina, the Senior Skins golf tournament, and the Cuisines of the Sun food extravaganza. The Mauna Lani Bay is jointly owned by Mauna Lani Resorts, Daiichi Seimei, and the Tokyu Corporation.

Ritz-Carlton, Mauna Lani (808/885-2000, 800/241-3333) ($225-$395, Suites: $500-$2,250). The Ritz opened in January 1991 and has received very favorable reviews from most people we know who have stayed there, including us. It is an excellent place for a convention, featuring the best movie/video theater in Hawaii among its exceptional facilities. It is less "Hawaiian"

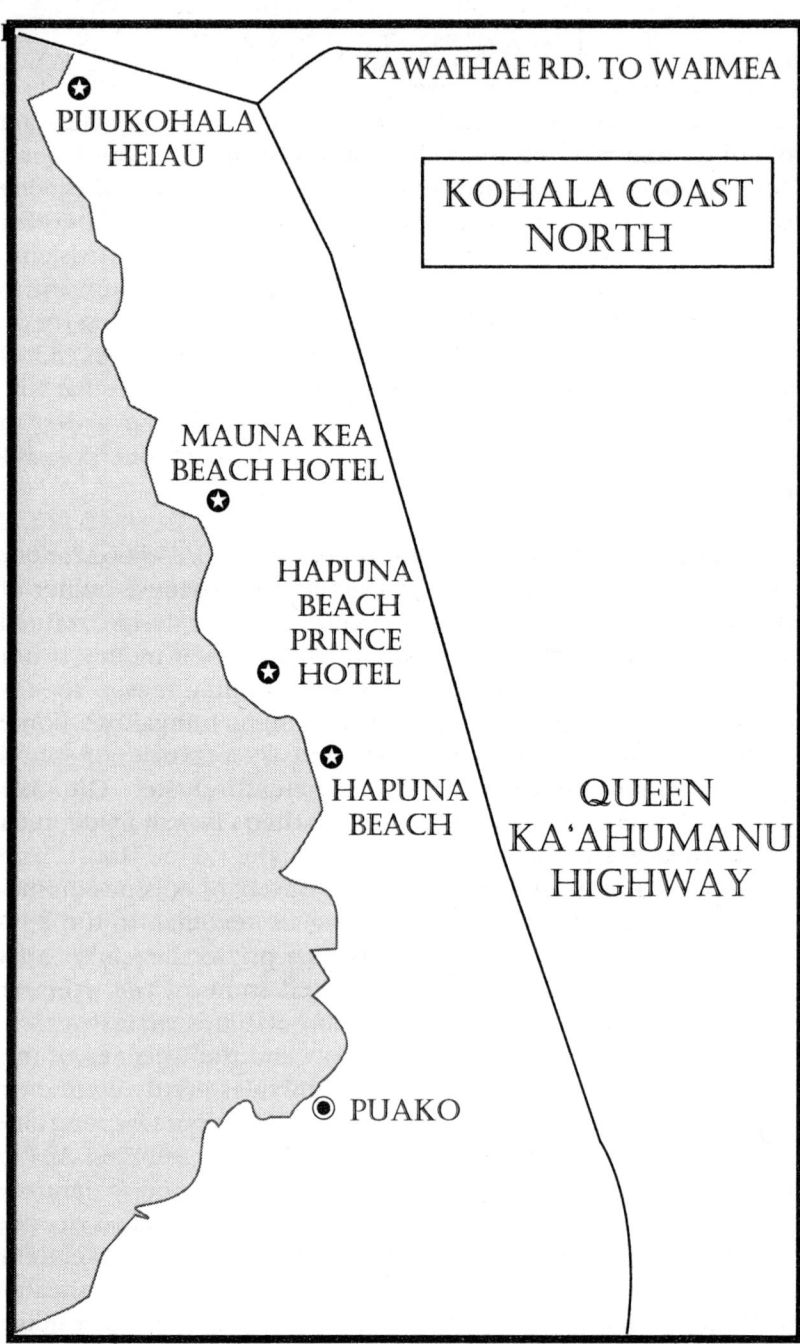

than the other hotels because it recreates the Ritz-Carlton look of French-Provincial elegance, but somehow it seems to fit. The hotel's three restaurants periodically change their menus and feature a variety of dining fare from Regional Hawaiian to grilled steaks and fresh fish. Try to see about an upgrade to the Club on the sixth floor, where you have access to a lounge with complimentary food and drink, day and night. The hotel is owned by a partnership of Ritz-Carlton, Shimizu, and Mitsui.

Kona Village Resort (808/325-5555, 800/367-5290) ($390-$665). For a change of pace, Kona Village is a secluded collection of luxurious thatched huts five miles north of the airport. The resort is very private, with no phones in the rooms, and each guest has an individual *hale* or Hawaiian house. It is very important to get a hale with a good location. These features make the Kona Village a favorite of visitors who want peace and privacy. Both the Kona Village and the Mauna Kea (see below) are more than twenty years old and lack some of the innovations of the newer hotels, however, if you want the maximum "Hawaiiana" experience, you will not be disappointed here. The Kona Village has two restaurants, both serving Pacific Rim specialties. The main dining room provides a set menu at $54 per person, while the Hale Samoa offers fine dining from $54 to $70. Room rates include food. The Kona Village is owned by a Japanese consortium.

Mauna Kea Beach Hotel (808/882-7222, 800/882-6060). David Rockefeller bought the best beach on the island for his hotel, now owned by Japanese interests, as are almost all of the luxury hotels in Hawaii. The Mauna Kea features an exceptional Asian art collection and the best golf course in Hawaii (but difficult). Many visitors have been coming here each year for twenty years or more. The hotel closed in July 1994 for restoration work, and is unlikely to be ready by its scheduled reopening date of December 1995. Long-time guests of the Mauna Kea are being booked at it's sister hotel, the new *Hapuna Beach Prince*, located next door, which opened in the summer of 1994. The Asian art exhibit will be displayed at the Prince during the Mauna Kea's renovation.

Hapuna Beach Prince Hotel (808/882-7222, 800/882-6060)

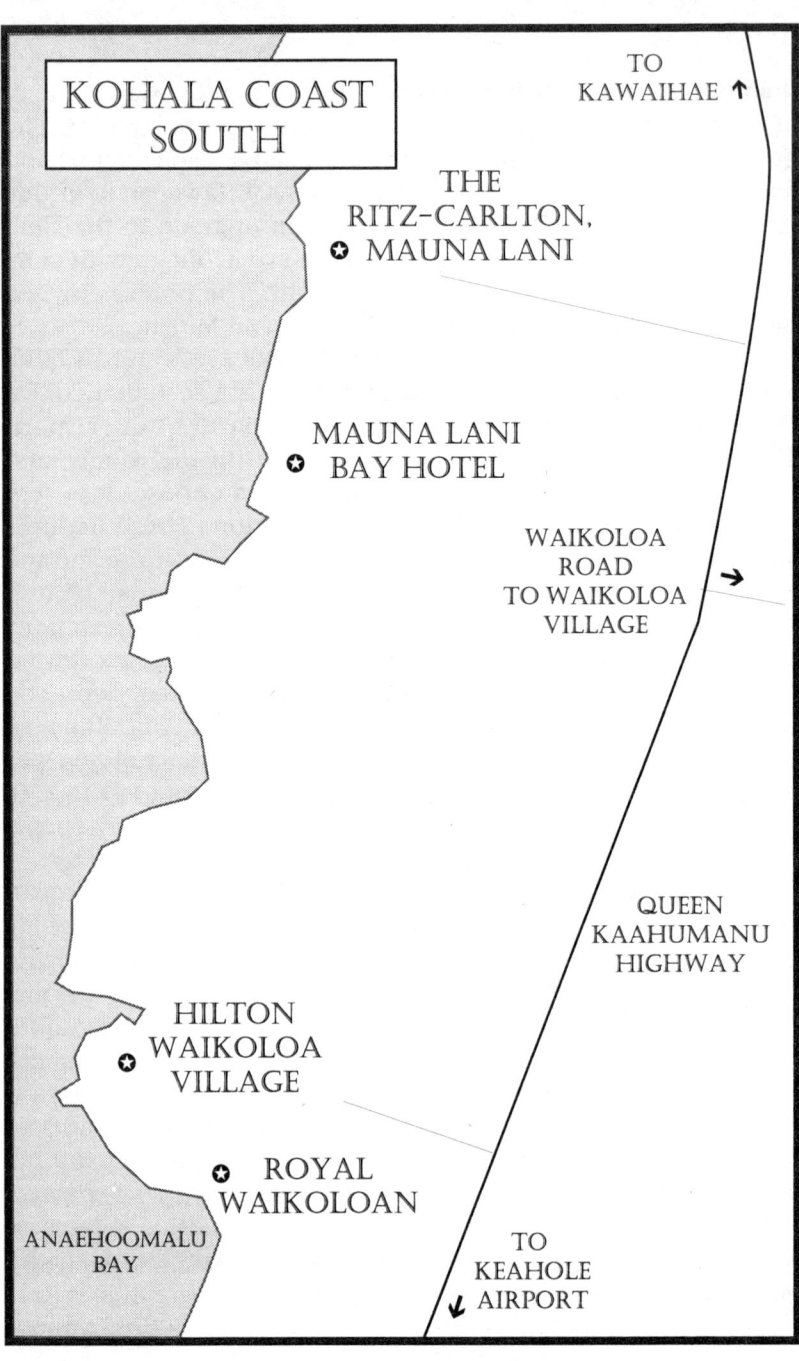

($300-$425, Suites: $800-$5,000). The Big Island's newest luxury hotel, which opened in August 1994, is located on one of the island's two nicest white sand beaches, and boasts that all its rooms have ocean views. Five restaurants offer everything from burgers and fresh seafood, to formal Japanese dining and Mediterranean fare. The steak, veal, lobster, local fish, salads, and everything else at the Coast Grille is excellent, done in Asian/French style; entrees are $20 to $38. The $5,000 per night Hapuna Suite is a separate mini-mansion, complete with its own private swimming pool and butler.

The Hapuna Beach Prince has stirred controversy from its inception, with angry residents protesting that it ruins one of the best beaches on an island that simply doesn't have many sandy spots along its rugged, lava-studded coastline. Tempers have cooled somewhat, however, and the hope is that with a little aloha, Hapuna will prove to be big enough for everybody.

Along with the Mauna Kea Beach Hotel, the Hapuna Beach Prince is owned by Seibu Railway's Yoshiaki Tsutsumi, said to be the richest man in Japan. The Japanese ownership may help explain the austere, minimalist decor.

Hilton Waikoloa Village, formerly the Hyatt Regency Waikoloa (808/885-1234, 800/228-9000) ($250-$350, Suites: $450-$3,000). This ostentatious extravaganza was built by a group led by now-departed Hawaii developer Chris Hemmetter in 1990 for a reported $360 million, and was sold in 1993 to Hilton and a group of Mainland investors for $60 million. It was the first undeniable admission by Japanese developers that they grossly overspent on one of their projects, and there will likely be similar sales in the future. Try to stay in the Lagoon Tower section of the hotel near the pools and retail shops. It's a long way from the Ocean and Palace Towers to the main pool, spa and shops. The Hilton Waikoloa is a unique and fanciful experience. We suggest checking it out, and recommend staying there if you have young children. Waterfalls, water slides, a ¾ size rapid-transit train, 30-foot teak launches that glide on tracks down canals *a la* Disneyland, and "Camp Hilton" day care will keep even the most energetic youngsters entertained. The Hilton's most famous attraction is the controversial Dolphin

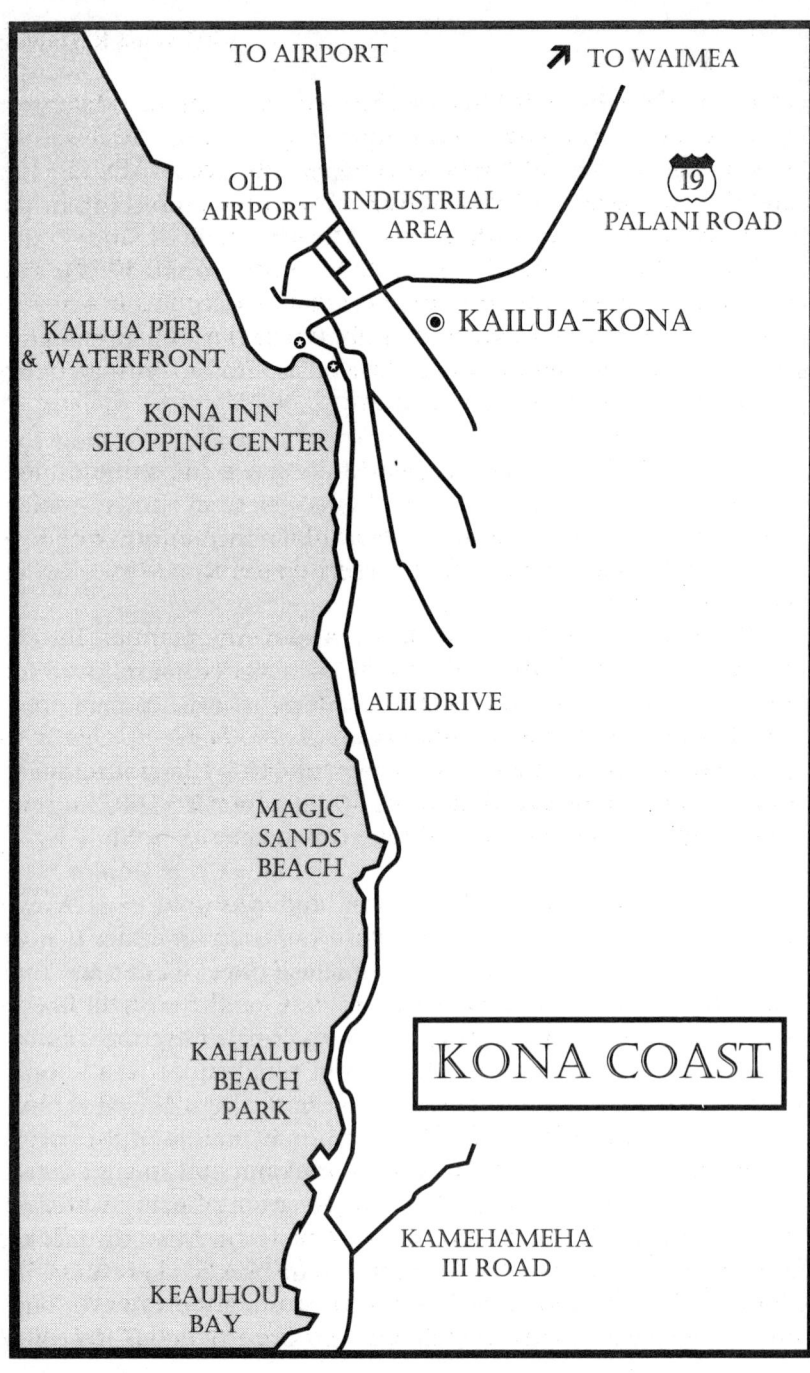

Quest (swim with dolphins for $50) which is opposed by those who believe that contact with humans may make the dolphins sick. Our criticisms of the hotel center on its size and gaudiness, and the comparison of its restaurants with the competition.

Royal Waikoloan (adjacent to the Hilton Waikoloa) (808/885-6789, 800/462-6262) ($115-$200, Suites: $350-$750). The oldest, least fancy, and least expensive of the Kohala hotels features a great beach, next to the public beach at Anaeho'omalu, the windsurfing center of the Kohala coast. The Royal Waikoloan is directly across from the Kings Shops at Waikoloa, an array of upscale retail stores.

Whichever Kohala hotel you choose, you are only minutes away from the other ones, and they all have courtesy vans to take you anywhere. The Royal Waikoloan is jointly owned by Transcontinental Development Company, Aetna, and the Outrigger Hotels.

There are several other mega-developments planned for the Kohala Coast, from the stalled Four Seasons Hotel next to the Kona Village, to Nansay's planned developments near Pinetrees beach and Chalon's in Mahukona up north. These are likely to proceed slowly, if at all, as they are funded by Japanese developers whose plans can change abruptly, depending on the state of the Japanese economy, and are now mostly on hold.

Hotels – Mid-Priced ($75 to $195, depending on season and whether room is single or double occupancy, and garden or ocean view. Kamaaina rates are available): There are four large hotels in or near Kailua-Kona. Before the Kohala hotels were built they were considered fancy, but all are now aging. Location is the major difference among them. *King Kamehameha's Kona Beach Hotel* (808/329-2911, 800/367-2111) ($105-$195, Suites: $300-$500) is in Kailua, right across from the pier, at the site of King Kamehameha's former estate and seat of power, which is now the location of many water activities, including the start of the Ironman Triathlon. The *Royal Kona Resort*, formerly the Kona Hilton (808/329-3111, 800/774-5662) ($75-$95, Suites: $210-$500) is a ten-minute walk south of the pier on Ali'i Drive, while the *Keauhou Beach Hotel* (808/

322-3441, 800/367-6025) ($96-$165, Suites: $235-$405) is four miles south on Ali'i Drive, and the *Kona Surf Resort* (808/322-3411, 800/367-8100 ($99-$175, Suites: $375-$650) is five miles south, at the end of Ali'i on Keauhou Bay.

Visitors who want to be able to walk to Kailua town might consider either the Royal Kona Resort or King Kamehameha. We prefer the Kona Surf, even though it is badly in need of renovation, because of its spectacular location, great saltwater swimming pool, and proximity to the *Kona Country Club* golf course and *Holua Tennis Club*. It's also the closest to coffee country, about a 15-minute drive.

The Keauhou Beach Hotel and the adjacent but closed Kona Lagoon Hotel are owned by the Azabu group, the biggest loser in the Japanese bidding war to buy Hawaiian property. The group now has assets of $3 billion, and debts of $6 billion, according to the Wall Street Journal, and its properties in Hawaii are not likely to be upgraded soon.

If you are interested in Hawaii's volcanoes, we recommend a stay at the *Volcano House* (808/967-7321) in Volcanoes National Park, Ka'u. The hotel is an old lodge with a big fireplace, a commanding view of the crater, and newly renovated rooms. This was a great deal at $50 per room, but they raised the rates ($79 for a garden view, $131 for a crater view) after the renovations. For the budget-minded, there are some basic A-frame cabins near Volcano House that go for around $35 per night and sleep four. As they are very popular, reservations need to be made well in advance through Volcano House. Linens are provided. There are no cooking facilities, other than a barbecue grill. Hot showers are located in a separate building.

Hotels – Bargain-Priced ($60 and less): There are two great old hotels which are a bit on the primitive side but capture the spirit of historic Kona better than any of the resorts, and they are right in the middle of the coffee fields. The *Kona Hotel* (808/324-1155) ($15 single, $23 double, shared baths only) in Holualoa (three miles uphill from Kailua) and the *Manago Hotel* (808/323-2642) ($35 single, $41 double) in Captain Cook, offer clean rooms (with no phone or TV) and interesting local surroundings. The view of Kailua from the back porch of the Kona Hotel is awesome. In Kailua, we suggest the *Kona Tiki* (808/329-1425) on Ali'i Drive for a budget oceanside hotel with kitchen facilities (around $60 per night).

If you're willing to spend a little time looking, you can sometimes find a bargain on a vacation rental by scanning the classifieds in *West Hawaii Today*, the local newspaper, or contact Joy Foster at *MJ Properties* (329-4813). She handles a nicely maintained studio in downtown Kona that rents for $46 per night, but you have to book a minimum of one week.

Tom Araki's *Waipio Hotel*, at $15 per night, is a former Peace Corps training camp in beautiful Waipio Valley (not far from Waimea) that offers clean, basic accommodations in a tranquil surrounding. Tom, who is in his seventies, loves to "talk story." Kerosene lamps provide lighting, and you need to bring your own food to prepare in the communal kitchen. For reservations, write Tom Araki, 25 Malama Pl., Hilo, Hi. 96720, or call (808/775-0368).

For a contemplative respite, you might consider a stay at the *Wood Valley Temple* (808/928-8539), a Buddhist retreat four miles outside the sugar cane town of Pahala, in Ka'u. Private rooms and dorm beds are available from $15 to $35 per person. Buddhist services are performed in Tibetan every morning on the 25-acre grounds. You need to make advance reservations, and a minimum stay of two nights is required.

As for Hilo hotels, we are still waiting for one we can enthusiastically recommend. Meanwhile, the *Hilo Hawaiian* (808/935-9361) on Banyan Drive is the best of a mediocre selection, and the *Hawaii Naniloa* (808/969-3333), also on Banyan Drive, while nothing special, offers great views of Hilo Bay, comfortable rooms, an adequately equipped fitness facility, and a reasonably priced Chinese restaurant.

Condos: There are a lot of condominiums on Ali'i Drive, and their desirability depends greatly on the exact location of your room. We especially like *Kona By the Sea* (808/329-0200) and the *Royal Sea Cliff Resort* (808/329-8021), both one mile south of Kailua, for their quality and good views. All the Kohala hotels have expensive condos in the vicinity, such as *The Shores* (808/885-5001) at Waikoloa. All three of these condos are managed by the Aston group (800/342-1551), which always has a good deal on rental cars.

If you're willing to sit through a time share sales pitch, the *Kona Coast Resort* in Keauhou is a high quality project and often has good deals (800/367-8047). Tennis players might want to call Marc Georgian at the *Holua Sports Shop* (808/322-0091) about the condos in the surrounding *Mauna Loa Village* (next to the Kona Surf Resort). Every group of buildings has its own pool complex, and you will be within walking distance to tennis, golf, the Kona Surf Resort, and water activities at Keauhou Bay.

Vacation Rentals: There are some very nice houses on the water which are available by the day, week, or month, as vacation rentals. Check the "Vacation Rentals" listings in West Hawaii Today. You can see many of them just driving down Ali'i Drive, or call C.J. Kimberly Realtors (808/329-4321). They also have a couple of oceanfront houses that are 35 minutes from Kailua and relatively secluded on spectacular Kealakekua Bay.

One vacation rental house that may be of special interest to those in the coffee industry is the three bedroom farm house at Kona Kai Farms. Although not the most secluded place in Kona, the house offers reasonable privacy combined with intimate access to all aspects of the Kona coffee business. You can call (800/826-5713) for more information.

Bed & Breakfasts: There are dozens of "Bed and Breakfast" accommodations on the Big Island, and each one is unique. If you've never stayed in a "B&B" you might want to try one, just for the experience, which is entirely different from what you find in a hotel.

Most B&Bs are private homes that are operated by the home owners, who generally live on site and are almost always gracious and accommodating. Their local knowledge and personal touch are invaluable, and oftentimes you will be the only guest. Most of the Big Island's B&Bs maintain a very high standard of cleanliness, and try to offer unique features. Rates start at around $35 for singles and $45 for couples.

In the Kailua-Kona area, one of the nicest is the *The Holualoa Inn* (808/324-1121, $125-$165). Located in coffee country on a 40-acre private estate owned by the kamaaina Twigg-Smith family adjacent to the artist's village of Holualoa, this B&B is about as deluxe as they come. Guests are suitably pampered by a friendly, efficient staff. The custom-built, elegant-yet-relaxed, modern red cedar home is nestled on a very quiet and peaceful mountainside a thousand feet above Kailua, and is surrounded by pastures, tropical fruit trees, and a coffee farm that produces the 100 percent pure Kona coffee served to guests. There are four bedrooms with private baths and several large common rooms. The only drawback (for parents) is that, to ensure a serene atmosphere, children are not especially welcome.

For individuals desiring to get away from civilization while remaining comfortable, the Holualoa Inn offers the *Owl Lodge*, ($150 per night, three night minimum) a secluded mountain retreat on a 300-acre ranch only fifteen minutes from the Inn. The lodge has all the comforts of home, except electricity, and sleeps four.

Of all the B&Bs we've seen in the Kailua-Kona area, our favorite is *Hale Malia* (808/326-1641) ($95 and $115). Located right on the ocean, a couple of miles from downtown Kona on Ali'i Drive, this private home is gorgeous, and the view is sensational. The only sounds you hear are the waves breaking on the lava rocks a stone's throw from your room, and the breeze in the coconut palms.

Because it is so nice and there are only two bedrooms, Hale Malia is generally completely booked up. Reservations need to be made well in advance.

Both bedrooms have private baths and their own TV's. The house, built ten years ago, is so well-maintained it looks brand new. It is bright and airy, with large rooms, and a 23-foot-high cathedral ceiling in the living room. There are no cooking facilities for guests, and people with children are gently persuaded to stay elsewhere.

Another beautiful B&B on Ali'i Drive is ***Kailua Plantation***

House (808/329-3727) ($125-$190), a modern two-story inn built in the old plantation style. It is right on the water and is very spacious and nicely designed. It was never a private home, but was built especially as a B&B.

It is excellently maintained and is as elegant as anyone might wish. There are five large bedrooms, sumptously furnished, all with private baths, three oceanfront with terrific views, and two in the rear, without views. The only drawback we noticed was that this B&B is not set back far enough from the street, so that guests staying in the two back rooms must keep their windows closed and airconditioning on in order to escape the loud road noise from busy Ali'i Drive. If you have children, be sure they're over 12 before trying to make reservations here.

Merryman's Bed & Breakfast (800/545-4390, 808/323-2276) ($75-$95) is located 12 miles south of Kailua-Kona, in the Kealakekua-Captain Cook area, just a few minutes away from Kealakekua Bay. The nicest thing about Merryman's, in addition to owners Penny and Don Merryman, is the tasteful country inn decor that gives the place a very cheery feel. Everything is pretty, bright, and clean, from the dust-free antique knick-knacks, to the tiled bathrooms. Penny is a gourmet cook who serves a full breakfast with a different "chef's special" every day, accompanied by fresh fruit, and pure Kona coffee.

The house is an attractive one, spacious and bright, made cozy and warm by lots of exposed cedar and oak. There's a covered lanai in the front that is so nicely done up in white wicker and floral fabric you feel almost compelled to curl up there with a cold drink and a good book. There are four guest rooms, two of which have ocean views. They all come with their own TV. Only well-behaved children are welcome.

Hale Maluhia Bed & Breakfast (800/559-6627, 808/329-5773) ($55-$125) located near the village of Holualoa, three miles from Kailua, is one of the few B&Bs that is truly kid-friendly. Owners Ken and Ann Smith have eight grown children, 22 grandchildren, and (at last count) two great-grandchildren. Their B&B consists of a cottage and two separate houses (offering lots of privacy) in addition to their own home.

A full breakfast is served, including pure Kona coffee, freshly baked breads and cinnamon rolls, fresh local fruit, ham (for the meat eaters, only), and fresh yard eggs from the Smiths' free-roaming chickens. In addition, guests may prepare their own meals in either of two kitchens, something many B&Bs do not allow. Hale Maluhia can accommodate groups of up to 20 persons. Ask about discounts and group rates.

Da Third House Bed and Breakfast (808/328-8410) ($60) is a very private studio apartment completely separate from the home of owners Robert and Carol DeFazio on a hillside overlooking the ocean and the City of Refuge in Honaunau, 18 miles from Kailua-Kona. It is clean and well-maintained with a wonderful view and lots of peace and quiet. Carol, who is a stained-glass artist, prepares a continental breakfast the night before and delivers it to her guests, so that they can sleep as late as they like the next morning.

Art and Ann Stockel, two of the original members of the local Sierra Club, have a reputation for lavishing so much hospitality upon guests at their *Three Bears' Bed & Breakfast* that most feel throughly spoiled.

The Stockels, who both speak German, serve a hearty European-style breakfast that always includes fresh island fruit, much of which they grow themselves in the yard of their hillside cedar home, 1600 feet above Kailua town. Their macadamia nut farm provides all the nuts you can eat.

Two bedrooms are available, both with private baths and TV, and guests who stay longer than two days are allowed to use the main kitchen. (800/765-0480, 808/325-7563, $65 and $75, private entrances, kitchenettes).

The Stockels also operate a reservation service that specializes in bed and breakfast accommodations on all the main Hawaiian islands.

The moment you walk in the door of the *Dragonfly Ranch Bed and Breakfast*, free-spirited hosts Barbara and David Link make you feel like you're part of their extended family which includes assorted cats and four tiny Pomeranians which look more like toys than dogs.

The Links describe their big, whimsical, rambling wooden home tucked into a hillside as "Swiss Family Robinson meets

Bali." It is quite comfortable and set in a lush jungle above the "Place of Refuge" National Park in Honaunau, about a half-hour drive from Kailua-Kona. It is unlike any other B&B we have visited.

The Dragonfly is very laid back, and a little magical. (800/487-2159, 808/328-9570, 808/328-2159) ($70 to $160, bedroom in main house, as well as private suites. Outdoor showers.)

In complete contrast to the Dragonfly is *Lion's Gate Bed and Breakfast*, also in Honaunau, near the City (or Place) of Refuge. Lion's Gate is owned and operated by big, friendly ex-Marine Bill Shriner, who along with his wife Diane maintains their large new home to a high degree of spit and polish perfection.

Three attractively furnished, very clean bedrooms are available ($65 for one night, $60 for two or more nights, per room. Ask about extended-stay and family rates.)

If you'd like to stay in an old coffee farm house, *Reggie's Tropical Hideway B&B* in Kealakekua might be just what you're looking for. Built in the forties and well-maintained, Reggie's even has the rolling roof that traditional coffee farmers use to cover up coffee beans drying in the sun whenever rain threatens.

Reggie's is more cozy than posh, with just one bedroom for rent. The room comes with its own large screened sleeping porch surrounded by tropical vegetation, and a private bath.

Reggie is a young, easy-going grandmother who caters to kids. She lets guests use her kitchen. The room goes for $45 without breakfast, and $55 with (808/322-8888).

Because Hawaii Volcanoes National Park is so isolated, many bed and breakfast inns have sprung up in the area, most of which are very nice.

Some of our favorites are *Carson's Volcano Cottages*, *My Island Bed and Breakfast*, *Hale Ohia Cottages*, *Chalet Kilauea*, and *Lokahi Lodge*.

The most secluded is Carson's Volcano Cottages (1/800-LAVA, 808/967-7683, $70-$125), surrounded by rainforest and very private, with a hot tub, and wood burning stoves for cold nights.

My Island Bed and Breakfast (808/967-7110, $35-$45 for singles, $55-$70 for couples, complete houses start at $90), an

1886 missionary house located on a five-acre estate, offers rooms in either the main house or garden apartments. Families are welcome.

Hale Ohia Cottages (808/967-7986, $75-$95) are private, with bonsai-style gardens and moss-covered grounds. The suites and cottages are comfortable and spacious. This is one of the nicest places to stay.

Chalet Kilauea (800/937-7786, 808/967-7786, $85-$225) has theme rooms, a tree-house suite, jacuzzi, fireplace, library, garden, candlelit gourmet breakfasts and afternoon tea.

Waimea (Kamuela) is said to have some of the best bed and breakfasts on the Big Island.

People we trust tell us that the booking agents *Hawaii's Best Bed and Breakfast* (800/262-9912, 808/885-0550) and *Three Bears' All Islands Reservation Service* (800/765-0480, 808/325-7563) are good resources for helping choose the B&B that best suits your taste and pocketbook. Both have very high standards and never book anyone into a B&B they haven't thoroughly inspected.

In Hilo, *The Wild Ginger Inn* (808/935-5556, 800/882-1887, $39-$59) is a quaint, 30-room bed and breakfast located at the north end of town, a couple of blocks walk from the historic downtown area. At $39 per night, including a serve-yourself breakfast, it's not a bad deal, if you can handle the street noise and no TV.

One of the nicer B&Bs in Hilo is the *Hale Kai* (808/935-6330). Located downtown on the edge of a cliff with a great view of Hilo Bay, Hale Kai's owners Paul and Yvonne consider their operation to be a "four-star" bed and breakfast. Everything is top notch and their home is filled with beautiful things. The bedrooms go for $85 a night each, and the cottage for $105. There is a three-night minimum.

Treehouses: No trip to the Big Island is complete without a visit to magical Waipio Valley. A very special place to stay, far beyond the reach of civilization, is the *Waipio Treehouse Retreat* (808/775-7160) which includes two separate guest cottages and a dream of a treehouse at the base of a 2,000-foot waterfall. The place is tucked away in the forest on the far side of the valley in a remote location accessible only by four-wheel-drive vehicle; a pickup service is available for guests at the lookout parking area above the valley.

The Treehouse sleeps three, the smaller cottage sleeps six, and the larger cottage sleeps eight to ten. Rates are $225 a night for the Treehouse and the Kahu cottage, per couple, and $175 per night for two nights or more. The Hale cottage is $150 per night for a two-night or longer stay, or $200 for one night, per couple. Weekly and group rates are available. (Rates include transportation from the lookout.) Small kitchens are provided, but you need to bring your own food.

Private estates, homes, villas: Have a hankering to stay in a $2-million beach house, a mansion on a golf course, or a mountain top retreat? It can be arranged, for a price ($300 to $3,500 per night, and up). Simply write or call one of the following: *C.J. Kimberly Realtors*, P.O. Box 5600, Kailua-Kona, HI. 96745, (808/329-4321); *Kona Vacation Resorts*, 77-6435 Kuakini Highway, Kailua-Kona, HI. 96740, (800/367-5168, 808/329-6488, FAX 808/329-5480); or *South Kohala Management*, P.O. Box 384900, Waikoloa, HI. 96738, (800/822-4252, 808/833-8500).

Hostels: Big Island hostels are not much like the European variety; they tend to be smaller, more relaxed, with less rules, and either non-existent or loosely enforced curfews. Because they are inexpensive and cater to a young crowd, you can expect them to be a bit funky and noisy, though they are generally clean and offer basic accommodations at rock-bottom prices.

Hale Lamalani (808/964-5401, 800/238-8BED, $15-$55) a bed & breakfast as well as a hostel, is located five miles north of Hilo, with great views, and "breakfast fixings." *Arnott's Lodge and Hostel* (808/969-7097, $15-$36) is a mile and a half outside Hilo, a block from the ocean. There are shared bunk rooms as well as private rooms. *Patey's Place in Paradise* (808/326-7018, $15-$45) is located in one of Kona's rowdiest residential neighborhoods (on Hamburger Hill behind McDonald's) but if you don't mind having to listen to the occasional Saturday night drunken brawl, you won't find a cheaper place to stay in Kailua.

The best thing about this hostel is its owner, Robert Patey, who is one of the nicest guys you'll ever meet and who goes out of his way to make sure his guests have a good time. The $15 rate is for shared, non-coed bunk rooms; private rooms go from $30 to $45. The shared kitchen has a stove and fridge, but not much in the way of cooking utensils or dishes, though if you ask, Robert will probably come up with whatever you need.

Camping: The Big Island offers twelve county campgrounds, six state campgrounds, and three federal campgrounds (located within Hawaii Volcanoes National Park).

The county parks have limited facilities and you need your own tent. Permits are required, and campsites are on a first-come, first-served basis – no reservations. Camping permits are issued for one week per park in summer months and two weeks per park in other months. The fee is $1 per day for adults, $.50 per day for juniors (13-17), and no charge for children 12 and under. For more information on county campgrounds, contact the Department of Parks and Recreation, County of Hawaii, 25 Aupuni St., Hilo, HI. 96720 (808/961-8311).

Facilities at state campgrounds range from A-frame cabins at Hapuna Beach and group lodges at Mauna Kea State Recreation Area to the primitive campground at MacKenzie State Recreation Area where no drinking water is available. There are no camping fees (except for cabin rentals), but permits are required, and five nights is the maximum length of stay allowed under each permit. To obtain permits, cabin rental rates, or more information, contact the Department of Land & Natural Resources, State Parks Division, P.O. Box 936, Hilo, HI. 96721-0936 (808/933-4200.)

All of the federal campgrounds on the Big Island are located within *Hawaii Volcanoes National Park*. No permit is needed and there is no charge for tent camping. Simple A-frame cabins that sleep four (you could squeeze in six, if four are little kids) are available at one of the campgrounds, and rent for $35 per night. They are very popular and reservations should be made well in advance of your visit. They are not heated and can get quite chilly, so bring extra blankets or sleeping bags. Cabin reservations can be made through *Volcano House Inn*, P.O. Box 53, Hawaii Volcanoes National Park, 96718, (808/967-7321.)

For more information on camping in Hawaii Volcanoes National Park, contact the Superintendent, Hawaii Volcanoes National Park, Volcano, HI. 96718 (808/967-7311).

Military Recreation Center: The *Kilauea Military Camp* located at Hawaii Volcanoes National Park offers 55 rustic, well-kept rental cabins (1,2,3, and 4 bedrooms) that are available only to active duty regular military, reserve, national guard, retired service personnel, or Department of Defense employees. Rates are very reasonable and are based on rank and grade. Advance reservations are required (808/967-8333, FAX 808/967-8343) in Honolulu, 438-6707.

The Aloha Theatre and Cafe, Kainaliu. Kona Historical Society

Places To Go

Kona Coffee Country Drive

Even a casual trip through the coffee growing area will tell you that the Kona coffee industry is undergoing a renaissance. There are at least a dozen companies buying coffee from farmers or selling roasted coffee to tourists, and new plantings abound everywhere. Before you begin your drive, perhaps a brief discussion of the mechanics of coffee growing and processing is in order.

Coffee trees bloom in spring, usually between March and May. The flowerings are intense, and the two or three peak days of each flowering are called "Kona snow" because the trees look as if they are covered with snowfall. The flowers are sweet smelling (coffee is related to the gardenia), but only last a few days. After the flowers drop, small green beans begin to form in their place. Seven to nine months later, these beans grow large and turn red, and are "coffee cherries." Each flowering or "round" must be picked separately by hand. The main picking season

CAPT. COOK TO HONAUNAU

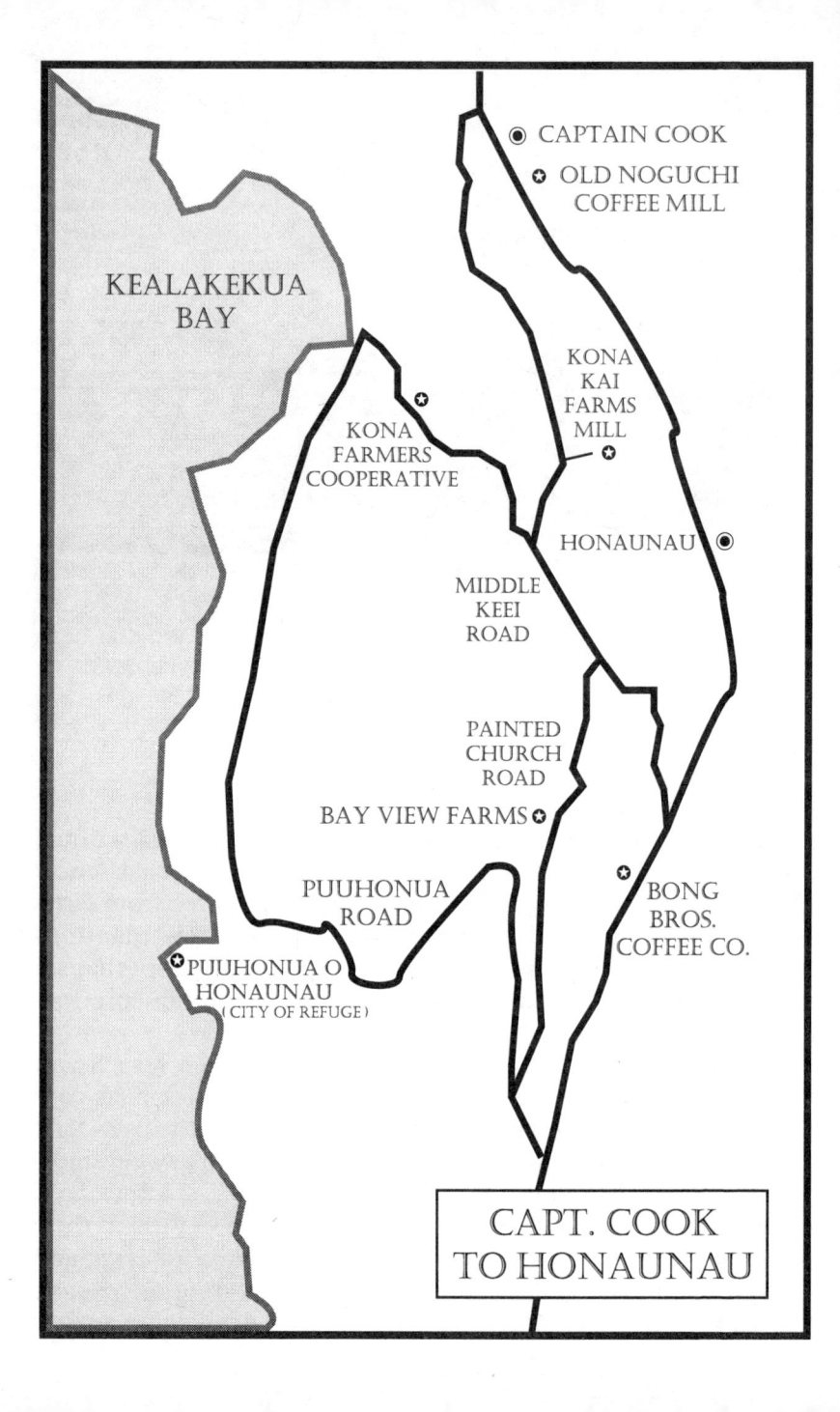

- ⊙ CAPTAIN COOK
- ✪ OLD NOGUCHI COFFEE MILL
- KEALAKEKUA BAY
- ✪ KONA FARMERS COOPERATIVE
- ✪ KONA KAI FARMS MILL
- ⊙ HONAUNAU
- MIDDLE KEEI ROAD
- PAINTED CHURCH ROAD
- ✪ BAY VIEW FARMS
- PUUHONUA ROAD
- ✪ BONG BROS. COFFEE CO.
- ✪ PUUHONUA O HONAUNAU (CITY OF REFUGE)

runs from September through January, but some coffee is harvested every month except April, May and June.

Once the ripe beans are picked, the outer "cherry" skin is removed in a pulping mill, and the seeds of the fruit are washed and put out to dry on decks with rolling roofs called "hoshidanas" (Japanese for "drying house"). These Kona inventions allow the coffee to be dried in the morning sun and then quickly covered when the afternoon rains begin. During mid-season, diesel-powered dryers are used to supplement sun drying.

After the beans (now called "parchment") have been dried to 12% moisture content, the outer skin and the inner "silver skin" are removed. Now called "green coffee," the beans are graded by size and density, and sewn up in 100-pound burlap bags for shipment to roasters the world over. "Extra Fancy" beans are $19/64$ inches round and contain less than 10 defects per pound, while "Number One" beans are $16/64$ inches round and contain less than 20 defects per pound. "Prime" usually denotes better cuts of meat, but Kona "Prime" is a lower grade coffee.

For a good overview of the coffee belt, we suggest this route: Leaving Kailua, drive up Palani Road (Route 190) past the traffic light for about seven miles to the junction of Mamalahoa Highway (Route 180). Turn right and drive south towards Holualoa. This is one of the best growing districts in Kona, and you can see lots of orchards from the road. A huge pink coffee cup on the makai side of the road marks Nikki Ferrari's *Hawaii Mountain Gold Coffee Museum*, a place that is hard to describe but definitely unique.

Continuing on, you come to the town of Holualoa. The art galleries are the main attraction here in this little coffee town, and there are many interesting ones to visit. The *Holuakoa Cafe* is a good place to stop for art, pastries, and espresso.

A couple of miles beyond Holualoa you will come to the *Old Donkey Mill*, which is not set up for visitors, but you can get a good look from the road. This was a co-operative that was sold to the owner of United Coffee, a San Francisco based coffee roaster, in 1982, and gets its name from the donkeys that were the main source of transporting coffee until the

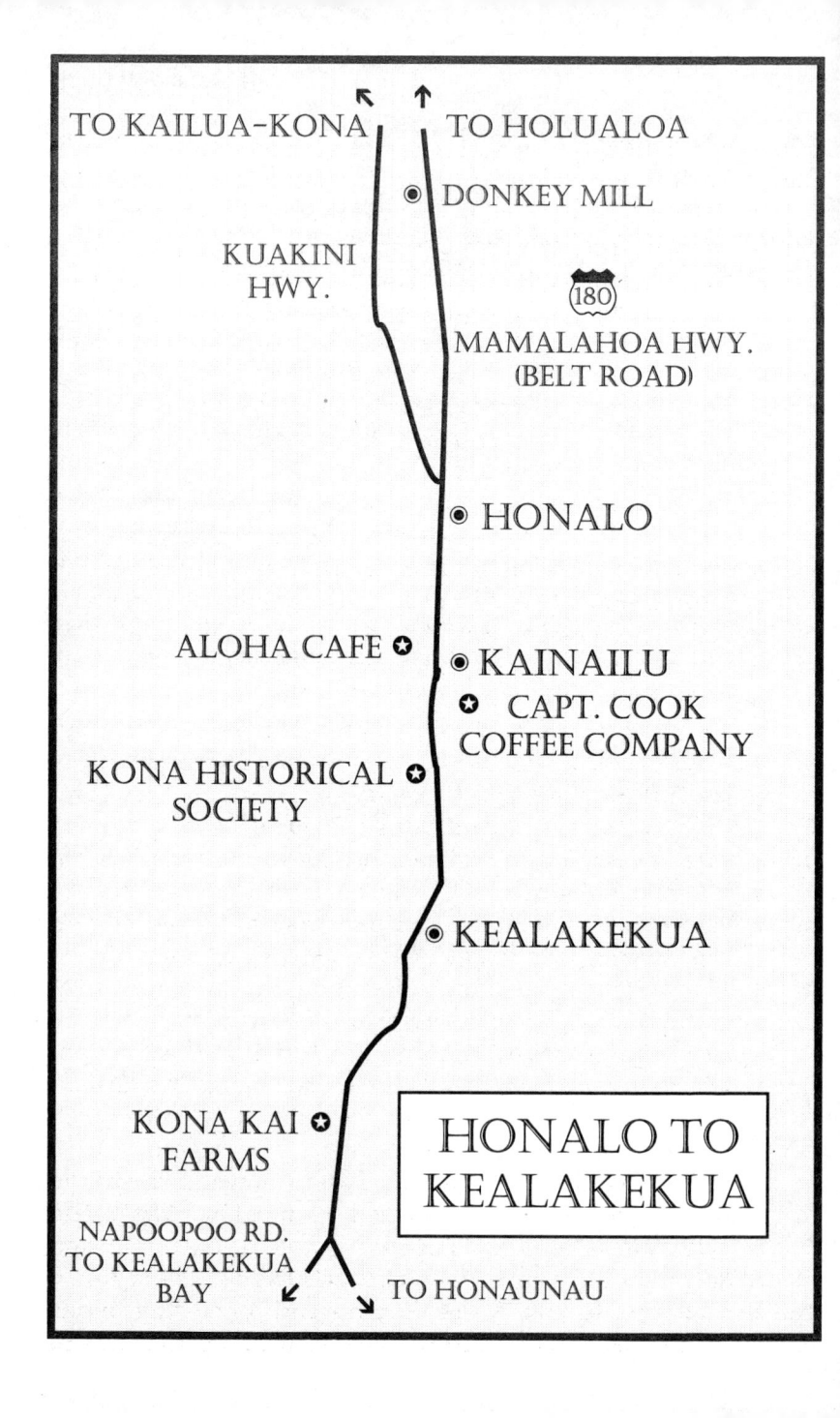

HONALO TO KEALAKEKUA

TO KAILUA-KONA
TO HOLUALOA
◉ DONKEY MILL

KUAKINI HWY.

(180) MAMALAHOA HWY. (BELT ROAD)

◉ HONALO

ALOHA CAFE ✪
◉ KAINAILU
✪ CAPT. COOK COFFEE COMPANY

KONA HISTORICAL ✪
SOCIETY

◉ KEALAKEKUA

KONA KAI ✪
FARMS

NAPOOPOO RD.
TO KEALAKEKUA
BAY
TO HONAUNAU

1960s. United Coffee is no longer in business, and the milling equipment inside the mill has been moved away.

Keep going and join up with the main highway at *Teshima's Restaurant* in Honalo, where you continue south. The next town is Kainaliu, and you should plan on eating breakfast or lunch at the *Aloha Cafe* inside the old theater building. At the other end of town is the old *Fujino Mill*, now operated by *Captain Cook Coffee Company* and the *Bad Ass Coffee Company*, a small retail-roasting outlet. *Kadooka's Orchid Nursery* at the north end of town is world famous because of the original orchids developed there.

Proceed south from Kainaliu through Kealakekua. One mile south of Kealakekua on the *makai* (ocean) side of the road you will see a native stone building circa 1870 which houses the Kona Historical Society (323-3222). This is a must stop for anyone interested in the history of the area – especially the photography collection which is one of the largest in the state. The KHS operates the Kona Coffee Living History Farm about two miles away – a perfectly preserved example of a Japanese family farm of the 1920s. You can sign up for tours over the phone.

Driving further south, past Kealakekua, you come to *Kona Kai Farms Tasting Room and Coffee Drop Off*, where farmers bring coffee cherry to be weighed during the harvest season. You can taste a half-dozen different kinds of Kona coffee, see many historical photographs, and purchase packaged coffee, burlap bags, seedlings, picking baskets, and other coffee-related items. If you are involved in the coffee industry, ask about a special tour of Kona Kai's processing plant and farms.

A quarter mile past the Kona Kai Tasting Room, turn right down the mountain at the "Kealakekua Bay" sign. The turn-off to Kona Kai's processing plant is 2.2 miles down this road, across from the Old Napoʻopoʻo School (now a county base yard). Keep going down the mountain and you will come to the *Royal Kona Coffee Historical Museum* operated by *Mauna Loa Coffee*, adjacent to the *Kona Farmers Co-operative* coffee and macadamia nut mill. This is the oldest and largest mill in Kona, and the museum has many old pictures and processing implements. Mauna Loa is scheduled to move to the main highway in

HOLUALOA

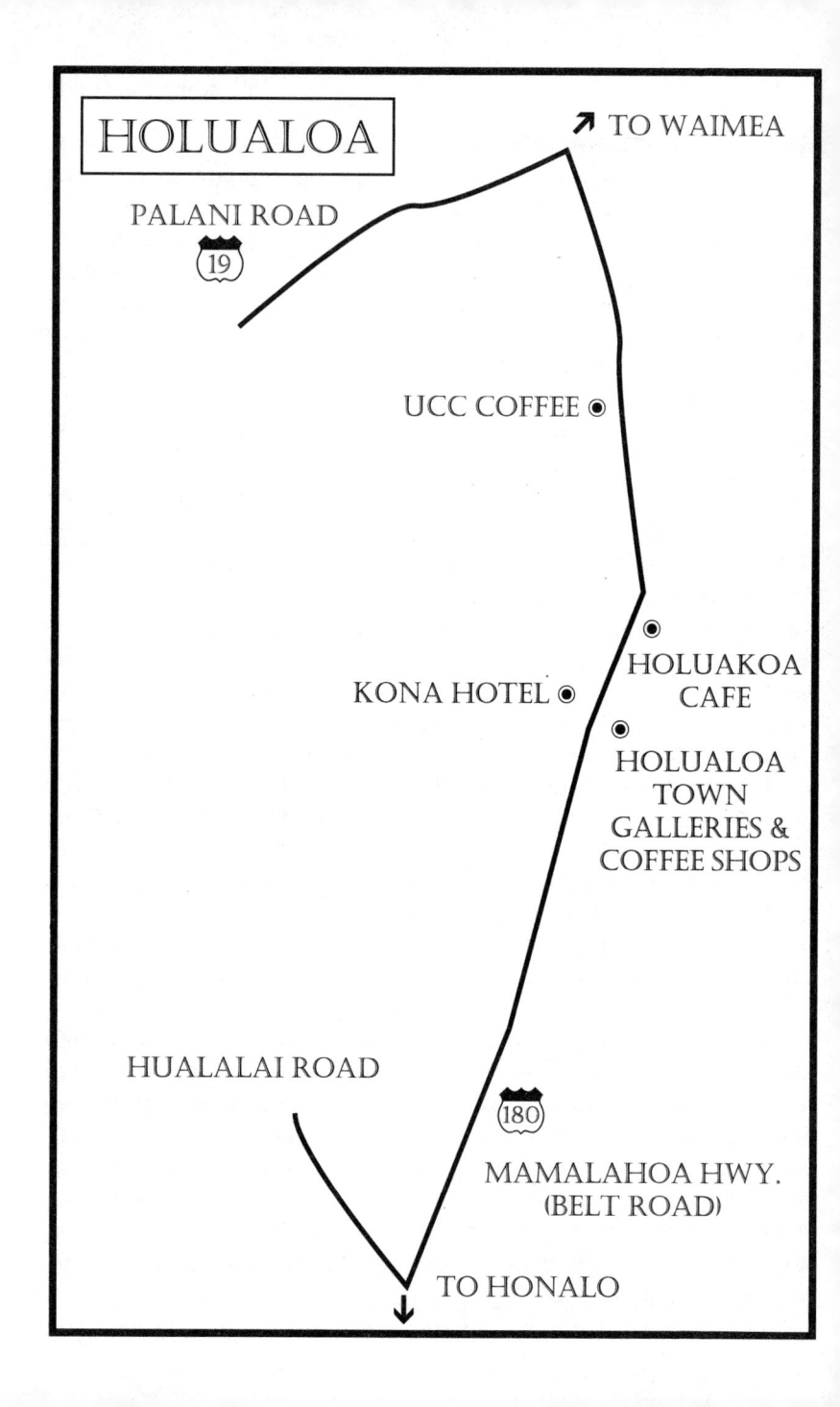

↗ TO WAIMEA

PALANI ROAD
(19)

UCC COFFEE ●

● HOLUAKOA CAFE

KONA HOTEL ●

● HOLUALOA TOWN GALLERIES & COFFEE SHOPS

HUALALAI ROAD

(180)

MAMALAHOA HWY. (BELT ROAD)

TO HONALO ↓

1995, to the Kona Country Fair location in Honaunau.

While you're in the area, keep going down to the bottom of the road, turn right, and drive ⅛ mile to the *Napo'opo'o Beach Park* at *Kealakekua Bay*. This is one of the most beautiful places in Hawaii. Captain James Cook "discovered" Hawaii here in 1778, and the white monument across the bay marks the spot where he was killed on February 14, 1779. Sometimes there is sand on the beach, sometimes just rocks.

After you've seen the Bay, go back up the same road about two miles to the junction of Middle Ke'ei Road and turn right. There's a great plumeria and vanda orchid farm on the corner. After about a mile, take another right on Painted Church Road One quarter mile on your right is Paleaku Gardens, a botnical garden dedicated to world peace. It contains a variety of rare Hawaiian plants, a meditation center, and several interesting religious monuments including a 21-foot Tibetan Buddhist stupa. For information on the various programs call 328-8084. Then drive two miles past the Painted Church, an interesting short stop, to the intersection of City of Refuge Road (Pu'uhonua Road). If you have extra time, turn right and go down to *City of Refuge National Park*. The more accurate translation of its Hawaiian name is Place of Refuge. It was never a city. It was like the Mexican border for ancient Hawaiians running from the King's soldiers: if you made it there, they couldn't follow. Now it is the closest thing to an old Hawaiian village on the island.

If you don't go down to *City of Refuge (Pu'uhonua o Honaunau)*, turn left up to the main highway and head back towards town. In a mile or so you'll pass *Bong Brothers Coffee Company*, which usually has some good local fruit and produce out in front. Another two miles north is *The Kahauloa Coffee Company*, formerly Captain Cook Coffee Company's retail outlet and now a deli and retail store, with a great view of the *Honaunau Valley* and *Kona Kai Farms*, right below. Another two miles north, just before the town of Captain Cook, is the old *Noguchi Mill*, formerly operated by the P*acific Coffee Co-operative,* but now vacant. There were 14 of these mills in the 1950s when coffee covered 6,000 acres.

Captain Cook itself isn't much of a town, but it does have the

Kealakekua Ranch Center shopping mall and across from it the old Kona Theater, now being renovated and featuring a gift shop, farmer's market and espresso bar/café (328-2244). Proprietor Ted Georgakis is a friendly source of information for travelers.

That completes your tour of Kona coffee country. The whole trip, from leaving Kailua to returning should take less than four hours. Morning is best, because it often rains in the afternoon "up mauka." There is a weekly tour of Kona Kai Farms which starts from our Kealakekua Drop Off Tuesdays at 10 a.m.

Kailua Bay and Ali'i Drive Circa 1910. Kona Historical Society.

HISTORIC KAILUA-KONA TOWN TOUR

A mini-Lahaina of tourist shops and restaurants today lines the waterfront at Kailua Bay. However, don't let the mass tourism facade deter you from taking in one of the most historic locations in all the Hawaiian Islands.

This is a walking tour, so drive into town and park. Usually there are open spaces in the free public parking lot along the makai (ocean) side of Kuakini Highway, near the Palani Road intersection. Walk through the row of shops to the waterfront at

Ali'i Drive and head for the luau grounds on the oceanfront of the King Kamehameha Hotel at the west end of the bay.

Here, in the shadow of the slopes of Hualalai, is Kamakahonu (the eye of the turtle), a few acres of land where pivotal events in Hawaii's history occurred. Kamehameha the Great, the Hawaiian warrior king who conquered and united all the Hawaiian Islands in the early 1800s, settled here in 1813, leaving Honolulu and years of battle behind. The tiny oceanfront oasis became the *ad hoc* capitol of Hawaii, and the site of Kamehameha's death in 1819.

The Ahu'ena Heiau, the recreated Hawaiian temple you can see adjacent to the luau grounds, was destroyed in 1819 but rebuilt in recent years. The stone foundation of Ahu'ena is believed to date from the 1400s, and human sacrifices may have been made on its altars. However, Kamehameha dedicated the heiau to Lono, a Hawaiian god of the harvest and peace, and used it as a meeting house to discuss the affairs of his kingdom.

A free in-depth presentation of historical exhibits that tells Kamehameha's story is given at King Kamehameha's Kona Beach Hotel (329-2911) weekdays at 1 p.m.

Leaving the hotel, walk east along the sea wall to the tall New England spire that marks the New England missionaries' Mokuaikaua Church, which is renowned as the first church established in Hawaii. Inside the church at the rear of the sanctuary is a history room that tells the missionaries' story.

Walk directly across Ali'i Drive to tour the handsome Hulihe'e Palace, built by Governor Kuakini in 1838 to become his personal estate. Instead, the then rock-walled building became a royal residence and summer palace for the Hawaiian monarchs of the Victorian Era. King David Kalakaua had the walls plastered smooth in 1885 to modernize the building.

In the decades following the 1893 overthrow of the Hawaiian Kingdom, Hulihe'e Palace and a number of other historic buildings of the monarchy fell into disrepair. In the 1950s, the estate was placed under the care of the Daughters of Hawaii who have faithfully restored it to past glory. The palace's collection combines European items gathered by Hawaiian monarchs, as well as interesting artifacts from the days of Kamehameha the

WAIPIO
VALLEY

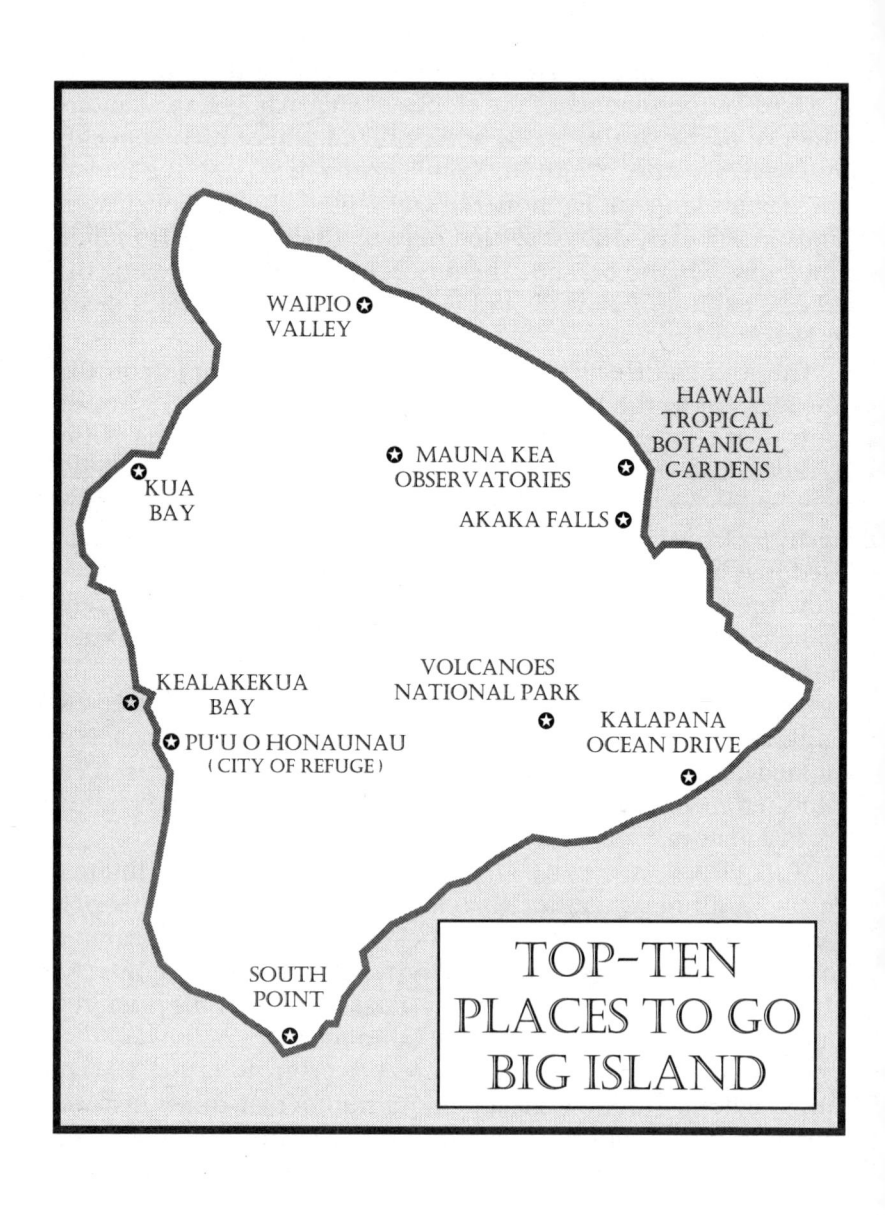

HAWAII
TROPICAL
BOTANICAL
GARDENS

KUA
BAY

MAUNA KEA
OBSERVATORIES

AKAKA FALLS

KEALAKEKUA
BAY

VOLCANOES
NATIONAL PARK

KALAPANA
OCEAN DRIVE

PU'U O HONAUNAU
(CITY OF REFUGE)

SOUTH
POINT

TOP-TEN
PLACES TO GO
BIG ISLAND

Great, such as war spears and other period pieces.

Some weekday afternoons local hula *halaus* (schools) of graceful dancers practice on the lawn of the palace, bringing the royal grounds to life again. Interpretive tours of the Hulihe'e Palace (329-1877) are held daily. Hulihe'e Palace is open from 9 a.m. to 4 p.m. weekdays, and 10 a.m. to 3 p.m. weekends. Tours are offered beginning at 9:30 a.m. on weekdays, and beginning at 11 a.m. on weekends. Admission is $4 for adults, $1 for children 11 and over, and $.50 for children under 11. Proceeds go to maintain the palace.

Adjacent to the Hulihe'e Palace is the *Kona Inn Shopping Village*, or what used to be the Kona Inn. This maze of commercial art galleries, souvenir shops, and clothing boutiques is the former site of a classic '30s resort hotel that was the center of action for all west Hawaii in the days when Ali'i Drive was a dirt road and it was more convenient to sail to Kona than to fly. Actor Richard Boone of "Paladin" TV fame came to Kona, staying at the Kona Inn in the '50s, and helped launch the world-famous *Hawaiian Islands Billfish Tournament*, which is still held every August at the Kailua Bay pier, though it is now called the Hawaiian International Billfish Tournament. Some of the bygone glamour of the Kona Inn in its glory days can still be captured by sipping a cup of Kona coffee while watching the sun set across Kailua Bay as you sit on the sea wall alongside the grass promenade fronting the shopping area.

KA'U DISTRICT – VOLCANOES NATIONAL PARK

Kilauea Volcano is the number one tourist attraction on the Big Island, and for good reason. It has been erupting continuously since 1983, and many of its lava fountains and flows are easily visible to someone traveling by car. You can also take one of the airplane or helicopter tours which fly over the volcano – spectacular, but on the expensive side.

Drive south on the main highway past City of Refuge Road. The next 20 miles are narrow and winding, until you reach *Mac Farms of Hawaii*, the world's largest macadamia nut orchard. The best food along the way is at the *Na'alehu Fruit Stand* in

Na'alehu, especially the fresh squeezed pineapple juice and John Santangelo's pizza. The side trip to *South Point* (just before Na'alehu) is a 24-mile detour into a unique and very spiritual place which was revered by the ancient Hawaiians, and is the southernmost point in the United States.

Those of you who are spiritually oriented might want to visit the buddhist temple at *Wood Valley Temple and Retreat Center (Nechung Dorje Drayang Ling) (928-8539)*, ten minutes out of *Pahala*. There are several times during the year when a Tibetan lama is in residence, and there are many retreats held there for meditative, spiritual, and healing groups from all over the world.

Continuing on past Pahala, you arrive at *Hawaii Volcanoes National Park*. On arriving at the park, check in at the visitor center where you can read up on the geology of volcanoes and see 15 minutes of the best eruptions over the last forty years. There's also a great arts and crafts shop right next to the visitor center. Then go over to the Volcano House hotel bar, which looks out on the great crater. Back in the car, take the Chain of Craters Road around the park for a tour of the results of past eruptions. We especially recommend the *Thurston Lava Tube*, a short walking side trip. For daily eruption information, call the hotline at 967-7977.

Unfortunately, the town of *Kalapana* and its lovely *Black Sand Beach* are now gone due to the recent lava flows. To get to the edge of the now-cooled flow, drive to *Kea'au* on the main highway, then cut down to the ocean. There's another black sand beach at SeaMountain Resort on the way back to Kona (just retrace your route).

WAIMEA (KAMUELA) – MAUNA KEA OBSERVATORIES

At first glance, *Waimea* is an upcountry, rural cowboy town, but if you stay awhile, you'll experience a surprisingly cosmopolitan atmosphere. Located on the rolling green plain between the *Kohala Mountains* and *Mauna Kea*, the town has long centered around *Parker Ranch*, the largest privately owned cattle spread in the United States. For decades, the laid-back little town

Observatory at Mauna Kea.

functioned mostly to service the ranch. Then, during WW II, when it housed 30,000 Marines, it was "discovered" by the outside world and has been a magnet for newcomers ever since. At 2,500 feet, the town enjoys a windy, cool, rainy climate that can often turn nippy, even in mid summer.

A wide variety of different sorts of people call Waimea home. Of the population of approximately 5,200, 17 percent are of Hawaiian ancestry and have lived in the area for generations. They believe in aloha, but the rapid changes transforming their once peaceful village are very disturbing to some. Not long ago, they could ride their horses anywhere, but now traffic is so heavy, they are being pushed ever farther out into the country.

Well-heeled retirees from Oahu and elsewhere, entranced by Waimea's beauty, are settling here in ever increasing numbers, fueling a real estate boom that has made property too expensive for the offspring of many long-time residents to buy, a problem that Hawaiians face throughout the islands.

Waimea is home, too, to a large number of astronomers and high-tech wizards from around the globe drawn by the world-class telescopes atop Mauna Kea. There are also preppies from Honolulu and other islands come to study at *Hawaii Preparatory Academy* (HPA), one of the state's top secondary schools.

Art and theater buffs, alternative lifestylers, hardcore counterculturists, and various free spirits lend the place something of a college town flavor, though there isn't a university nearby.

Waimea's weather – alternating between a clear blue sky with high western clouds, sweeping rain showers and misty mornings, warm sunny moments during the day, but mostly brisk (for Hawaii) mountain weather – makes for an inviting change from the dry Kona coast, as well as from tropical east Hawaii. The town is about evenly split for weather – the east side is commonly known as the wet side, and the west side is the dry side. If you're getting drenched downtown, just drive a mile or less west for the sun.

Paniolo culture is popular in Waimea, as evidenced by the rodeos, western outfitting stores, checkerboard *Palaka* shirts, horseback riders, broken old wagon wheels and dilapidated buggies scattered here and there, and locals who favor cowboy boots, western shirts and Stetson hats over t-shirts and rubber slippers.

Waimea is sometimes called *Kamuela*, but Kamuela is really just the name given the local post office in the days before zip codes, to prevent mail from winding up in Waimea, Oahu, or Waimea, Kauai. Waimea is the ancient Hawaiian name for the village, and means "reddish-waters," a reference to the color of mountain streams after a heavy rain. Kamuela means Samuel in Hawaiian. Samuel was one of the sons of John Parker, founder of Parker Ranch.

The most direct (and scenic) route to Waimea from Kona is up Palani Drive along Highway 190, the Hawaii Belt Road, or Mamalahoa Highway, for about 45 minutes. It's a quick ride with light traffic and long stretches of open space. Watch for radar traps.

On the edge of town is the *Waimea-Kohala Airport*, the town's main rodeo arena, and *Pu'u'opelu*, Parker Ranch's main house which houses a fine collection of European and American art.

Created by the late Richard Smart, heir to the Parker Ranch and a former professional stage actor on Broadway, the gallery at Puʻuʻopelu and nearby *Mana Home*, the original Parker Ranch homestead (885-5433), are open daily to visitors from 9:30 a.m. to 4:30 p.m. Admission is $5 for adults and $2.50 for children.

Parker Ranch Tours (885-7655) will take you in comfortable vans on a tour of the ranch itself. The tour goes 12 miles upcountry to the original two acres of land where John Parker started ranching. Riding at *Mauna Kea Stables* is available as is a special helicopter tour with Mauna Kea Helicopters. If it's raining hard, the rough ranch roads become impassable and tours are canceled.

Waimea town is a short drive from Puʻuʻopelu. Life in Waimea is very much centered around the local population. Visitors are welcomed, but only as part of the local scene. The one major deviation from this is the *Parker Ranch Visitors Center* in the *Parker Ranch Shopping Center* near the main crossroad in town. This second Parker Ranch museum completes the story of the family with photos and artifacts of the of six generations of the Parker family, as well as the surrounding cowboy lands. Admission can be combined with the art museum. For surfing buffs, a side room is full of memorabilia from the life of Duke Kahanamoku, the famed Hawaiian surfer and Olympic swimming champion from Waikiki.

If you are traveling with children, especially on a lengthy drive to the volcanoes or to Hilo, a must stop is the incredible all-wood *Anuenue Playground* adjacent to the baseball field at *Waimea Park*. Two thousand of the town's people with support from local businesses and foundations came together to build the playground (at a cost of $340,000). Some families drive all the way from Hilo or Kona just to bring their kids here to play. It is as much a work of art as a playground, and offers plenty of benches for mom and dad to rest on while the youngsters go wild.

Dining and shopping are major attractions in Waimea. We particularly like the several rooms of Hawaii-made products at *Cook's Discoveries* in the historic *Spencer House* at Waimea Center, right next to McDonalds. The items are well chosen and are things local Hawaii residents would buy to wear, decorate a home, or give as gifts.

For dinner, try the German or Continental fare at *Eidelweiss*, west of town, or *Merriman's,* which offers Hawaiian, Oriental, and Western cuisine, near the park, or *Hale Kea's* wide variety of steaks, seafood, chicken, and pastas, served in a setting of antique elegance. Hale Kea, located two miles west of town on Kawaihae Road in a rambling old ranch house that used to be a Rockefeller estate, also offers a Sunday brunch that is popular with Waimea residents. If it's not raining, be sure to walk behind Hale Kea's complex of buildings for an outstanding pastoral view of a waterfall, rushing mountain stream, and horses grazing along the Kohala Mountains.

For a good cup of coffee, try *Waimea Coffee*, in Parker Square, which features many of Kona's best estate grown coffees.

Theater productions, dance and musical performances, and many community events occur year round in Waimea. To find out when and where, pick up a copy of the *Waimea Gazette*. It's a quality, black and white magazine-size publication that would be worth paying for if it weren't free, which it is. It's available at many stores in Waimea, and at some galleries in Kona and Holualoa.

The best way to experience unspoiled backcountry Waimea as it's always been is from horseback. Local Hawaiian cowgirls Jodi Sylva and Nanea Chambers are the owners of *Pu'u Haloa Trail Rides* (885-8480) and they will skillfully guide you through some of the prettiest country you'd ever want to see.

From Waimea, you can either drive to beautiful Waipio Valley, to Hilo, or to the top of awesome Mauna Kea.

You'll need a four wheel drive vehicle to reach the 13,000 foot summit of the mountain, but once there, you'll probably be glad you took the trouble. It is recommended that children under 16 not go to the summit, as the altitude is potentially harmful to youngsters. To get there, take Mamalahoa Highway out of Waimea, heading back toward Kailua. Seven miles from Waimea you'll come to the Saddle Road turn off. Take the Saddle Road up to Mauna Kea. It's about a one-hour drive from Waimea or Hilo, and about two and a half hours from Kona (one way).

You don't need a four wheel drive vehicle to reach the

Visitor's Information Center (961-2180) at 9,300 feet. It is open to the public on Friday, from 1 to 5 p.m., and Saturday and Sunday from 8 a.m. to noon, offering information, programs, and tours, all free of charge. Guided tours of the summit are given on Saturday and Sunday afternoons. To go on one of these tours, you need to show up at the Visitor's Center with a four wheel drive vehicle, no later than 1:30 p.m. on Saturday or Sunday. Every Friday and Saturday night the Visitor's Center offers a stargazing program that is open to all ages beginning with a lecture and video from 7 to 8, followed by stargazing (weather permitting) until 10 p.m. Eleven-inch Celestron telescopes are provided, and the stars are brighter here than anywhere else on earth. It is suggested you call ahead to confirm.

There are currently nine observatories on top of Mauna Kea, and a tenth is under construction by the Japanese. The recently completed W.M. Keck I telescope, the world's largest, will be joined in 1996 by the Keck II, which will double the light-gathering power of the observatory. The Keck I can already peer more than 12 billion lightyears into space, which is almost impossible to grasp, as one lightyear equals approximately 5.878 trillion miles.

Astronomers seldom look directly through these telescopes, but instead use sophisticated cameras that are much more sensitive than the human eye to record the images upon which the telescopes focus. The astronomers then watch these images on TV monitors.

The landscape at Mauna Kea's summit looks like the moon, and during winter the snow can be deep, although some years it never snows. High winds, freezing fog, snow, and sub-freezing temperatures are frequently encountered, at any time of year. Blizzards are not uncommon, even in July. It is best to prepare for high mountain conditions, as weather can change suddenly and unpredictably. A wool hat, sweater, mittens, scarves, long underwear, windproof jacket, sturdy boots or shoes, sunscreen and sunglasses are recommended. Do not go up in beach wear!

You may feel short-term effects of altitude sickness, including dizziness, dehydration, headache, or nausea. It is suggested that before your trip to the top, you stop at the *Visitors Center* and rest for an hour or so to "climatize." Be sure to drink plenty of water, and don't smoke for at least 48 hours before going up.

Children under 16, people with respiratory, heart, or obesity conditions, or pregnant women are advised not to go higher than the Visitors Center at 9300 feet. Scuba divers must wait at least 24 hours after their last dive before ascending the summit.

No gas, food, water, or other supplies are available on Mauna Kea, so be sure to stock up before going. It's also a good idea to call the Visitors Center to check on road and weather conditions, particularly during winter months.

Because of the high altitude, the air holds only 60 percent of the oxygen found at sea level. Scientists working at the summit constantly battle mental exhaustion and impaired judgment. But in the near future, this will no longer be a problem. Soon to be linked by fiber optics, most of the telescopes' operations will be computer-controlled, allowing a majority of the scientific work to be performed an hour's drive away, at the observatories' Waimea offices.

Morning is the best time to go to the top of Mauna Kea, and an hour or so is all some people need before they become dizzy.

Hamakua Coast & Waipio Valley

The sea cliff towns of the *Hamakua Coast* stretch from *Honoka'a* above Waipio Valley, south to Hilo. With a backdrop of sometimes snow-capped Mauna Kea, the tradewind-swept Pacific, and miles of sugar cane fields, Hamakua is a picturesque district known best for its spectacular waterfalls and tropical plants.

From Kona to Honoka'a is about an hour-and-a-half drive and well within range for a one-day visit. Honoka'a is today the scene of a dramatic struggle for economic survival following massive layoffs due to the closing of sugar cane plantations and mills. A somewhat isolated town, Honoka'a is searching for ways to survive while striving to maintain an idyllic rural lifestyle reminiscent of the Hawaii of the 1920s and '30s. Downtown Honoka'a has a sleepy main street lined with small restaurants, and you can

Waipio Valley Overlook

find decent espresso, cappuccino, and pastries at the *Mamane Street Bakery & Cafe* (775-9478). There are also a couple of antique shops, as well as the *Honoka'a Peoples Theater* (775-0000), an old but still operating plantation movie house, and a growing number of tour operators who will take you down into Waipio Valley. It's fun to spend a lazy afternoon of antique browsing here, followed by dinner, and topped off with an evening at the movies, or just to stock up with drinks and snacks before heading down to Waipio.

Waipio Valley is today a quiet, incredibly scenic valley where a handful of Hawaiian and Japanese taro growers, counterculturists and dreamers live without electricity and minus most modern conveniences. In the days of ancient Hawaii, it was a capitol of the ali'i with a population estimated at 40,000. In those days, it was the political and cultural center of the Big Island.

The view from the lookout at the end of highway 240 is awe-inspiring, but only a glimmer of the experience waiting 1,000 feet below in the valley. Access is down a very steep four wheel drive, narrow, paved road. You can hike in, or catch the *Waipio Valley Shuttle* (775-7121). The road is treacherous if it rains hard, and if you drive in, don't come to a complete stop going up or down. Deep in the valley you ford streams to get around.

At the bottom of the road turn left for a view of the double waterfalls of *Hi'ilawe Falls*, which plunge 1,200 feet, six miles back from the coast to form Waipio Stream. Turn right for the gray sand beach which stretches across the mouth of the valley. Joining an organized tour of the valley is advisable if you want to know about its history, natural wonders, and people. But if you just want to wander in a lush, mystical, ancient Hawaiian valley brimming with archaeological remains and seemingly removed from the modern world, go exploring on your own. Waipio reminds us of one of those Amazon jungles in the movies where explorers go through a waterfall and discover dinosaurs – it just feels prehistoric.

For experienced hikers, the twelve-mile trek up the north valley wall of Waipio and over the top into *Waimanu Valley* is rated one of the best trails in Hawaii. Waimanu is very isolated and like Waipio was once inhabited by Hawaiians who departed long ago, leaving behind a myriad of archaeological remains. Be sure you are in good condition for this hike, it's strenuous.

Returning to Waimea after your visit to the Waipio Valley, take Kawaihae Road down toward the beach. You'll come out near the Kohala hotels and the island's two best, easily accessible beaches – *Hapuna State Park* and *Anaeho'omalu State Park*. It's a straight 45-minute shot back to Kailua on the Queen Ka'ahumanu Highway.

Just before you get back to Kona, there is one more attraction to see, the *Ocean Thermal Energy Conversion* project (OTEC), at the *Natural Energy Lab* (329-7341), just south of the airport, where electricity is produced by pumping cold water up from 2,000 feet (the reef drops off dramatically just off shore). The difference in temperature between the cold and warm water creates steam which powers a generator. There are other high tech companies at OTEC including a maker of spirulina, some of which use OTEC's excess cold water to raise varieties of edible algae and other forms of sea life. Tours are Thursday mornings at 10, and although there is no charge, you do need to make reservations.

KOHALA COAST

Lavish resorts and championship golf are the big draws along the Kohala Coast, an oasis of luxury hotels, golf courses, and white sand beaches about 20 miles north along the Queen Ka'ahumanu Highway from Kona.

Staying at the Kohala Coast can be a self-contained experience. Golf and tennis packages are offered by most of the resorts, and there are enough tennis courts, white sand beaches, ocean activities and hotel restaurants and bars to keep you entertained for weeks if you enjoy resort life. The area is also rich in Hawaiian history, with large petroglyph fields, ancient trails, and ruins of old coastal fishing villages within easy reach of the hotels.

Kawaihae, a small port town just north of the Kohala Coast is where barges of goods bound for Kona arrive at *Young Brothers* terminal each week. This is not a very scenic spot, but the recently opened *Kawaihae Center* on the way to the docks provides two levels of interesting shops and restaurants with a rural flavor, and a store where you can buy something cold to drink. Local fishing gear, hand carved koa wood sculpture, and classic Hawaiian furniture are some of the better products available.

Waterworld, which will be either a blockbuster hit that put Kevin Costner's career back on track or one of the biggest financial disasters ever in the film world, was mostly shot at a huge floating sci-fi set at Kawaihae Harbor. Of the film's estimated $175 million cost, $25 million was spent on lodging and other expenses on the Big Island.

The *Pu'ukohola Heiau* at Kawaihae just above *Spencer's Beach* is the last major heiau constructed in Hawaii. The heiau has become a focal point for the Hawaiian sovereignty movement, and on some Hawaiian holidays Hawaiians in ancient dress mount the summit of the temple to reenact ceremonies of the Hawaiian religion.

NORTH KOHALA

The green rolling hills, country roads, refreshing trade winds, historical Hawaiian heritage, and laid-back lifestyle of North Kohala make this district one of the most picturesque on the island. Rural North Kohala is also a place back in time. Very little changes here, and what change occurs happens slowly.

Start early for North Kohala. It is a daytime place, an isolated rural area where you aren't always sure you'll find an open gas station or restaurant.

There are two ways to approach *Hawi*, the sleepy main town of North Kohala. Head north from Kona along the coast and turn left just before Kawaihae, where Highway 19 ends at a stop sign. The second choice is to turn right here, drive mauka towards Waimea and turn at Waiakea onto Highway 270, the Akoni Pule Highway, which heads up into the *Kohala Mountains* and over to Hawi.

The drive along the *Kawaihae Coast* passes mostly arid brush land and the white-capped blue Pacific with a perfect view of *Haleakala* on Maui, and on really clear days even East Maui. During the humpback whale mating season, from late fall to midspring, you're likely to see the huge mammals leaping and spouting fairly close to shore. The one highly recommended stop here for a picnic, a look at ancient Hawaiian life, or a bit of snorkeling is the *Lapakahi State Historical Park* and the adjacent state underwater park. The two parks are at one site; gates open at about 8 a.m. and close at 4 p.m. sharp, daily, except holidays. Lapakahi is a 600-year-old Hawaiian fishing village that was abandoned in the last century when its freshwater springs went dry. Over 20 stops along a one-mile, well-marked trail through the village will show you how the ancient Hawaiians lived and worked. Just offshore of the village is an excellent snorkeling spot with protected reefs and a marine life sanctuary.

A few miles before Hawi, the landscape suddenly turns green as you enter the heart of North Kohala. The turnoff for *Upolu Point Airfield*, a short runway used by private planes, will take you to a dirt road that runs along an isolated stretch of coastline to the archaeological sites at the *Mo'okini Heiau* and *King*

Kamehameha's Birthplace. Built in the fifth-century A.D., Moʻokini stands as a silent memorial to the ways of ancient Hawaii, and is believed to be the oldest existing heiau in Hawaii. Up to the 1800s, Moʻokini was the site of human sacrifices and is maintained by a family who traces their lineage to the kahunas, or high priests, who oversaw the temple from its inception. On the right side of the heiau as you enter the grounds is a large vertical stone with a human head-sized indentation in it where sacrifice victims are said to have placed their heads as they were tied to the rock. They were dispatched quickly by a heavy blow from a club that smashed the skull.

The atmosphere amidst the high rock walls of Moʻokini, with its undulating terrain and isolated, windswept location is spiritually-charged, reminiscent of the mystical air surrounding England's Stonehenge, set apart on the equally remote Salisbury Plain.

Back on Highway 270, continue on into Hawi, the capitol of North Kohala. Hawi's main street is a funky collection of local mom & pop stores, a good coffee house at *Kohala Coffee Mill*, the interesting *Bamboo Restaurant*, which combines a 1940s Hawaii decor with reasonably priced Pacific Rim and Thai food, a New York-style neighborhood bar and pizza parlor at *Ohana Pizza*, a health food store, galleries, and boutiques. The flavor of Hawi is representative of North Kohala's population of native Hawaiians, third and fourth generation descendants of the sugar cane workers who labored at the now-gone Kohala Plantation, and a core population of counter culture types still living out the dreams of the '60s tucked away in the hills of Kohala, plus a growing number of retired mainlanders with a taste for rural Hawaiian life. Try to visit Hawi during the day; like rural Hana, Maui, the sidewalks roll up here early and the action happens before sundown.

The statue of King Kamehameha at *Kalahikiola Church* in *Kapaʻau*, a few miles east of Hawi, is the predecessor to the famous golden Kamehameha statute in Honolulu across from Iolani Palace. The Kapaʻau Kamehameha sank with the ship carrying it off the Falkland Islands in 1880 on its way to Hawaii. Created by Boston sculptor, T.R. Gould, from Russian artist Louis

Choris' life drawings of Kamehameha made at Kona in 1817, the statue was later salvaged and spotted at auction by a passing sea captain who brought it to the Big Island.

Highway 270 ends at the *Pololu Valley Lookout* and turnaround. Pololu is the northernmost along the stretch of steep coastal valleys that begins at Waipio to the south. The valleys are similar to Kauai's famed Na Pali Coast, but much less visited. A trail drops down into Pololu, where Hawaiian fishing villages and taro fields once flourished. The two-hour hike is an excellent opportunity to see one of Hawaii's majestic coastal valleys without boarding a sightseeing helicopter or riding aboard a tour boat.

Route 250, the 20-mile-long back road between Hawi and Waimea, is a country road which climbs to the summit of the Kohala Mountains and winds through green grazing lands along the leeward side of the Kohala mountains. One of most picturesque roads on the island, with expansive vistas ranging from the often snow-peaked top of Mauna Kea down to the wide Pacific, this refreshing drive will take you past horse ranches, high-tech windmills, gated estates, and even a field of llamas. *Chalon International's Kohala Trailriding in Hawi* (889-6257) and *Paniolo Riding Adventures* (889-5354) offer guided horseback tours in this area.

Hilo

Hilo is a sleepy South Pacific-like town of 45,000 that suffers from a reputation as the rainiest city in Hawaii. Downtown Hilo, where the county seat of the Big Island is located, is reminiscent of pre-WW II Hawaii with dozens of wood-frame and stucco buildings containing mom & pop stores and a wide variety of shops, all tied together by a relaxing way of life rapidly disappearing from Hawaii. Country folk from Puna and Hamakua come in to Hilo to shop, and Saturday matinees for kids are still a way of life. Many of the buildings are restored, and a self-guided walking tour brochure of the more prominent historic buildings is available from *Destination Hilo* (1-800-HILO-DAY).

Close enough to Hawaii Volcanoes National Park to be a base

for exploring the park, Hilo is a good place to stop over for a night on a round-the-island jaunt. We occasionally drive over from Kona for a taste of a different climate, some shopping at *Prince Kuhio Mall*, the only major shopping mall on the island, and to do some Hawaiian antique hunting in little shops like the *Mid Pacific Store* across from *Lyman House Memorial Museum*.

Though two major tidal waves swept through Hilo in mid-century, most of the historic sights in town are intact. The Lyman Museum is worth a visit. On the grounds are a well-preserved New England missionary family's home, and a modern two-story museum focused on Hawaii's natural history, and the story of the Hawaiians and Hawaii's immigrant peoples. The *Naha Stone*, located in front of the Hilo public library, was said to have been lifted by Kamehameha when he was a boy to prove his worth as an ali'i or ruler, in a story reminiscent of King Arthur's pulling the sword from the stone. The waterfront area along the bay is also worthy of a stroll.

Dining in Hilo has improved greatly over the past decade. Joining the many local-style restaurants are trendy eateries like *Lehua's Bay City Bar & Grill* featuring California-style fare, and *Roussel's* with its Cajun-style local seafood. *Nihon*, a Japanese restaurant overlooking Hilo Bay and the *Lili'uokalani Gardens*, serves credible meals in a peaceful setting. The Hawaiian dishes and crowd at *Kimo's Ono Hawaiian Food* will give you a taste of Hawaiian ways. We like hanging out at the hip *Jasper's Cafe*, 110 Kalakaua, not only for the inexpensive, hearty, healthy, home-cooked food, and the good coffee and espresso, but also to watch the interesting clientele, and to sit in on the poetry readings.

If you get up early enough, the daily fish auction at *Suisan Market* at 85 Lihiwai on Hilo Bay, beginning at around 7 a.m., is a window into the world of local commercial fishing. Glimmering mahi mahi, big yellow fin tuna, squid, and a variety of tropical fish are set out for sale. The auction is conducted in rapid pidgin with competitive bidding by buyers from local restaurants and markets. This is the only open fish market left in Hawaii.

Hilo abounds in local delicacies, commonly known in Hawaii

as *omiyage*, the Japanese word for gift. Anyone from Hawaii traveling from island to island feels gently obliged to bring omiyage home. Omiyage takes the form of beef jerky, macadamia nut products, taro chips, stone cookies from *Mountain View Bakery*, special pies, and other goodies you'll see prominently displayed in shops.

If you are interested in Hawaiiana, Hilo is a good place to browse in bookstores and Hawaiian shops. *Basically Books* on Waianuenue Avenue has a well-selected collection of Hawaiian books and maps, plus a shelf of rare, used Hawaiiana. The Lyman Museum's bookstore offers a thorough selection of Hawaiiana plus some unique koa wood gift items.

Especially if you are traveling with children, the *Panaewa Rainforest Zoo*, about three miles outside of town on Mamalahoa Highway on the way to the volcanoes, is an interesting stop. Hawaiian nene geese, Hawaiian hawks, owls, and other rare Hawaiian birds join water buffaloes, wild pigs, monkeys, a tiger, a pygmy hippo, an anteater, Axis deer, and other rainforest dwellers from around the world at this small, but interesting and beautifully landscaped zoo. Admission is free.

Hilo's biggest event of the year is the *Merrie Monarch Festival* beginning Easter Sunday. This is the most prestigious hula competition in all Hawaii, and hula troupes practice throughout the year to create unique dances for this grand event. Held in honor of King David Kalakaua, a Hawaiian monarch credited with reviving the hula in the 1870s, the festival is also a coming together of the Hawaiian people in an attempt to restore their culture. Tickets are hard to get and Hilo's hotels are sold out during the Merrie Monarch, so make reservations for hotel rooms well in advance.

Heading south from Honoka'a past miles of cane fields and a seemingly endless series of long curves past deep valleys, the tiny coastal towns of *Papa'ikou*, *Kawainui* and *Pepe'ekeo* zip by. The main attractions along the coast, however, are waterfalls. Watch for the turnoff for Route 220 to *Akaka Falls*. Keep going on the road, it's a bit of a drive mauka. Stop at Honomu on the way for refreshments and browsing at the *Akaka Falls Flea Market*. Once parked at Akaka Falls an easy hike along a loop trail takes you past two falls: Kahuna Falls and Akaka Falls. Akaka is spectacular with a 420 foot drop that mists up before it hits the pool below. The trail winds through towering bamboo, vermilion torch ginger shooting up over 15 feet, fragrant white and yellow ginger, splashes of bright impatiens, and a very lush overgrowth of tropical foliage.

Another exquisitely beautiful place is the *Hawaii Tropical Botanical Garden* (964-5233) on *Onomea Bay*, seven miles north of Hilo. Coming from Kona, follow Route 19 past Waimea towards Hilo, past the towns of Honakaa, Hakalau, and Honomu. Five miles past Honomu watch for a blue sign on the right that reads: "Scenic Route 4 Miles Long." This is the north end of the scenic route, which emerges back onto Route 19 just past the pink Pepeekeo Post Office building. The old yellow church which serves as the botanical garden's office is on the southern side of the scenic route, which in itself is well worth the detour.

The 17-acre botanical garden, featuring 1,800 species of plants, is located in the valley adjacent to Onomea Bay within a tropical rainforest with waterfalls, streams, and rugged ocean coast. You'll see a great variety of local plants and flowers together with a selection of tropical plants from around the world. These include many species of palms, bromeliads, gingers, heliconias, exotic ornamentals, medicinal plants, and rare and endangered species. Wildlife includes African bessor flamingos, South American macaws, Hawaiian shore birds, and giant sea turtles. The overall feeling is one of peaceful awe, inspired both by the beauty of the natural setting as well as by the care and taste of the people responsible for the plantings.

Admission to the garden is $12 for adults, with children under 16 admitted free. The kama'aina rate for local residents is $8. If you don't want to spend the money (even though it's well worth it) or are pressed for time, there is a breathtaking view of the gardens and Onomea Bay from the scenic route, about a mile north of the garden offices.

Around the Island Drive

Driving the Big Island is a top attraction for people from other islands and visitors from the mainland. Unlike the rest of the main Hawaiian Islands, which are so much smaller, you can drive for hours on the Big Island without going in circles. City-bound Honolulu drivers love to escape to the Big Island, rent a car and take off.

Big Island drivers are generally courteous, but it's advisable to drive defensively especially along the long stretches of highway where both visitors and locals speed along well over the speed limit of 55. The dry weather and long road stretches of West Hawaii makes it one of the best places in all Hawaii to cruise on a motorcycle. There are no helmet laws and new Harleys are available for rent.

If you are interested in sightseeing, look for the red and yellow Hawaii Visitor Bureau Hawaiian Warrior road markers. Most historical sites and visitor attractions are pointed out by the roadside markers.

From Kona, the most popular ride is a circle-island trip of about 225 miles, with a one-night stopover in either Hilo or Hawaii Volcano National Park. Heading north to Waimea, the first stop on the way to Hilo, there are two routes – along Highway 19, the coast road past Waikoloa, or up mauka along the Hawaii Belt Road. Without stops this is about an hour drive from Kailua-Kona. You'll pass the luxury resorts along the Kohala Coast, then turn north just before Kawaihae for a short drive up to Kamuela. On the Hawaii Belt Road the drive goes through long stretches of ranch land and offers an up-close look at sometimes snow-capped Mauna Kea.

Puna Drive

Puna is a coastal district south of Hilo worth a side trip if you are staying a while at Volcano or in Hilo. Puna is well-known in Hawaii for the destruction of homes there by lava flows and real estate is affordable because of the risk of future flows. The tradewinds blow comfortably across Puna and the area is known for its orchid growers. Highways with quaint, old Hawaii shops and sleepy villages begin at the little town of Kea'au. Turn off Highway 11 onto Highway 130 for a scenic drive along rugged coastlines and through rural areas lush with tropical fruits and flowers. At Pahoa, Highway 130 continues south to Kalapana and Highway 132 heads north to Kapoho. A series of picturesque beaches, some with black sand, line the coast. The road at Kalapana was cut off by a lava flow in 1983 which also buried the famous Kalapana Black Sand Beach.

The "New Tourism"

Mark Twain, Robert Louis Stevenson, Isabella Bird and other nineteenth-century visitors to Kona came to experience the Hawaiian culture, explore the unique environment, and to travel as the locals did, riding horseback on mountain trails or cruising the coast in inter-island steamers. With no grand hotels, rental car companies, or fine restaurants in place, these writers relied on the hospitality and warm aloha of Kona's Hawaiians to meet their needs, and the resulting experiences were recorded as high points in their travel journals.

The latest travel trend of the 1990s is a return to what Mark Twain and others found delightful in visiting Hawaii. Troupes of local hula halaus performing culturally authentic dances are replacing the schmaltzy, Waikiki Polynesian shows; experts in Hawaiian history and culture are lecturing to enthralled visitors; hotels are replanting with indigenous flora and adding native Hawaiian foods like taro to their menus; hikes along ancient Hawaiian trails and horseback rides through native forests are being offered as alternatives to resort golf and tennis and other non-Hawaiian activities that can be enjoyed at resorts anywhere. Perhaps most importantly, hotels are beginning to train their employees in Hawaiian culture and ways of hospitality to enhance the visitor's experience and to build the self-esteem of the workers through honoring their native cultures.

In part, this trend is tied to the rebirth of the Hawaiian culture which began in the 1970s, when after decades of neglect the hula, non-commercial Hawaiian music, the Hawaiian language, and native arts became once again focuses of mainstream life in Hawaii. More recently, the Hawaiian sovereignty movement – a political and social movement among native Hawaiians to reclaim their lands and culture – has added new dimensions to this trend.

Hopefully, combing tourism with authentic Hawaiian experiences won't degrade the reemerging culture or overrun off-the-beaten-track "special places" of local people.

Hawaii Forest & Trail (329-1993): A Kona-based company that sends you in a van to the jumping-off point for hiking excursions with an experienced naturalist to remote wilderness locations. The focus is on Hawaii's indigenous birds, plants, animals, geology, and climate. Locations vary from rainforests to mountainsides to valleys and deserts. Walks are moderate and children are welcome.

Ke Aloha Na Kupuna "The Love of our Grandparents": *Kupunas* (Hawaiian grandparents) gather every Tuesday and Friday from 10 a.m. to 2 p.m. in the lobby of King Kamehameha's Kona Beach Hotel to perform Hawaiian music and hula, talk story, and sell their arts and crafts. A talk on various Hawaiiana subjects is offered the first week of each month by well-known local experts; check with the hotel for dates and subjects. A tour of historical exhibits focusing on King Kamehameha, who lived at Kamakahonu where the hotel's luau grounds are today, and ancient Hawaiian culture, are given each weekday at 1 p.m. Both events are free.

The environment of the Big Island of Hawaii is one of the most diverse in the world. There are deserts, high mountain peaks, tropical shorelines, volcanoes, rainforests and more – all within a reasonable driving time of each other. To open up these different worlds up visitors, Dr. Hugh Montgomery, a psychologist who lives in the invigorating foothills environment of Waimea, has created an eco-tourism company called *Hawaiian Walkways (885-7759).* He offers a variety of hikes throughout the year. The hikes range from half-day to full-day.

Activities

Not surprisingly, the best activities in Kona have to do with the sand, sun and surf. Tourist guide books are filled with ads for these attractions, and we have certainly not experienced even a quarter of them. Those listed below are the ones with which we are familiar, and where we and others we know have had a good time. It's not an exhaustive list, by any means, and we encourage you to investigate other activities not mentioned here.

Fair Wind Cruise: If you take the four-hour morning voyage of the Fair Wind trimaran from Keauhou Bay (by the Kona Surf Resort at the end of Ali'i Drive) to Kealakekua Bay, your sailboat will anchor near the Captain Cook monument, where you'll find the best snorkeling in Kona. The trimaran is big enough to have what you want, and small enough not to be crowded.

The new Fair Wind II sails seven mornings a week, departing at 9 a.m. and returning at 1:30 p.m. The cost is $59 for adults and $33 for children 12 and under, and includes a barbecue cheeseburger lunch, and snorkeling gear.

Afternoon cruises are now offered seven days a week from 2 p.m. to 5:30 p.m. Prices are $38 for adults and $25 for children. S.c.u.b.a. (and snuba) instruction and equipment are available for an additional charge. A separate three-hour cruise departs the Keauhou small boat harbor at 1:45 p.m. on Sunday, Monday, Wednesday, and Friday afternoons. Although lunch is not included, a light snack is served (322-2788).

Captain Cook Cruises: The Capt. Cook VI is a comfortable 73-foot motor vessel that offers a choice of two different cruises. The four-hour day cruise takes you to Kealakekua Bay for snorkeling or s.c.u.b.a. diving, and an onboard barbecue, while the two-hour evening cruise takes you to Keauhou Bay to view the underwater antics of manta rays through the glass viewing portals in the boat's hull, while you enjoy mai tais, pupus, and light entertainment.

The day cruise operates seven days a week, while the manta

ray cruise is available Friday evenings only. The cost of the day cruise is $54 for adults and $27 for children, which includes lunch, snorkeling gear, and light entertainment. For an additional $65, they'll teach you how to s.c.u.b.a. dive and send you out with a certified instructor. The mai tai/manta ray cruise costs $30 for adults and $20 for children, and departs the Kailua pier at 6:30 p.m. Reservations for either cruise should be made at least one day in advance (326-2999).

Captain Bob's Glassbottom Boat: Snorkeling is, of course, the best way to view the undersea world, but for those who don't want to get wet, Captain Bob's is the next best choice. Bob Chapman has been skippering his glassbottom boat in Kona Bay for the past 25 years, and has been feeding the reef fish for so long, they start congregating en mass the moment they hear the sound of his engine. The price of the cruise is one of the best bargains in Kona, at $14.95 for adults, and $7.50 for children. You'll see plenty of fish, and various types of coral, and since the boat never leaves the protected waters of the bay, the trip is almost always smooth. One-hour tours are scheduled at 10 a.m., 11:30 a.m., 1:30 p.m., and 3 p.m., every day, except Saturday and Monday. The boat leaves from Kailua Pier, and you can just show up there (reservations aren't necessary) or call Captain Bob at 987-8588 (days) or 322-3102 (evenings).

Rava Kai: If you're looking for something other than the typical tourist experience, you might consider sailing with Skipper Doug Rideout on his 48-foot motorsailor, the Rava Kai. Doug is an easy-going Californian who has been sailing for 30 years, made numerous ocean crossings, and has at one time or another skippered most of the commercial boats you see in Kailua Bay. His ketch is equipped with a pilot house and overnight accommodations for six passengers. Doug is happy to take you out for a day, a month, or as long as you'd like, and to show you the Kona coast, or his favorite unspoiled islands in the far reaches of the South Pacific. His boat is rigged for deep sea fishing and whale watching, as well as for long distance cruising. Contact Rava Kai at P.O. Box 5444, Kailua-Kona, HI 96745. Rates are negotiable.

Atlantis Submarines: For $79 (adults), and $39 (children)

you get a one-hour tour, 120-150 feet beneath the surface of Kailua Bay in a high-tech sub. Tours depart Kailua Pier every hour, Monday through Friday, from 9 a.m. to 3 p.m. Children must be at least three feet tall for safety reasons, and reservations are required (329-6626).

Boats: Water craft range from outrigger canoes, kayaks, and rubber "zodiacs" to state-of-the-art marlin rigs and luxury yachts. Many companies run s.c.u.b.a., snorkeling, and sightseeing tours out of Anaeho'omalu Bay, Kealakekua Bay, Keauhou Bay, Kailua Bay, or Honokohau Harbor. Besides those listed in the s.c.u.b.a. section below, we recommend *Captain Zodiac* (329-3199), *Kona Aggressor* (329-8182), *Body Glove* (326-7122), *Ocean Sports Waikoloa* (885-5555), and *Red Sail Sports* at the Ritz Carlton (885-2000). If you want to rent a kayak or a foot-propelled paddle boat, check out the beach concession at the King Kam hotel. If you want to skipper your own 16-foot dive boat, *Hawaiiana Boat Rentals* at Keauhou Bay (322-8006) will let you take the Green Flash for $240 per day, which includes gas and fishing gear. For a complete list, look in the yellow pages under "Boats."

Whale Watching: Humpback whales, which spend the summer and fall feeding in Alaskan waters, travel to Hawaii in the winter months to mate and bear their young. Their presence here peaks from December through March, though they begin arriving around Thanksgiving and remain in smaller numbers until May.

Six other species of whales live in Hawaiian waters all year long and can be observed at any time. These include the pygmy killer whales and Hawaiian melon-headed whales, which are six to eight feet in length and often congregate in groups of from 200 to 400 individuals, the false killer whales, beaked whales, pilot whales which are 15 to 18 feet long and swim in pods of up to 40 or more animals, and sperm whales which grow 50 to 60 feet long and are also found in large pods. Pilot whales are the most commonly seen. Dolphins, cousins to the whales, are also frequently observed.

It is against federal law to approach too closely to whales, or to harass them in any way. It can also be dangerous, as they are wild animals possessing large mouths full of sharp teeth. Humpbacks, of course, don't have teeth, as they strain the tiny organisms they eat through baleen plates, but most of the other whales found in Hawaii are of the toothed variety. An underwater photographer was recently fined $10,000 in federal court for getting too close to a group of pilot whales off the Kona coast. His assistant experienced an equally unpleasant ordeal. She was bitten on the thigh by one of the whales which held her forty feet underwater before bringing her back to the surface and releasing her.

Whales can often be seen from shore, up and down the coast, and for a closer look there are a number of whale watching cruises. *Captain Dan McSweeney* (322-0028), considered the guru of whale watching because he's a marine biologist who has been studying whales off the Kona coast for 20 years, is happy to share his expertise with the public. Because he is so familiar with the big mammals and knows where they are likely to be found, he says his customers have a 90 to 95 percent chance of sighting whales, any time of year.

Tours: There are many types of tours – van, bus, limousine, helicopter, plane, submarine, boat, walking, hiking, hunting, bicycling, and many others. It is possible to organize a custom tour through almost any of the tour companies, and it's a lot more fun when you are on a bus with friends. Most visitors we know prefer to rent cars and make up their own tour.

Helicopter tours are a fast way to see the island, but expensive. To give just one example, a two-hour, deluxe tour from *Mauna Kea Helicopters* in Waimea (885-6400, or 800/400-HELI) which takes you over a large part of the island including coastal valleys, rainforests, waterfalls, and active areas of the volcano, will cost you $235 per seat, while their 45-minute excursion to only the volcano runs $125. There are several helicopter companies to choose from, and their prices do vary, so it's a good idea to shop around. Ask about specials, which during the off-season can run as low as $79. For a complete listing, look under "Helicopter" in the yellow pages.

If you're considering an organized bus tour of the island, you might want to consult with a large tour company we have used,

Jack's Tours in Kailua-Kona (329-2555). Other tour companies are listed under "Tours" in the yellow pages.

Holidays: There are a few uniquely Hawaiian holidays which are occasion for celebrations and parades: Prince Kuhio Day (March, during Spring Break), Lei Day (May 1), Kamehameha Day (June 11), Admissions Day (August 21), and Aloha Week (late September).

Activities for children: Kids in Kona love to snorkel when it's calm and ride their boogie boards when the waves are up, or simply splash in the water or play on the sand. The two safest beaches for children on the island are the beach in front of the King Kamehameha Kona Beach Hotel in Kailua, and Spencer Park in Kawaihae. When the water is calm, Hapuna Beach State Park near the Mauna Kea Beach Hotel, and Anaeho'omalu Beach, next to the Royal Waikoloa Hotel, (both in South Kohala) are great places to take the kids, but it's best to keep them out of the water when the surf is breaking, as the waves can be dangerous.

Always use sunscreen, as it takes only an hour or two of strong tropical rays to cause a painful sunburn.

Exploring tide pools is another activity kids love, and most grocery stores and drugstores carry small, inexpensive dip nets that are perfect for capturing minnows and other marine organisms. Don't forget a bucket. *Long's Drugs*, and other stores, carry special reef-walking footwear in childrens' sizes, and it's a good idea to get these for your little ones as most of the beaches on the Big Island are not sandy, and lurking unseen underwater are all sorts of sharp corals and spiny sea urchins that can cause painful wounds. Sneakers work fine, too.

Another favorite of kids is spending a few hours at the *Hilton Waikoloa Village*, riding the Disneyland-like trains and canal boats, and watching the tame dolphins do tricks in their large, natural-looking enclosure. You don't need to be a guest of the hotel to enjoy these free amenities, as the management welcomes the public.

Sports

The internationally televised *Ironman Triathlon* is Kona's most famous professional sporting event. The town virtually stands still on race day with many stores closing and hundreds of local volunteers working at aid stations along the route. Some call the 17 hour-long race "Kona's Super Bowl."

Don't plan on doing much in Kona the day of the race, for Ali'i Drive and most major streets are blocked off by police barricades, and the rest are choked with traffic. If you are in town for the Ironman you can join in the excitement by volunteering to help out at one of the many aid stations, handing out water, Gatorade, and wet sponges (call 329-0063).

The 4,000 volunteers are given an official race t-shirt and tickets to a volunteer party, held at the King Kamehameha Hotel a week or so after the race, where prizes are given away, a hefty buffet is served, and ice chests overflow with all the Gatorade you'd ever want to drink.

Held in mid-October, the Ironman draws over fifteen hundred of the top triathletes in the world. Everything begins just after dawn on Saturday when a human wave of swim-capped competitors plunges into Kailua Bay, in front of the King Kamehameha Hotel. They swim two-and-a-half-miles out around a buoy and back, then jump on their high-tech racing bikes and head for Hawi in faraway North Kohala. One hundred and ten miles later, the triathletes arrive at the Kona Surf in Keauhou, throw on their running shoes, and cap the day off with a marathon foot race (26+ miles) to Keahole Airport and back through Kona to the jam-packed finish line at the King Kam, where they're greeted with flower leis, cheering crowds, flaming tiki torches, blaring music, and a massive party.

Local radio and television stations run live coverage throughout the race, adding to its all-encompassing effect, while national network television films the event for airing a few months later.

The early-morning start and the finish around 4 p.m. are the Ironman's most exciting moments. It's really something to watch these superbly conditioned athletes push their bodies to the limit as they strive to set new course records in one of the most grueling athletic events in the world. Though most are no doubt driven primarily by the keen thrill of competition, they also probably can't help but think about the more than $20,000 in prize money, plus a wealth of endorsement opportunities.

Perhaps the most inspiring scenes in the race come during the late-night finishes of the stragglers. Triathletes as old as 76 compete, but must cross the finish line by midnight to be considered official finishers. The partying crowds cheer them to the end, psyching up completely exhausted racers, some of whom literally drag themselves across the finish supported by family and friends. Seeing a 60-year-old nun finish after 15 hours on the course makes you wonder how she did it, or why you can't!

The Ironman got its start on the island of Oahu when Navy Commander John Collins and some of his buddies began wondering what it would be like to combine three of Oahu's major races – the Waikiki Rough Water Swim, the Around Oahu Bike Race, and the Honolulu Marathon – into one mega endurance contest. They held the first Ironman Triathlon on Oahu in 1978. Fifteen men entered, and twelve finished. In 1981, the Ironman moved to the Big Island to escape Oahu's highly congested traffic conditions, and it's been going strong here ever since.

Other triathlon and running events: The *Keauhou-Kona Triathlon* is held in late May. Limited to 500 triathletes, the race is based at the Keauhou Beach Hotel and draws competitors from Oahu and other Hawaiian Islands, Japan, and the mainland. Call 329-2692, or write to P. O. Box 2153, Kailua-Kona 96745 for an entry form.

Local events are held year-round, as Kona is very much a town of joggers, and many triathletes reside here because of the Ironman. Look in the newspaper or contact one of the following shops for race dates.

B&L Bike & Sports (329-3309), located at 74-5576B Pawai Place in Kona's Old Industrial Area, offers a good selection of race clothing, equipment, and qualified repair service. *Dave's Bike & Triathlon Shop* (329-4522), across from Hulihe'e Palace on Ali'i Drive in Kona, rents equipment, sells triathlon clothing, and provides repair services. *Action Sports Hawaii* (329-1861), in Kopiko Plaza just below Longs Drugs, carries a large selection of premium running shoes, as well as running clothes and gear.

Kona is a sports-conscious place, and there are both amateur and professional events almost every week. Visitors can usually find a tennis or golf tournament they can enter, while such sports as canoe races and polo matches can be enjoyed from the sidelines. The Konawaena Wildcats are the local high school team, and football games are real community events.

Basketball: The local pickup court is "The Ghetto" on Kuakini Highway next to Ali'i Sunset Plaza. It is lighted for night play, and is often crowded. Other outdoor courts are located at the Old Airport park. One of Kona's best kept secrets is its new county gym (on Kuakini just past West Hawaii Motors near the Old Airport). The gym is open to the public, yet often deserted during the day (when school is in session) so you can have the court all to yourself. Hours for free play are from 2 p.m. to 6 p.m. Monday through Thursday, and from 8 a.m. to 4:30 p.m. on Fridays. When the kids are out for summer vacation, though, the gym can get crowded. The gym parking lot is also the premiere rollerblading spot in Kailua-Kona.

Bicycling: Each year careless motorists injure several triathletes training on their bikes; Nick Rott, a much-loved member of the triathlon community, and several other local cyclists have been killed during the last few years. The most dangerous spot for cycling is along Queen Ka'ahumanu Highway between Kailua and the Keahole Airport. Still, many cyclists are willing to accept an element of risk as they ride the Ironman Triathlon course to Hawi, or head south to Kealakekua Bay. The shoulders along Ali'i Drive and Queen Ka'ahumanu Highway are wide enough to cycle on, but they're a far cry from bike lanes. They are unevenly paved, strewn with gravel, and pitted with pot holes. We've biked there ourselves, but with the rough surface and cars zinging past just inches away, it's not a very relaxing experience.

There's a much more fun way to bike the Big Island. *Mauna Kea Mountain Bikes* in Kamuela (885-2091) offers various off-road cycling tours of rainforests, beaches, and mountain areas for all levels of ability, and if you'd rather go exploring on your own, they'll rent you a bike and give you some pointers on where to go.

Paddling: Outrigger canoe racing is a uniquely Hawaiian sport, with roots going back thousands of years to the days when paddling was done more for purposes of transportation and warfare than for sport. The paddling season is a long one, kicking off in March and ending in October with a tough 40-mile race across the choppy channel between the islands of Molokai and Oahu.

Local paddlers of all ages take paddling very seriously and train hard. Paddling requires not only great physical stamina, but also tremendous precision, timing, and cooperation, as all six paddlers must dig their blades into the water in absolute unison. When paddling all out in an important race each member of the team feels an almost mystical union with the others.

There are canoe clubs at most coastal towns on the Big Island and races are held regularly throughout spring and summer, for all ages, from eight-year-olds to grandmothers. Kona's *Kai O Pua Canoe Club*, which keeps its canoes on the lawn fronting the King Kamehameha Hotel, is a perennial winner and, because of its traditional hospitality and aloha spirit, is a favorite with canoe clubs from other islands who come here to compete.

Hundreds of paddlers from all over the state and from as far away as California and Tahiti come to Kona over Labor Day weekend for the *Queen Lili'uokalani Race*, a two-day competition. At twilight the paddlers gather at the pier, light kerosene torches, then march in a torchlit parade through downtown Kailua to the beat of drums pounded in exotic rhythms by burly Tahitians.

Surfing: Surfing in Kona's clear blue waters with colorful reef fish zipping by underwater is a refreshing experience. Beware, though, for unlike the world-famous waves of Oahu, most surfing waves here tube over lava rock reefs rather than white sand or coral reef. Intermediate and advanced surfers will enjoy Kona's surf once they get the rock bottoms wired. Beginners are advised to stick to small wave days or travel north for bodyboarding at Hapuna Beach on the Kohala Coast.

Longboarders, shortboarders on potato-chip-thin rippers,

bodyboarders and wave skiers vie for waves in Kona. The challenge of surfing along the rocky coast has produced champion surfers and bodyboarders who compete in international competitions.

Waves break year-round at *Banyans* on Ali'i Drive by the Banyan condos and mini-mart, and at nearby *Lymans*, just south and across the bay. Lymans (it's named for a family estate overlooking the spot) is where Kamehameha the Great spent his teenage years in the late 1700s surfing the waves of Holualoa Bay. A mysterious, overgrown *heiau* (Hawaiian temple) looms along the coast, enhancing the ancient Hawaiian atmosphere in the water, and other stone ruins hidden by brush and weeds are a reminder of long ago days when the waves were ruled by the ali'i who claimed the best surf spots as their personal possessions and punished anyone foolish enough to intrude by smashing their skull with a club.

Kahalu'u Beach Park, four miles from town on Ali'i Drive, is another ancient and popular surf spot where Hawaiians once slapped the ocean with vines as they prayed for big surf. Avoid the rip moving north along the rocks.

White Sands Beach Park, north of Kahalu'u on Ali'i Drive, is a small, pocket beach considered one of the hottest bodysurfing spots in all Hawaii, with ridable waves up to six feet in winter. White Sands Beach, also known as *Disappearing Sands*, or *Magic Sands*, often vanishes overnight, washed away by big waves. Those uninitiated in the art of bodysurfing larger waves should avoid White Sands when it is up, as it can be deceptively powerful and dangerous. Small days are a blast, but watch out for the rocks lurking just under the surface, especially on the north end of the beach.

Other surf spots dot the Big Island but are much more widespread than those on other Hawaiian islands, and more fickle due to wind conditions. To catch the best waves outside Kona it's vital to hook up with knowledgeable local surfers. Well-supplied surf shops are located in Kona, Waimea, and Hilo.

Windsurfing and Sailing: Anaeho'omalu Bay at Waikoloa is the best spot near Kona for sailboarding, and rental equipment and lessons are available from *Ocean Sports Waikoloa* (885-

5555). For the beginner, the calm morning wind and water conditions combined with the sheltered location make the area a fine place for learning. A typical morning consists of nice flat water and about a three-to-five knot onshore breeze. The wind tends to pick up in the afternoon. Seasonal conditions do vary enough to offer a little bit of everything for all levels of windsurfers. In the fall, lighter onshore winds tend to prevail, but moving into winter, Kona storms can bring southwesterlies ranging from 18 to 35 knots – definitely not for the beginner. In spring, trade winds begin to dominate, and during April and May the trades can really let go and rip. It's not uncommon for days on end to see the winds pick up to 20 or 30 knots. When the trades are blowing, sailing is advised for the advanced shortboard sailor only. With the winds blowing offshore, the sailing can be extremely dangerous and tricky. Local concessions don't rent equipment when the trade winds blow, so if you're planning a visit during this time of year, you'll need your own board and rig. Sometimes in spring the wind and waves come together just right when the last of the winter swells combine with either offshore or cross-shore trade winds. When this happens, the best wave sailing (and a bunch of happy local windsurfers) can be found on the south point of the bay.

Summertime usually brings with it a combination of light onshore breezes and thermal wraps from summer trade winds, calling for slalom boards and large cambered sails. During the heat of the day, the trades can wrap to an onshore wind that blows 12 to 18 knots.

Because Kona is in the lee of Mauna Loa and Mount Hualalai, the howling trade winds which provide world-class windsurfing at Maui's Ho'okipa are blocked. However, on northwind days excellent windsurfing and sailing conditions can happen along the Kona Coast. If you are adventurous, hire a four-wheel-drive vehicle and drive north or south to coastal areas exposed to trade winds and look for good launching sites. Local windsurfers rave about secret spots they've discovered.

Some insist the Big Island's best windsurfing is found at *Ka'alu'alu*, a long drive from either Kona or Hilo on the island's southeast shore near South Point. It's for experienced sailors only, with water starts a necessity, and is at its best when summer trade winds blow. It's never crowded. Head south from Kona on Highway 11, turn right on South Point Road for four miles, then turn off on Kipuka Maheo Road. This is a long drive, but worth it as the wind is usually up and conditions are generally good. You launch off flat, smooth lava rock to a small flat water bay; about 100 yards offshore is the surf. Other than summertime, when large south swells curl in from the South Pacific, the surf is generally small and fun. You can camp at Ka'alu'alu, but bring plenty of water and food and a first-aid kit to this wilderness location. If you make the trip you will be able to say you've windsurfed at the southernmost spot in the United States.

Always put safety first in windsurfing in Hawaii. Hawaiian waters can be treacherous for the uninitiated and for windsurfers accustomed to lake sailing. Once you are offshore in Hawaii you are in the middle of the ocean; strong currents and high winds can sweep you away from shore along uninhabited coastlines beyond swimming distance as you struggle to raise a mast. Veteran windsurfers use a buddy system. A windsurfing report airs on radio KAOI (95.1 FM) twice a day.

Those who prefer their sailing sitting down may charter Ralph Blancato's 50-foot *Maile* for a sunset sail (326-5174), or catch a twenty-dollar ride on the 65-foot *Lanakila* (987-3999), the prettiest catamaran in Kailua Bay.

Kayaking: Over the past decade paddling along isolated coastlines in hard shell plastic kayaks has become a popular activity in Hawaii. The kayaks are very transportable, inexpensive to rent or buy, fairly easy to handle, and if you are at all fit you can cover a lot of territory that is not easily accessible otherwise. Perhaps the most popular kayak trip near Kona is the paddle to the monument which marks the spot where Captain Cook was slain at Ka'awaloa Point in 1779. You launch from the old pier at Napo'opo'o and can either hug the coast or cut straight across Kealakekua Bay to the monument. We've paddled through pods of spinner dolphins and had a massive whale breech a few hundred feet away. Bring along flippers, mask and snorkle, sun screen, plus something to eat and drink. Once at the monument you will discover perhaps the best diving conditions in Hawaii.

The waters near the monument are protected and abound with dozens of species of colorful reef fish, as well as sea turtles and other marine life. The corals along the steeply shelving bottom are spectacular, too. You can either rent a kayak in Kona or arrange with one of the rental companies to meet you at the Napo'opo'o pier.

Kona Kai-Yaks (326-2922) offers around the island tours, day and overnight trips, plus introductory lessons. They charge $19.95 per day for single kayaks, and $49.95 a day for doubles.

Snorkeling: Although we've lived in Hawaii for over a dozen years, we haven't yet tired of putting on our swim mask, snorkel, and fins and slipping into that aquamarine wonderland that surrounds us. It is an entirely different world where fish flash colors brighter than neon and coral formations look like stone vegetables from outer space. There is so much to see and marvel at, you tend to forget all your worries and cares.

Even if you've never tried it before, snorkeling is easy to learn–you can master the basics in about five minutes. The great thing about snorkeling is that there are more fish in shallow water near shore than out where it's deep, so even if you aren't a strong swimmer you can enjoy this relaxing sport. (More than 400 species of fish can be found in shallow water in Hawaii). The best way to find out if snorkeling is something you want to try is to rent some gear (very inexpensive and available at dive shops and beach concessions everywhere) and experiment with it in shallow water where you can stand up if you start to get nervous. Once you've discovered what a snap it is and have built up a little confidence, you're ready for the many great snorkeling spots around the Big Island.

The best place to learn is *Kahalu'u Beach Park*, four miles south of Kailua on Ali'i Drive. The water is generally calm, as it is protected by a breakwater, and there is an alert lifeguard on duty most of the time. It's a good idea to wear the type of swim fins that enclose your entire foot, or some other sort of foot protection as there is little sand and the bottom tends to be littered with rough rocks and sharp fragments of coral. The water is very shallow, and you can stand up in most places. There are lots of fish and they are very tame, as they are used to being fed. The whole issue of feeding the fish is controversial, one opponent is Big Island marine biologist Bob Nishimoto.

"It's not healthy for the fish and I think it's totally wrong to do it. You're creating a zoo atmosphere even though you want to see things in their natural habitat. It's like going to Africa and hand feeding lions, then expecting them to be wild. It really upsets me when people treat the ocean like a big petting zoo," Nishimoto says.

Feeding fish can also be dangerous, he adds, as some have sharp teeth and a tendency to bite. He says a tourist on Maui recently had his ear bitten off by a moray eel he was hand feeding.

You can demonstrate your environmental good sense by not feeding the fish, and by not touching or standing on the coral, as it dies and turns white when it is handled too much.

Sea turtles are spotted regularly at Kahalu'u and they are so used to people they will not swim away, but will continue grazing placidly on seaweed as you watch. They are protected by federal law and it is a crime to approach too closely to them or to harass them in any way.

The only drawback to Kahalu'u is that it is very popular and generally quite crowded. Some days so many people are snorkeling it's almost as hectic as maneuvering through rush hour traffic. On such days there is so much suntan oil in the water it becomes cloudy.

It's generally less crowded at the tiny beach in downtown Kailua next to the pier, and there are plenty of fish, but no lifeguard.

When the ocean is calm, snorkeling is good at White Sands (Disappearing Sands, or Magic Sands), not far from Kahalu'u, on Ali'i Drive, and there is a lifeguard. But it can be dangerous when the waves are up.

Our favorite place to snorkel is Kealakekua Bay. There's an abundance of fish, crystal clear water, and a dramatic cliff that rises sheer above the bay and slopes steeply below the surface. This sloping shelf is adorned by many varieties of coral that look like exotic plants in a terraced garden. You need to be a strong swimmer if you attempt to snorkel here from shore, but if you're not in good shape, you can paddle out on a boogie board, surfboard, or kayak, or take one of the many snorkel cruises offered by a number of different boat companies. However you do it, always take a buddy along.

Other good snorkeling spots include *Kona Coast State Park*, two miles north of the airport, Honaunau Bay (City of Refuge), twenty miles south of Kona, Anaeho'omalu Bay, and Hapuna Bay.

For everything you ever wanted to know about snorkeling, (and then some) check out *Snorkel Bob's* (329-0770) next to Huggo's on Ali'i Drive.

S.C.U.B.A. diving: The waters off the Kona coast offer some of the best diving in the world. The most spectacular part of the marine environment is the array of beautifully colored reef fishes swimming almost everywhere. It's also quite a thrill to explore lava tubes and caves far beneath the surface, swim over convoluted canyons and abysses in the reefs, check out a shipwreck, or observe white-tipped reef sharks as they glide through the water with incredible power and grace. As most divers know, white tips won't hurt you, they're more afraid of you than you are of them and will flee the moment they catch sight of you. We've found that one of the best things about diving is the feeling of utter weightlessness it gives, as if you're floating in outer space. The undersea world is like an entirely different planet, much more peaceful than the one we know, and much quieter. Every time we go down there, we don't want to come back up, it's that beautiful, soothing, and exotic.

Although there are plenty of great shore dives (one of the best spots is at Honaunau Bay just north of the Place of Refuge), most visitors prefer to use one of the many dive boat services that are available. These offer classes for persons wanting to become certified divers, as well as courses in night diving, deep diving, cave and wreck diving, and other specialties. One exceptional night dive takes you to see manta rays attracted to the lights off the Kona Surf Resort. Swimming toward you through the water, mantas look like enormous black butterflies fluttering their wings in slow motion. Despite their large size and formidable appearance, they are harmless.

If you've always wanted to try s.c.u.b.a. but haven't yet had the opportunity, Kona is a great place to learn. The water is always fairly warm (averaging around 72 degrees) and very clear. Nearly everybody has anxious thoughts when they first contemplate taking the plunge, but once you're under there and you realize how reliable the equipment is and what a fantastic experience you're having, the fear quickly fades, and before you know it, you're hooked. And you don't have to worry about sharks. The only time we've ever seen them is when we went looking for them. They are generally territorial creatures with habitual hangouts. Dive operators know where their hangouts are, and avoid them unless requested to go there. Swimming with sharks is quite an experience. There's something infinitely fascinating about a creature that possesses the gracefulness of a ballerina, and the ability to bite your head off.

For equipment rentals, lessons, and charters, we recommend *Ecoscapes* (329-7116), *Kona Coast Divers* (329-8802), *Body Glove Cruises* (326-7122), and *Jack's Diving Locker* (329-7585). Many more dive companies can be found in the yellow pages under "s.c.u.b.a."

If you like your diving on the luxurious side, you might want to consider spending a week aboard the *Kona Aggressor II*. This 80-foot, powered catamaran is equipped with five staterooms, each of which has a private bath and hot shower. There's a hot tub on the sun deck, and even an onboard darkroom complete with photo experts who'll help you improve your underwater photography skills. The Kona Aggressor departs each Saturday evening from the Kailua pier and returns the following Friday. The cost per person is around $2,000 and includes four or five dives per day, and a night dive every night. Reservations need to be made well in advance, as the boat is frequently booked up (329-8182).

If you're not looking for luxury and want to go diving without spending a lot of money, there are a good number of close shore dives. One of the best guides to shore diving the Big Island's west side is *Let's Go Shore Dive'n' on the Kona Coast*, by Dick Dresie. Unfortunately, it's out of print, but you can find it at the local library, and since it doesn't have a lot of pages, it's worth photo-copying the whole thing. It describes 27 of the best Kona shore dives, detailing entry and exit points, what sort of terrain and sea life you're likely to encounter, and how to find each dive spot.

There is another Kona shore dive guide available, and although it is carried by most dive shops, it only includes seven dives. It is entitled (with tongue in cheek) *The Ultimate All Inclusive Shore Dive Guide to Hawaii* and was written by Greg Slingluff.

The *Kona Reefers Dive Club* meets every third Friday of the month and goes diving each Sunday following the meeting. Visitors are welcome to come along. For more info call Roy Damron at (325-5422), or Linda and Nick Caleo at (929-7653).

Hiking: There are a couple of good books on hiking the Big Island that you can pick up at a local bookstore or study at the public library. (To check books out of the library non-residents have to pay a fee of $25 to get a library card.) One of the books is *Hiking Hawaii: The Big Island*, by Robert Smith, and the other, more recently published, is *Hawaii Trails: Walks, Strolls, and Treks on the Big Island,* by Kathy Morey.

The most popular of Kona's few-and-far-between public trails runs 2.5 miles (and takes about two hours to hike) to Captain Cook's Monument at Kealakekua Bay. It's steep, strenuous, and dry, so wear good walking shoes and take plenty of water and snacks. Add a mask and snorkel to your day pack, so you can reward yourself with a swim after your sweaty descent; there are lots of fish, turtles, and eels, and the water is crystal clear.

To get there, drive 14 miles south from Kona on Route 11 to the town of Captain Cook and take the turnoff to Kealakekua Bay, then drive one-tenth mile (about 500 feet) to a jeep road on the right, which is the trail. It's a little hard to find, but don't give up, it's worth it. From the trailhead, the jeep road descends about 50 yards to where the road turns right into private property, and the trail goes left into tall grass. Go left, heading towards the coast, following a stone wall on the left. The trail can sometimes be overgrown and hard to see, but it opens up farther along. Once you reach the beach, follow the coast to the left for a few hundred feet to the monument. There are numerous caves along the walls of the cliff. If you choose to explore, don't disturb any finds. There was once a large native village here, and it is believed the area contains ancient burial sites.

On the Hilo side, we enjoy the easy stroll along paved pathways through a luxuriant rainforest to *Akaka Falls*. Not only are the falls spectacular, (there are two of them) but flowers bloom all along the way, rare Hawaiian birds chirp in the treetops, and a grove of enormous bamboo towers 50 feet over your head. If you visit in summer you will be treated to the heady aroma of white and yellow ginger in bloom.

The *Kona Hiking Club* organizes hikes the first Saturday and third Thursday of every month, and is always happy to have newcomers join in (328-8192 or 322-3094).

One of the most interesting places to hike is Hawaii Volcanoes National Park. There are many trails, of varying difficulty, and maps may be obtained from park headquarters.

Some of the best hiking on the Big Island is on privately-owned land that is not generally open to the public, but there is a way to get to see this unspoiled terrain; contact Rob Pacheco of *Hawaii Forest & Trail* (329-1993).

Horseback Riding: There are a number of stables offering trail rides through a variety of terrain, and your best bet is to look in the yellow pages under "Horseback Riding" to determine which outfit is right for you. *Kings' Trail Rides O' Kona Inc.* guides horseback tours down the trail to the Captain Cook Monument, and because the trail is steep and difficult, it is for experienced riders only. The views are spectacular. David "Bones" Inkster, operator of Kings, is a former coffee farmer and quite a character.

Fallbrook Trail Rides, ten minutes from Kailua, will mount you up on their well-mannered, youthful horses whether you're experienced or not, for a ride through a rainforest and a Hawaiian farm (329-0543).

Pu'u Haloa Trail Rides (885-8480) offers an "inner healing" tour that will restore your spirit as you ride through pastures and forests, and past rushing mountain streams and waterfalls in the Waimea area. Owners Jodi and Nanea are knowledgeable

Hawaiian paniolos who grew up in the area, on horseback.

There are polo matches at *Waiki'i Ranch*, the island hosts rodeos, and Kona has a chapter of the Arabian Society.

Shore Fishing: There are some exciting game fish you can hook from the shoreline, but you have to have the right equipment and know-how, and it's best to get some local advice on where to go. (OTEC is a favorite spot close to Kona.) We haven't been so lucky, but we've seen others hook into some real fighters, even right off the rocks in downtown Kailua. Some local favorites are *ulua*, *papio*, *wahanui*, and *omilu*, fast, streamlined predators which you can sometimes see chasing bait fish along the sea wall, though the bigger ones are usually out in deeper water. Sharks and barracudas are also caught, but they aren't such good fighters.

Basic shore fishing takes just a bamboo pole, some monofilament line, a tiny hook, and either squid or shrimp for bait. All can be purchased very inexpensively at grocery stores, or fishing stores. No license is necessary for salt water fishing in the state of Hawaii. Catches include a variety of reef fish, an occasional flounder, mullet, and even moray eels in the rocks.

Certain times of year, mostly in summer, huge schools of various species congregate along the pier and sea wall and every time you drop in your hook you can catch something, with a little practice. Most of these fish are very small, and are either used as bait, or eaten bones and all, as the bones get soft if the fish are fried very crisp. These include the *o'ama* (baby weke, or goat fish), *halalu* (baby akule, or mackerel) and *papio* (baby ulua, of the Crevalle, jack, or pompano family.)

Spear fishing and throw-net fishing are popular pastimes, as are catching freshwater prawns, and hand-grabbing "bugs" (spiny lobsters and slipper lobsters) from their hideouts in the reef.

Yama's Specialty (329-1712) can supply all your fishing needs, and their friendly employees, when not too busy, will be happy to give you a few pointers.

Deep sea fishing: The last time we went out after big fish, we hooked up two marlin (between 200 and 300 pounds) and both immediately leaped and twisted high in the air, shook their heads violently, instantly threw the hook, and disappeared back into the depths before we had a chance to say "Wow!"

Marlin is caught regularly from charter fishing boats. We've seen a couple weighed at the Kailua pier that topped 1,000 pounds. Although the major tournaments are held in summer, marlin are caught all year long in the waters off Kona.

Some skippers still leave from the pier, but to avoid congestion most launch out of *Honokohau Harbor*, the small boat harbor located between Kailua and the Keahole Airport. There's a big selection of charter boats to choose from, and it's really hard to know which one has the best chance of finding fish, since a lot depends on pure luck. It's a good idea to ask around town before making your choice (especially at the pier or harbor) as some charter captains have developed reputations as exceptionally skillful (and lucky) at finding and landing the big ones.

You can make reservations with any of the activities desks, with individual captains (listed in the yellow pages under "Boats-Charter"), by calling *The Fuel Dock* (329-7529, 800/648-7529) at Honokohau Harbor, or by contacting the *Kona Charter Skippers Association* (329-3600). Remember to bring sunscreen, ultra-violet proof sunglasses, a hat with a brim, and some sort of seasickness medication if you are prone to that malady.

Rates vary according to the size of the boat, how many people are in your party, and the experience and reputation of the captain and crew. For example, a 27-foot boat that can accommodate one or two fishermen will run $225 for a half day, and $325 for a full day. That's the price for the boat, whether it carries one or two passengers, so if you and a buddy want to go, you can split the cost. A thirty-foot boat that carries three passengers will run $275 for a half day, or $375 for a full day. Once again, that's the full price, and those in the fishing party can split the cost. A boat that carries four passengers will cost $300 for a half day and $400 for a full day, while a boat over 38 feet that can hold six will cost $360 for a half day, and $540 for a full day. (Those are prices for the boat, not per person.)

A few charters are willing to sell individual space on their boats, and that runs around $50 for a half day and $100 for a full day, per person.

Jackie Ferrier, a perennial tournament winner, and the person you're likely to speak to if you call the Kona Charter Skippers Association, warns that although you can find cheaper charters, boats that greatly undercut the competition usually do so because of inferior equipment or lack of ability.

"They don't care whether you catch fish or not, they just want your money," she says.

In our experience, your chances of catching a marlin, swordfish, ahi, mahimahi, or other gamefish are somewhere between 25 and 50 percent. Don't be surprised if the crew keeps your catch; this is a common practice that helps pay their expenses, though you may be given some choice fillets.

The International Billfish Tournament is Kona's most prestigious fishing event, drawing some of the world's top fishermen. August is a busy month for tournaments, with tournaments back-to back. Many marlin are tagged and released, which is becoming standard practice for smaller marlin in many tournaments. If you show up at the Kailua pier around 4 p.m. on a tournament day you may see a real monster hanging on the scale.

The *Pacific Gamefish Research Foundation* (329-6105), which promotes a marlin tag and release policy, works closely with the larger tournaments.

Golf

West Hawaii's dry, warm weather is perfect for golfing year-round. Dramatic backdrops ranging from snow-capped Mauna Kea and Mauna Loa to wide expanses of coastline fringing blue Pacific waters add to the experience at a variety of challenging, world-class courses. Most of the Big Island's courses are on the Kona side, with six others, mostly public, located on the windward side in Hilo and Hamakua, an area of much higher rainfall.

The problem of creating acres of greens and fairways atop fields of lava was solved by renowned golf course designer Robert Trent Jones, Sr. of Palo Alto, California, who devised an innovative underground watering system that allowed grass to flourish amidst the lava. The Big Island has abundant supplies of fresh underground water, which is tapped for about a million gallons a day for watering one 18-hole course. Soil for some courses was made by crushing lava rock and dredged coral with D-9 Caterpillars. Before golfers could play the Mauna Lani links, course designers pushed 750,000 cubic yards of lava rock aside, brought in 600,000 cubic yards of sandy loam for soil and installed a computerized network of 2,200 sprinkler heads.

Golf is a hot topic in Hawaii because so many courses have been built recently and many others are on the drawing boards. They are constantly the subject of political struggles with the Planning Commission because of environmental and other development related problems.

Resort courses offer discount rates for guests at adjoining hotels, and sometimes for locals with a Hawaii drivers license. Special three-night golf packages are put together by many resorts, and are a good deal if you're planning a resort stay. If you play a lot of golf, a local drivers license will save you hundreds of dollars (the state Department of Motor Vehicles, located at the Old Airport, will require you to surrender your mainland license when you apply). Play where the weather is best, because wind or rain can ruin your day. Weather varies from town to town on the Big Island, so at least one course should have good weather.

Besides the pro shops at the courses, there is a *Golf USA* discount store (329-2292) on Luhia Street in the Kona Industrial

Area, and the more upscale *Keauhou Golf & Racquet* (322-0020) at the Keauhou Shopping Village. Rentals at most courses are about $30 for clubs and $10 for shoes. For lessons, the most respected local teaching pro is Kenny Springer who operates his *Golf Swing Development Course* (322-3369) at Holua, right next to the Kona Country Club.

Kohala Coast

The top resort golf courses on the island are located within the Kohala Coast Resort area, an eight-mile stretch of coastline about 30 minutes north of Kailua-Kona. A variety of green fees and packages are offered. Golf carts are required and included in the green fees.

Mauna Kea Beach Golf Club (882-7222 or 800/882-6060). Designed by Robert Trent Jones, Sr., the Mauna Kea is the island's premiere course, not recommended for beginners. Though the Mauna Kea Beach Hotel is closing for renovations until at least December 1995, the course will remain open. Set amidst rolling hills along the ocean, it is beautifully designed and maintained. A shot across surging ocean waves on the 3rd hole is one of the highlights. This 72-par course is 7,114 yards long from the black tees. Green fees are $130 for 18 holes, or $80 if you are staying at the hotel. Pro shop, restaurants, bar.

Hapuna Course, Hapuna Beach Prince Hotel (882-1035 or 800/735-1111). An 18-hole, Arnold Palmer-designed course recently opened to the public. The adjoining hotel opened in the summer of 1994, and is one of a chain of upscale Japanese-owned hotels in Hawaii. The course is planted with indigenous Hawaiian plants, and is known for its challenging narrow fairways. It's a great course for kama'ainas at $45. Green fees are $110 for visitors, and $70 for guests at Mauna Kea and Hapuna Beach, and includes the cart fee. A par-72 course, 6,875 yards from black tees.

Francis H. I'i Brown North & South Courses, Mauna Lani Resort (885-6655 or 800/845-9905). The original 18 holes are not as difficult as Mauna Kea, but many seem even more beautiful. In October 1991 they split the original 18 holes and added 18 more. The North Course features rolling terrain and a kiawe tree forest; the par-3 signature 17th hole sits at the bottom of a deep lava bowl. The South Course snakes through jagged a'a lava; the oceanside 15th hole is a challenge.

The late Francis I'i Brown is a legend in Hawaii golf. Grandson of an orator at Kamehameha's royal court, he balanced the excesses of a lavish competitive golfing life with simple Hawaiian living at a remote country home along the coast at Mauna Lani. Green fees: visitor $150, guest at resort $80, kama'aina with Hawaii drivers license, $70. Both courses are par-72. The South Course is 7,029 yards from the black tees, and the North is 6,993 yards. Tee times are taken one day in advance for off-resort golfers.

King's Course & Beach Course, Waikoloa Beach Resort (885-4647 – King's Course, 885-6060 – Beach Course). Located on Anaeho'omalu Bay, the 18-hole Beach Course was literally carved out of lava rock by Robert Trent Jones, Jr. in 1981. Hawaii's second largest petroglyph field lies between the 6th and 7th holes of the beach course. The Beach Course was designed in the Scottish links fashion with straightaway fairways; the 12th hole features a tough shot across ocean water to the green. The 18-hole King's Course was designed by Tom Weiskopf and Jay Morrish. Golfers are tested by six major lakes, 70 bunkers and an undulating landscape; the par-5 18th hole winds along an ancient lava flow. The popular John Jacobs School of Golf is located at Waikoloa. Green fees: visitor $95, resort guest $80, and $50 for off-island kama'ainas; a special Big Island resident program costs $10 to join then $35 per round (kama'aina rate available after 10 a.m.). The Beach Course is a par-70, 7,704 yard course; King's Course is par-72 and 6,566 yards.

Waikoloa Village Golf Course (883-9621). Waikoloa Village is a resort community ten minutes up the mountain from the Waikoloa Resort. This Robert Jones, Jr.-designed 18-hole course is a favorite of ours when the wind isn't blowing (it can really howl). Call before you leave home for the latest weather information. Green fees: $65 includes cart, $70 special adds breakfast or lunch; after 2 p.m., $40. Kamaaina, $35, $25 after 2 p.m. A par-72 course, 6,687 yards from championship tees.

Kona

Though perhaps not as fancy as the courses along the Kohala Coast, Kona's courses offer a local flavor and unique settings.

Makalei Hawaiian Country Club, Hue Hue Ranch (325-6625). Kona's newest course, eight miles up Palani Road from Kailua, is distinguished by its high elevation and beautifully landscaped terrain. It was designed by Dick Nugent, the designer of the famed Kemper Lakes Course. A cart is included in the $110 fee; $45 if you have a Hawaii driver's license. Par-72, 7,091 yards.

Kona Country Club & Ali'i Country Club, Keauhou Resort (322-2595). The closest course to Kailua now has 36 holes, set along the ocean and on plateaus above the Keauhou Resort. The upper course, *Ali'i Country Club*, is very hilly with great ocean vistas. The Kona Country Club runs along the ocean and is notable for its light winds, as Keauhou is in the lee of Mauna Loa. Probably the most crowded of the Big Island's courses. Green fees for 18 holes: $65 for visitors, $38 for kama'ainas. After 12 p.m. green fees are $50; a special kama'aina rate of $28 is offered after 11 a.m. on the mountain course only. Both are par-72.

Ka'u

SeaMountain Golf Club, Punalu'u, Ka'u (928-6222). A really nice little 18-hole ocean course, if you're willing to drive 90 minutes south from Kailua. Set above black sand beaches, below Mauna Loa. Another place to check the weather before you leave. Green fees: $50, kama'aina $26 weekdays, $28 weekends.

Volcano Country Club, Volcano, Ka'u (967-7331). Can be chilly and damp, but a wonderfully unique course at 4,500 feet above sea level, near the Kilauea crater on the grounds of Volcanoes National Park. A round or two here combines well with a trip to see the volcano, or a night spent at Volcano House. Originally built by Scots in 1922, the course was renovated in 1983. Check the weather. Green fees, with shared cart, are $52 for visitors and $40 for off-island Hawaii residents. Big Island residents are $28 weekends and $26 weekdays.

TENNIS

Kona offers a wealth of opportunities for tennis players from beginners to enthusiasts. Major hotels all have tennis centers with several courts, a pro shop, and professionals available to give lessons, find matches, or provide equipment. Since tennis is not as big a tourist preference as golf or the beach, hotel courts are usually not too crowded. Tennis is popular among Big Island residents, and most of the best dozen or so players work as professionals at the tennis clubs. There are many private courts at the various condominiums. Court fees vary, ranging from $5 a day to $10 per person per hour, with special deals for weekly use and hotel guests. Most hotel tennis clubs offer memberships for much less than equivalent clubs on the Mainland.

There are two tennis centers not associated with hotels, and they are probably the most popular courts in Kona: Holua at Mauna Loa Village, and the Old Airport public courts.

The Holua Tennis Center (322-0091) in the middle of Mauna Loa Village (look for blue roof condos and waterfalls just before the entrance to the Kona Surf Hotel in Keauhou Bay) is probably the best tennis complex in Hawaii, with 14 courts, seven of them lighted (the lower six courts do not have windscreens). As is typical for Kona, the courts are medium speed hard courts (the Hilton Waikoloa has two clay courts and the Mauna Lani has two grass courts).

Holua's Director of Tennis, Marc Georgian, played at Cal State Hayward and on the European satellite tour, and is one of the best players in the state. The head tennis professional is Barry Cutler, who directs the junior tennis summer camp and numerous clinics and mini-tournaments. Neil Ohata, the shop manager/assistant pro runs most of the officially sanctioned USTA or HPTA tournaments in Kona.

Pure Kona coffee is available at Holua every morning, and every spring Holua is host to the Kona Kai Farms/Holua Hawaii Grand Prix Tennis Tournament, featuring the best players in the state. Holua offers a full service pro shop with guaranteed same day stringing.

Serious tennis players should consider staying at the condos surrounding the tennis courts, called Mauna Loa Village – the tennis shop can set you up with the best room packages available. Court fees are $5 per day for Big Island residents or $10 per day for non residents. Memberships are $300 per year (single) and $500 (family), and three month memberships are available for $100 and $250.

The *Old Kona Airport* has four public lighted courts, which are the only decent public courts in Kona (those at Konawaena High School are a disgrace). They are heavily played, and used for lessons by independent tennis professionals such as the venerable dean of Kona tennis, Bruz Freeman – a gifted tennis professional and jazz drummer from Los Angeles who has made Kona his home for the past fifteen years. Although the public courts are free, they are crowded, and extremely hot during the middle of the day. Because of the heat, the courts are often deserted at midday and this is the easiest time to get on a court without waiting, but watch out for sunstroke. You'll find public restrooms and outdoor showers, but no pro shop or other amenities.

Hotel tennis clubs can be divided into two groups – those in or near Kailua town, and those at the Kohala hotels. The tennis centers at the Kohala hotels are generally newer, have more courts, larger staffs, and are more expensive. It can, however, be extremely windy in Kohala, especially in the afternoons. The midday sun is hot everywhere – many experienced mainland players, even professionals, wilt in the Kona heat, so sunscreen and water are used plentifully by most players. The following is a geographical listing of tennis courts, beginning from the south:

Kona Surf Hotel (322-3411). Fifteen years ago, the Surf had the best tennis program in Kona, and even hosted a real professional tournament where Bjorn Borg defeated Ilse Nastase in the finals. Unfortunately, the general decline of the hotel under the Otaka ownership has resulted in the total abandonment of the tennis program. There are now only the dilapidated courts and no staff. Fortunately, Holua is right next door, so guests at the Kona Surf have a great place to play with special guest rates.

Keauhou Tennis Ranch at the Keauhou Beach Hotel (322-3441) offers six courts (two lighted). Three are near the ocean, three near the parking lot, and all but one have windscreens. There's a small pro shop, and restrooms and showers downstairs. Courts were resurfaced in November 1993. Court fees are $3 per person, per hour, and $5 per day (hotel guests) and $6/hour or $10/day (drop-ins). Keauhou has eleven USTA league teams, daily tennis aerobics, and a junior summer camp for ages four through 18.

Royal Kona Resort (329-3111, formerly the Kona Hilton). New owners Dennis Correa and Al Chan have resurfaced the four plexipave courts (three lighted). Court fees are $4 per hour per person or $6 per day. Matt Johnson is head pro and Cindy Chan runs the shop. There are drop-in clinics, men's night, ladies night and mixed doubles night, as well as programs for kids. Open 8 a.m. to 8 p.m.

Royal Waikoloan Tennis Club (885-6789). New head pro Harold Lowe supervises six plexipave courts between the parking lot and the hotel. All are screened, none are lighted, and they were resufaced last in 1989. The resort is part of John Williams Tennis International (a management company with resorts in tropical locations all over the world), and offers a full tennis program, with court fees of $5 per hour per person. Memberships for local residents are $300 per year single and $550 family.

King's Sport and Racquet Club at King Kamehameha's Kona Beach Hotel (329-2911). There are four newly resurfaced courts adjacent to the parking lot, but only one is lighted. The small pro shop with restroom and shower is close by in the hotel. Lianne DePontes is director of tennis, Jaime DePontes is head professional. This tennis club, the only one run by a woman, gets a lot of play from the better female players in Kona, as well as some good local men. The closest club to Kailua town; you can walk to a variety of restaurants for lunch.

Kona Village Tennis at Kona Village Resort (325-5555). Play here is reserved for hotel guests and their friends on three lighted, screened, hard-surfaced courts that were built in 1991. Director of Tennis Andy Klug, one of the best players in Hawaii, provides lessons, equipment, and free daily mixers and clinics,

Mondays through Fridays. There are no court fees, but in keeping with the extremely private atmosphere of the resort there is no outside play or tournaments. One of the most beautiful tennis settings in Hawaii.

Kohala Tennis and Spa, Hilton Waikoloa Resort (885-1234). Director of Tennis Tripp Gordon, and Head Pro Tim Di Donato, oversee eight courts, two of which are Fast-Dry green clay, the only clay courts on the Big Island. All courts are screened, but none have lights. Court fees are $20 for 90 minutes per court. The stadium court is probably the nicest center court in Kona, with 500 individual seats in a garden setting. The full-service pro shop is adjacent to a 25,000-square-foot spa which has rates of $15 per visit, or a book of 10 visits for $80. The Kohala Spa is a great place for friends or family to idle while waiting out a tennis match. The Hilton Waikoloa hosts a Hawaii Grand Prix tournament each year, as well as age group and class tournaments.

The Tennis Garden at the Mauna Lani Bay Resort and Bungalows (885-6622). These ten hard-surfaced courts, built in 1992, are all screened; none are lighted. Court fees are $7 per hour, per person. A full service pro shop and locker room facilities are available. Director of Tennis Craig Paulter is on duty weekdays, and some weekends. A kids' summer camp, daily clinics, and lessons, are just some of the activities that take place here.

The Racquet Club at the Mauna Lani Bay Resort and Bungalows (885-7765). The site of the 1992 Davis Cup match between the U.S. (Sampras, Agassi, and McEnroe) and Argentina is probably the classiest tennis resort in Kona. There are six plexi-paved courts (three lighted, $7 per hour, per person) and two grass courts ($10 per hour, per person), a full service pro shop, health club, and one of Kona's better restaurants (The Gallery) overlooking center court. Club manager Guy LaGuire offers lessons and clinics Tuesdays through Saturdays, from 8:30 to 5. Club facilities include a weight room, a 25-meter lap pool, steam room, and jacuzzi. Memberships, include access to the nearby Beach Club (restaurant/cafe and private beach) and can be purchased for $1,600 per year (family) or $1,100 (single). The courts are reserved for hotel guests, club members, and their friends. If you've never played on grass courts, why not give it a shot?

The Tennis Pavilion at The Ritz Carlton, Mauna Lani (885-2000). Eleven hard courts, seven lighted, all screened, are offered here. There is a full-service pro shop, and showers are located at the hotel spa. Court fees are $10/day for hotel guests, $12 for others. Memberships for the tennis club and spa are available for $1,000 (family) or $750 (single). The excellent staff includes Director of Tennis Richard Stumpf (along with Marc Georgian, our recommendation in Kona for advanced teaching), Head Pro Bill Imwalle, and Assistant Pro Dan Klug. At least one pro is available every day, and there is the usual compliment of classes, clinics, and lessons. The Ritz Carlton hosts several excellent tournaments each year, especially the Hawaii Grand Prix, and a Jr./Sr. Vet tournament.

The Tennis Garden at the Mauna Kea Beach Hotel (882-7222). Director of Tennis Jay Paulson is the "senior" teaching pro in Kona, and has been a great tournament player for years. Kerry Crowell is the assistant pro. She works Saturdays through Wednesdays and Jay is available Tuesdays through Saturdays. There are 13 courts, none lighted, all with screens. Showers are available in the locker rooms. Court fees are expensive: peak hours from 7 to 11 and 3 to 6 are $18/hour per court for guests and $20/hour for outsiders; at other times it's half price.

For all the tennis info in the state of Hawaii, including current open, junior, and veteran rankings, you might want to take a look at the *Hawaii Tennis News*, a semi-monthly newspaper edited by Cheryl Shrum which is available at all tennis centers. The *Hawaii Pacific Tennis Association* (HPTA) publishes a yearly guide to all the sanctioned tournaments in the state.

Other Sports

Volleyball: You can usually find a pickup game at the beach court at Keauhou Bay, or Anaeho'omalu Beach, always on Sundays. And there's often a game at Disappearing Sands Beach. (White Sands, or Magic Sands.)

Bowling: The modern *Kona Bowl* (326-2695) in the Frame 10 Center adjacent to Lanihau Shopping Center has a smoke-free bowling policy. Friday night Rock 'N Bowl is a favorite among Kona's bowlers, which seem to include almost every long-time coffee farmer we know. The adjacent diner has good food.

Baseball: The Hilo Stars are one of the teams that comprise Hawaii Winter Baseball, a four-team league that draws major league prospects from the mainland, Japan, Korea, and other nations to Hawaii for off-season training and play from mid-October to mid-December. Games are exciting, and the international rosters add an interesting element. It's likely you will see a future major league star in action, as 20 major league teams now send players, and several from the inaugural year of play are already in the majors. Games are played at the University of Hawaii at Hilo's Vulcan Field outside Hilo. Saturday and Sunday games begin at 1 p.m., with weekday games starting at 6 p.m. The team travels to Oahu, Maui, and Kauai for games, so check in advance for home dates. For ticket information call 969-9033.

Following Honolulu's University of Hawaii baseball team (the Rainbows) is a passion for many local baseball fans. Hawaii's former AAA minor league team, The Islanders, departed over a decade ago and UH has taken up the slack. They play from late winter through the spring, and many games are televised. Diehard fans might want to see a Rainbows game at their top-notch stadium located at UH's Manoa campus on Oahu. Tickets are available at numerous locations in Honolulu.

Massage, Fitness and Well Being

Kona is fast becoming one of the massage capitals of the world, and there are scores of massage therapists practicing here. *Auntie Margaret Machado* at Keei Beach (328-2472) holds world-famous classes in Hawaiian lomi lomi massage, and many of her students are working all over the island. For a convenient massage in a wonderful oceanfront setting, we suggest Lisa Pyne at *Kona Rub-A-Dub* on Alii Drive (329-1002) just south of the Royal Kona Resort ($40 per one hour session). In Waimea, call Margaret Horwatt at the *Center for Well Being* in Opelu Plaza (885-7711) for acupuncture or massage ($50 for one hour). Every hotel has a massage staff, and although they charge a lot ($50 per session minimum) the massage therapists are usually excellent.

The new Kohala hotels have integrated body and mind therapies into their spas, and several have made them a featured part of the hotels. The largest, fanciest spa is the 25,000-square-foot Kohala Spa at the Hilton Waikoloa. The daily rate for use of the facilities is quite reasonable ($15, $10 after 4 p.m.), which includes the use of the steam room, sauna, whirlpool, weight room, dressing room, lounge and all the towels you can use. The rates for massage, aromatherapy, facials, leg waxing, manicures, pedicures, salon, and other services are expensive, although no more so than the other hotels. The "Day at Kohala" package includes a fitness class, massage, facial, body polish, shampoo and blow dry, pedicure, manicure and lunch for $250. There is also a half day package and a "Sampler" package

The spa and fitness center at The Ritz Carlton, Mauna Lani is for guests only, with no use fees. Their full-service facility is smaller than the Hilton's but usually not very crowded. They offer seven types of massage and seven types of body treatments.

The new Four Seasons hotel next to the Kona Village is expected to set a new standard as a health and fitness resource. They are now negotiating with a European company to offer the most modern and complete health therapies, and are using local health professionals as consultants to plan their facility and services.

The local gyms don't offer the same kind of upscale facilities as the hotels, but they are inexpensive and available. There are usually classes in aerobics, yoga, dance, and tai chi. Schedules vary, so call first. The most popular place is *The Club* fitness center next to *Subway Sandwiches* just makai of Kuakini Highway in the center of Kailua (326-CLUB). The Big Island Gym (329-9432, on Alapa Street in the Old Industrial Area) is especially popular with weightlifters, as is the YMCA is on Pawai Place in the Old Industrial Area (329-9622). Up in coffee country there's the Mauka Gym in Kealakekua across from the Post Office (322-8495) and dance and yoga classes at P.A.C.E.S. in Kainaliu (324-7116).

Yoga devotees can take drop-in classes at the YMCA or the West Hawaii Dance Academy in Kailua or up mauka at the Big Island Yoga Institute in Kealakekua next to the library, above Dr. Peebles' office (323-3758) or at P.A.C.E.S.

The following are some health professionals in various disciplines who we can recommend. There are plenty of others in the phone book. Acupuncturist: Marga*ret Horwatt* in Waimea (Opelu Plaza, 885-7711). Chiropractic doctors: *Karl Hynes* on Lunapule Road in Kailua (329-6888). Naturopathic physician: *Michael Traub* in Kailua (329-2114). General practitioner and clinic: *Kevin Kunz* at *Kona Kohala Medical Associates* on Hualalai Road in Kailua (329-1346). As long as we're referring doctors, we might as well give you a legal contact: *Meredith Lenell*, Pottery Terrace, Kailua-Kona (326-1010).

The *Kona Community Hospital* in Kealakekua just north of the Post Office on the mauka side of Mamalahoa Highway (322-9311) always seems to have funding problems, but is fairly modern considering the small size of the resident population. The new *North Hawaii Community Hospital* is being built in Waimea with money raised by dedicated volunteers, and is expected to offer many forms of complementary medicine as well as state-of-the-art hospital services when it opens in late 1995.

BEACHES

There aren't as many sandy beaches on the Big Island as on Kauai and Maui, and because of their scarcity they are often crowded. But if you're willing to do a little driving or hiking, you can usually get away from the crowds and find your own isolated pocket of sand hidden amidst the rocky coastline. Certain beaches are noted for snorkeling or surfing, others for swimming or fishing. Those with easy access are well-visited, have ample parking, and most likely will have picnic tables, showers, or other facilities. Many beaches are archaeological sites where Hawaiian fishing villages and *heiaus* (temples) once stood.

It's advisable to pack some basic gear for beach excursions. Bring sun screen (especially for visitors from non-sunny climates), a small beach chair, a water container, or a cooler with drinks, thick rubber-soled slip-on beach shoes or Japanese *tabi* for walking on rocks or reefs (available at Longs Drugs and other stores), sun glasses (make sure they filter out ultraviolet light) and a wide-brimmed hat. You might want to bring enough food so you can skip supper and stay for the sunset, almost always guaranteed to be spectacular.

Beware of dangers found both in the water and on land. Waves and rip currents can be dangerous if the surf is up; beware, too, of cutting your feet on coral, sea urchins, or underwater rocks. On land, be careful about parking at isolated beaches – don't leave valuables in sight, or better still, leave them at home, if possible. Theft at Hawaiian beaches is an increasing problem, and occurs in Kona too frequently, even from locked car trunks.

KAILUA-KONA

King Kamehameha's Kona Beach Hotel: This white sand beach with it's calm, shallow water, in downtown Kailua, is great for young children. While there, check out the restored Ahu 'Ena Heiau where Kamehameha the Great once held council meetings, located adjacent to the Kailua Pier. A tiny crescent of sand on the street side of the pier is a popular swimming spot for kids and snorkelers, and marks the starting line for the Ironman Triathlon held in October. Tour boats moor at the pier, and outrigger canoe teams practice in the bay. Athletes, both professional and casual, daily swim the one-third mile course marked by white buoys.

Old Airport Beach: This long beach has lots of sand, wide-open spaces, and adequate public facilities, but isn't good for swimming. An outer reef makes for protected pools close to shore, but stay off the reef when waves are breaking, as it can be dangerous. Follow Kuakini Highway through Kailua towards the old industrial area, keep going past the West Hawaii Today building, the new county gym, and the baseball fields until the road runs into the runway of the old Kona Airport. Drive on the runway (it's no longer used by airplanes) until you see covered picnic tables and restrooms along the ocean. Park anywhere. Tide pools line the coast and contain reef fish, sea urchins, crabs and other critters. The wide, straight runway is a great place for rollerblading and biking.

Disappearing Sands Beach (Magic Sands, or White Sands): Popular with locals and visitors, this beach actually disappears in winter when big waves wash away its sand. Only rocks remain until spring, when the beach mysteriously reappears. It's a good boogie boarding beach for beginners when the waves are small, and is a public beach park with some facilities. A young crowd hangs out here to play volleyball, "talk story", drink beer, listen to loud radios, and generally hang out, but don't let that deter you; families and visitors peacefully enjoy the beach, too. Located about three miles south of Kailua on Ali'i drive.

Kahalu'u Beach Park: A great snorkeling beach with dozens of colorful reef fish in shallow water just offshore, Kahalu'u is four miles south of town on Ali'i Drive. Green sea turtles, which you can watch but not touch, are protected by federal law, and often spotted here. They aren't afraid of people and will let you watch them as they nibble seaweed. Also known locally as "Children's Beach" because the area is protected from rough seas by a breakwater, this is a public beach park with a lifeguard, showers, covered picnic tables, and a large pavilion that is often the site of local wedding receptions and birthday parties.

North Kona and Kohala

Honokohau Harbor: A five-minute walk north of the boat harbor takes you to this isolated nude beach, three miles south of the airport. The Pai Family, a Hawaiian clan, is living along the beach here near the small boat harbor to claim ancestral land they feel belongs to their family; watch dogs patrol near their compound. The beach is usually not very crowded and is good for swimming, but not snorkeling. Surfing waves break off-shore.

Kaloko: A National Parks Service nature refuge. The turn-off is located makai (ocean side) of the New Industrial Area north of Kona. Kaloko is only open mornings and early afternoons. This is a historic landmark that once was home to a Hawaiian fishing village; petroglyphs and the remains of a Hawaiian fish pond are still visible. There's good snorkeling here when the surf is flat. Look for indigenous fish and native plants in and around the brackish pond. We recommend wearing beach shoes.

Natural Energy Lab: This white sand beach just south of the airport has safe tide pools for kids to play in, but no real swimming or snorkeling. It's a favorite with locals for picnics and barbecues, or just relaxing at a spot not far from town. As you're driving north from Kailua toward the airport, take a left at the Natural Energy Lab sign, about five miles north of town.

Pinetrees (OTEC): This pleasant local surf spot is about two miles south of the Ocean Thermal Energy Conversion research facility, just south of the airport. Take the Natural Energy Lab turn off, then turn left onto the sand when you reach the ocean. It's a four-wheel-drive road, although enterprising surfers in VWs and trucks can make it through the difficult spots. Once you reach the clump of trees which mark the surf break, you'll find about six campsites. A good place for beginning surfers, boogie boarders, and small kids. Unfortunately, Pinetrees is now threatened by developers, as resort plans have passed the preliminary approval stage. Beach shoes advisable.

Kona Coast State Park: The only road to this beach is rough, but it's worth the bumpy ride. The entrance is well marked, about a mile or two north of the entrance to the airport. A white sand beach speckled with black lava, it's good for snorkeling, swimming, and lightweight boogie boarding. A picturesque bay to the north is good for long swims. The outside point occasionally has good surf.

Anaeho'omalu Bay Beach Park, Waikoloa: Just south of the Royal Waikoloan Hotel, this palm-lined state park has ample public parking. A beach service rents windsurfing equipment, snorkeling gear, and kayaks. If you're interested in trying windsurfing, this is the best beginner's spot on the island. Though seemingly a resort beach, it's nevertheless popular with locals who readily join guests from the Royal Waikoloan. Its safe swimming, its range of beachgoers, and its palm trees are reminiscent of Kahala Beach in Honolulu. The hotel is a short walk away for drinks or lunch. Charter catamarans offer rides.

Spencer Beach State Park, Kohala: Set in the lee of wind and waves, Spencer Beach is almost always calm, and perfect for young children or anyone who likes to swim. Camping is allowed here, and you'll find Europeans, Japanese, Mainlanders, backpackers, and locals enjoying themselves. Below the classic 1930s pavilion good snorkeling can sometimes be found, though the water is often murky. Sea turtles are frequently spotted here. Pu'ukohola Heiau, the last major *heiau* (Hawaiian temple) ever built and a national monument, is a short walk above the beach and well worth a look.

Hapuna Beach State Park, Kohala: Rated one of the best beaches in all the Hawaiian Islands by visitors, local residents, and magazines like *Condé Nast Traveler*, Hapuna is a long, wide stretch of white sand with excellent swimming and snorkeling when it's calm, and great boogie boarding and body surfing when the surf's up. A popular getaway far from any towns, it has lots of parking, showers, lunch tables, grass, sun, and shade. Watch out for a fairly dangerous undertow when the surf is up and for waves that are a great deal more powerful than they look. More people have drowned here than at any other beach in Hawaii, mostly when overcome by waves. The new Hapuna Beach Prince Hotel recently opened fronting the north end of the beach, and although it has made the beach somewhat more crowded, there still seems to be enough room for everybody.

Kauna'oa Beach (Mauna Kea): If you don't want to take the

short walk to get here along the ocean from Hapuna Beach, you can try to get one of the "public access" parking places at the Mauna Kea Beach Hotel, though there are only a handful of these and they are usually all taken well before mid-morning. (You have to tell the security guard at the hotel gate that you're going to the beach). Once you get here you'll find white sand, clear water, good snorkeling, and clean facilities.

Kua Bay: To get to this little-known, beautiful beach take the gravel road about ¼ mile south of the Kona Village Resort (five miles north of the airport), near a conspicuous cinder cone. Drive as far as you can, then park and walk the rest of the way. Lava caves, surf, boogie boarding and a great natural location will keep you entertained. As there are no shade trees, make sure you bring sun screen and a hat.

South Kona

Kealakekua Bay, Napoʻopoʻo: One of the prettiest places in Hawaii, with its dramatic cliff and aquamarine water, Kealakekua Bay is a protected marine preserve teeming with reef fish, eels, turtles, dolphins, and incredible coral formations. A white marble obelisk on the far shore marks the spot where English explorer Captain James Cook was killed in 1779, and an ancient Hawaiian temple, Hikiau Heiau, rises from the near shore. Some say human sacrifices were carried out here. Ancient burial caves are located in the cliff above the bay. Henry ʻOpukahaʻia (Obookiah), the Hawaiian credited with inspiring the first missionaries to Hawaii, was born nearby in 1792. The Captain Cook monument, at the site of the vanished village of Kaʻawaloa, can be reached in about 45 minutes by swimming, if you're in good shape, or you can rent a kayak, or take the strenuous trail down the cliff. The bay is a great place for snorkeling, but unless you're in top shape and willing to swim a long way out from shore, we recommend taking one of the many boat cruises to the bay which provide snorkeling gear and anchor right in the middle of the best snorkeling spots. Sometimes the bay is fringed by a nice sandy beach, but at other times there's nothing but boulders. Generally the surf is flat and the beach of smooth ocean

Kealakekua Bay

lava rocks is a favorite for a swim or sun bath. Beware, however, if the surf is up as the rocks can be slippery underfoot.

Pu'uhonua O Honaunau National Park (Place of Refuge): The clear water makes for great snorkeling; you can enter the water off natural steps in the lava rock shoreline. This is a fun, somewhat isolated picnic and luau spot with authentic replicas of Hawaiian grass houses and temples, and interesting recorded interpretative info that tells how things used to be in ancient days. There's a $2 per person entrance fee from 7:30 a.m. to 5:30 p.m., but the grounds remain open until midnight, and are free after 5:30. It's a great place to watch the sunset.

Ho'okena Beach Park: Although the gray sand here isn't as attractive as white sand, good snorkeling, swimming, and body surfing more than make up for it. The beach is a couple of miles beyond Pu'uhonua O Honaunau, 20 miles south of Kona.

Black Sand Beach, Punalu'u: Now that Kalapana has been covered by lava, this is the only accessible black sand beach left on the island. Adjacent to SeaMountain Resort, an hour's drive south of Honaunau, it's a good place to take a break when driving around Ka'u to the volcanoes.

Hilo

None of Hilo's beaches are very pretty or inviting, but beachgoers young and old don't care, they just want to have fun, and can do so, just about anywhere. Several beaches can be found east of the city along Kalaniana'ole Avenue, which runs six miles from downtown Hilo to where it dead ends at Lelei Point. Some beaches aren't marked, but you can tell where they are by the parked cars.

Hilo Bayfront Park: The water is so murky here and probably polluted you won't want to swim, but it's a good place to picnic and fish.

Coconut Island Park: Long ago this was a place of refuge, and it's now the only decent place to swim in Hilo Bay. It's reached by a footbridge from a spit of land just outside Lili'uokalani Gardens on the bayfront and has restrooms, a pavilion, and picnic tables shaded by ironwoods and tall coconut palms. Long a popular picnic spot, there's a diving tower and a sheltered natural pool.

Onekahakaha Beach Park: When Hilo families want to go to a nearby beach, this is the one they choose because it's safe for kids, has white sand, lifeguards, park facilities, and camping.

You might want to also check out James Kealoha Park in the winter for its surfing and for snorkeling in the summer, and Richardson's Beach for some of the best snorkeling on the Hilo side.

The most comprehensive guidebook on the subject is John Clark's *Beaches of the Big Island*, published by the University of Hawaii Press, and available from local bookstores and at the public library.

DINING AND FOOD

INTRODUCTION

A few general tips apply to all Hawaiian restaurants: Local food, simply prepared, is best. Try to order what is grown, caught, or raised on the Big Island or some place in Hawaii. The fresh fish ("catch of the day"), undercooked rather than overcooked, with the sauce on the side, can never be too wrong. And, it really is true that ocean views make the food taste better!

We have not spent much time in hotel restaurants and coffee shops except the very best ones. They tend to be very similar, and not terribly distinctive in terms of quality, service and value. Most hotels will have a coffee shop breakfast restaurant, an all-purpose medium priced restaurant, and a fancy restaurant. They are frequently disappointing compared to the other alternatives, and that applies to some of the Kohala hotels as well. It definitely applies to the hotels in the Kailua-Kona area, where it is unusual to find even the high-end restaurants serving pure Kona coffee (the *SS James MaKee* Room at the Kona Surf is an exception).

COFFEE

Since this is the middle of coffee country, you would expect the coffee to be uniformly great, to set an example of what coffee should be for the specialty coffee industry. We are sorry to disappoint you, but it is rather hard to get a decent cup of coffee in Kona, although a recent proliferation of Kona coffee retail outlets and espresso shops has eased the coffee crisis here.

Almost all food service (hotel & restaurant) coffee is a "Kona blend" type of pre-packaged, 1.75 ounce or less, ground coffee, no better than you would find at most chain restaurants on the mainland. State law now requires that these blends contain at least 10% Kona coffee; no major brand contains more. The better restaurants will have whole bean "Kona blend" coffee and portion control grinders. There is an increasing coffee consciousness in Kona restaurants, but progress is still disappointingly slow.

The newer hotels and restaurants are installing espresso machines as part of their coffee service, but espresso coffee is unusually hard to find everywhere else.

What should Kona coffee taste like? Kona coffee is known for its slight acidity, sweet, mellow flavor, and spellbinding aroma. For regular coffee drinking, we prefer the Kona Fancy grade beans with a "full city" roast. For darker roasts, try the Kona Peaberry (a round bean, formed in five per cent of all coffee cherries). For a full explanation of Kona coffee see the *Guide to Making Good Coffee* at the back of this book.

Here are our recommendations for serious coffee drinkers:

Kailua-Kona: *Kona Kai Cafe,* Kona Inn Shopping Center (329-2262), *Under the Palm,* Alii Drive (329-7366).

Kainaliu: *Aloha Cafe*, at the north end of town next to the theater (322-3383).

Kealakekua: *Kona Kai Farms Tasting Room,* just past the 111 mile marker (323-2115).

Holualoa: *Holuakoa Cafe,* across from the Kona Hotel (322-2233).

Waimea: *Waimea Coffee & Co.* in Parker Square (885-4472).

Hawi: *Kohala Coffee Mill,* Route 270 (889-5577).

Breakfast

This meal starts early in Kona, and it is hard to find anything special to eat. The one consistently good place is the *Aloha Cafe* (322-3383) in Kainaliu, where ahi and eggs is our favorite of the several morning specials. Try to get a seat at the makai end of the long outside lanai. The coffee and papayas are from Kona, the oranges are from Kaʻu and fresh squeezed, and the muffins baked every morning. The *Aloha* opens at 8:00. Breakfast menu closes at 11:30 and they have a Sunday brunch in season. *Edwards at the Terrace* (322-1434) at the Kanaloa Condominiums on the ocean across from the Keauhou Shopping Village is hard to find but worth the effort. Breakfast there is served from 8 to 11 Tuesday through Sunday. If you are not interested in a view, try *Sam Choy's Restaurant* on Kauhola Street in the Kaloko Industrial Area between town and the airport (326-1545,

Monday thru Saturday, 5 a.m.-2 p.m.).

The rest of the breakfast places serve food comparable to a Denny's type restaurant, serve tasteless Kona blend coffee and do not have espresso. A few of these places are better than the others because of location, service, or low prices but you can probably do as well or better at your hotel. The *Kona Ranch House* (329-7061) on Kuakini Highway at the Palani junction (next to the Shell station) has a wide menu, low prices, and good service. *Seafood Pasta Palace* (upstairs at Waterfront Row, 329-4436) has a $3 Wiki Wiki special breakfast beginning at 7 a.m. (scrambled eggs, potatoes, sausage), a 2-for-1 coupon, and a nice view. The oceanfront *Captain's Deck* at *Fisherman's Landing* in the Kona Inn Shopping Village serves inexpensive breakfasts from 7 a.m. to 10:30, and the *Jolly Roger* (329-1344) on the ocean just south of the Kona Inn Shopping Village is an exquisite location for breakfast, marred only by greasy food and substandard coffee.

Brunch

There are many good Sunday brunches at Kona and Kohala hotels; most are "all you can eat" buffets with a wide range of food priced from $12 to $18. None are especially distinctive in terms of cuisine, but they are pleasant, and food is plentiful and usually served on a terrace overlooking the ocean. In Kailua village the *Keauhou Beach Hotel* probably has the best location, while the Kohala hotels such as the *Mauna Lani* or *Ritz Carlton* serve more interesting food (the brunch at the *Mauna Kea Beach Hotel* was a local favorite for many years, and will resume when the hotel re-opens). If you have the time for a leisurely Sunday brunch, the Kona Village is a great spot. Besides, if you're not staying there the only way you can see the hotel is to have meal reservations. Check *West Hawaii Today* for hotel brunch specials. For excellent brunches at more down home places than the hotels, try the *Aloha Cafe* in Kainaliu or *Bamboo* in Hawi.

LUNCH

Most of the restaurants mentioned in the dinner section also serve lunch. Lunch specials featuring the catch-of-the-day are recommended. Sometimes you can get fruit salads with local fruit such as papayas, mangos, bananas, pineapples or cheramoya, but more often they will feature mainland melons and strawberries. Our favorite sit-down lunch spots are *The Aloha Cafe, Huggo's, Quinn's* (Aliʻi Drive across from the King Kamehameha Hotel, 329-3822), *Under the Palm* and the *Kona Inn.*

For a quick New York-style sandwich, there's *A Piece of the Apple* in the Alii Sunset Shopping Plaza, right behind *Lava Java* (329-9321).

In Waimea, try Ann Sutherland's *Mean Cuisine* (885-6325) in Opelu Quare or *Island Bistro* (885-1222) on Kawaihae Road as well as *Merriman's* and *Eidelweiss.*

PIZZA

Of the many pizza places in the Kona area, two are especially notable. *Cafe Pesto* (882-1071) is located up north in the Kawaihae Shopping Center, in the town of Kawaihae just past the Mauna Kea Beach Hotel. It's a simple place in a drab shopping center with no view, but great California-style pizza and other Italian cuisine. *Bianelli's Pizza* in the Pines Plaza on Hualalai Road above the theaters (326-4800) also has no view, but provides good pizza and Italian dishes, with a wide selection of imported beers and a warm atmosphere (with sports TV at the bar). It also deserves kudos for being Kona's first large all no smoking restaurant! Of the rest of the pizza spots, *Basil's* is a small, open air cafe on Alii Drive (326-7836) that is often crowded and *Tom Bombadil's* (across from the Royal Kona Resort just off Aliʻi Drive, 329-1292) has a sports bar with satellite TV and a view.

DINNER

Three Star Restaurants

There are two superior restaurants in West Hawaii which we rate as consistently very good to excellent. Anyone who is interested in the best cuisine that Hawaii has to offer should make an attempt to visit one of them, even though they are at least an hour's drive from Kailua village. If you have to choose only one, the oceanfront setting of *The Canoe House* makes it our first choice.

*** *The Canoe House* at the Mauna Lani Bay Hotel (885-6622) features Alan Wong's Pacific cuisine in a fabulous oceanfront setting, combined with attentive service. We had a memorable dinner there with Mimi Sheraton, food critic of *Condé Nast Traveler* magazine, who ordered every pupu on the menu. The restaurant is a stand-alone building on the north side of the hotel right on the ocean, and features extensive use of koa, including the Hawaiian canoe hanging from the ceiling. This restaurant is normally very crowded, especially on weekend nights, so make your reservations early.

*** *Merriman's* at Opelu Plaza in Waimea (885-6822) features the Hawaii regional cuisine of owner/chef Peter Merriman, with the best use of local ingredients on the island. Both Merriman and Wong are active in the *Hawaii Regional Cuisine* group of twelve Hawaii chefs which tries to promote use of locally produced food in Hawaii restaurants. Other Big Island chefs in HRC are Sam Choy *(Sam Choy's)* and Amy Ferguson-Ota of the *The Grille* at The Ritz Carlton, Mauna Lani.

Two Star Restaurants

** *Bamboo* (Route 19, Hawi, 889-5555). Tuesday thru Saturday 11:30 a.m. until 9 p.m., Sunday brunch 9 a.m. to 2 p.m. Smoking allowed. No Amex. Easy on street parking.

Hawi is a long way from central Kona, but only about a half hour from the Kohala hotels. Wherever you are coming from, it's well worth the drive to have dinner at this original, fun, and delicious restaurant/gallery. Jim and Joan Channon, who also own the historic building that houses *Bamboo,* have created something special that is pleasantly different from any other place on the Big Island. A large, high ceiling dominates the dining room, decorated with tropical plants, furnishings, and paintings featuring the work of Jim Channon. The north side of the room houses the Kohala Koa Gallery, featuring local woods and local woodworkers. We hardly noticed that the restaurant has no view because the inside was so interesting.

Bamboo's menu, created by Doug Seymour and Jim Hamel, is not long or extremely creative as a whole, but we were able to find several dishes among the best we've ever tasted in Hawaii. The tequila grilled *Margarita Shrimp* ($7) and the ample *Bamboo Special Salad* ($6) were excellent starters, and the catch-of-the-day entrees ($14 to $18) featured Nohu, a rare, delicate white bottom fish similar to a moonfish, along with excellent ono and ahi. Dessert was a guava cheesecake ($6). The house special wine was a blend of sauvignon blanc and chardonnay (at $29 the priciest wine on the list) that fit our food perfectly.

The service at Bamboo is not sophisticated, but the waiter, hostess, and chef were nicely attentive and appreciative of our patronage, and we felt they were genuinely concerned that we have a great time at their restaurant. The drive from the Kohala hotels to Hawii is particularly beautiful at sunset. To avoid the long drive back to Kona, try staying in one of the several nearby bed and breakfasts.

** *Cafe Pesto*, Kawaihae (882-1071) and Hilo (969-6640). Moderate $$.

Kawaihae is the port where the Matson barge docks in West Hawaii, ten miles north of Waikoloa. It's not exactly a town, but it does have one shopping center and boasts the best pizza and Italian food on the Big Island. It takes an hour to get there from Kona, so you will probably want to combine a meal at Cafe Pesto with some other activity in Kohala. Or, if you're staying at one of the Kohala hotels, you might want to eat here every day.

The restaurant itself is a simple, black and white affair with no view, but there's a warm atmosphere that seems to come from being a good restaurant in the middle of nowhere. If you're there for lunch, you might want to visit the adjacent Kohala Gallery to view a fine collection of the best local artists.

Cafe Pesto has a second location in Hilo in the beautifully restored Y. Hata Building with a large room with twenty foot ceilings with people walking past down Kamehameha Avenue.

** *The Coast Grille* at the Hapuna Beach Hotel (880-1111) is just getting established, but already Executive Chef Corey A. Waite and Chef Jean Marc Heim have impressed us with such creations as the Thai Lobster Cone appetizer (a mixture of shitake mushrooms, grilled eggplant, roasted corn and salsa seasoned with ginger and Thai spices–$10) and their East-Coast-style Oyster Bar. Entrees start at $20 for the Center Cut Pork Loin, and go up to $38 for the Steamed Keahole Lobster with Black Angus Tenderloin of Beef. The menu has an interesting combination of Asian and French influences, and the presentations are creative.

** *Edward's at the Terrace.* (322-1434), Kanaloa Condominiums across from Keahou Shopping Villiage. Tuesday through Sunday, breakfast 8 to 11, lunch 11 to 2, dinner 5 to 9. Moderately expensive. The condominium does not favor advertising for the restaurant, so you have to look hard to find that it's in the back by the pool. Once you are there, you will find a very relaxed, open air setting with an ocean view and suprisingly good mediterranean style cuisine.

***Eidelweiss,* Kawaihae Road, Waimea (885-6800). Rustic location, excellent German cuisine, great service, moderate prices. If you like high cholesterol classic German dishes, this place is for you.

** *The Gallery Restaurant,* Mauna Lani Bay Hotel, Kohala Coast (885-7777). California cuisine on the golf course.
Everything about the Mauna Lani is stylish, but expensive.

** *The Grille Restaurant*, Ritz Carlton Mauna Lani Hotel, Kohala Coast (885-2000). A quiet, elegant, and slightly formal restaurant inside the Ritz-Carlton, this is one hotel dining room we can recommend enthusiastically. Although the setting could be a Ritz-Carlton anywhere, the menu is distinclty Hawaii regional cuisine.

** *La Bourgogne*, Kuakini Highway between Honalo and Kailua (329-6711). Dinner Tuesdays through Sundays, 6 p.m. to 9 p.m. Expensive $$. Reservations required. Visa, MC, no Amex.

If you're looking for an intimate little French restaurant with excellent food but no view (really, not even any windows) *La Bourgogne* will serve you quite well. Although the original founding owners are no longer there, their tradition is being perpetuated by Colleen Moore and Roger Gallaher, who moved from Honolulu to purchase the place in 1993. Colleen runs the front of the house and Roger runs the kitchen. The menu is French, but with a touch of Hawaii.

** *Palm Cafe*, Ali'i Drive, Kailua-Kona (329-7765). Expensive $$$. Non-smoking area available in open air restuarant. Visa, MC, Amex. Reservations recommended.

There's a beautiful rock building on the mauka side of Ali'i Drive at the south end of town, across from the sea wall. The second story houses the *Palm Cafe*, which has developed into the most popular "fine dining" restaurant in Kailua village. The Palm is only three years old, and has just added a stepchild, *Under the Palm*, downstairs which features coffee, a full bar, continental breakfast, pizza, salads, and sandwiches prepared in the kitchen upstairs, at prices between six and nine dollars. *Under the Palm* has an open-air sidewalk cafe, live music most evenings, and is an especially good place to go after 10 p.m. when most other restaurants are closed.

There are several things to like about the *Palm Cafe*. It has a big, airy open dining room with beautiful floral arrangements. There are booths and tables to choose from, several overlooking the water. The aesthetics of the restaurant – colors, plates, tablecloths, etc. – are pleasing. You can sit at the official bar, or at the secondary bar and eat by yourself. The staff is probably the most knowledgeable about food in Kona, and Daniel Thiebaut is becoming recognized as one of the hot chefs on the Big Island, especially for the pupus like the blackened ahi or Vietnamese spring rolls, and his consistent use of local produce. As always, the fresh fish is usually your best choice, and the Palm offers at least three preparation styles.

The only drawbacks here are the electric wires on Ali'i Drive which detract from the otherwise great view, the less than perfect coffee service, and the expense of the experience. Otherwise, you will have to drive to Waimea or Kohala to find a better restaurant, and it's a really long drive back to town from either of those places. We suggest you reserve a table close to the ocean, and try to get there for sunset.

** *Sam Choy's Restaurant,* Kauhola Street, Kaloko Light Industrial Park, Kailua-Kona (just south of the airport, 326-1545). Breakfast and lunch 6 a.m. to 2 p.m., Monday thru Saturday. Dinner Wednesday thru Saturday only, 5 p.m. to 9 p.m. No credit cards, personal checks OK, no non-smoking section. Easy parking. Moderate/expensive prices.

Sam Choy has a solid reputation as one of Hawaii's premier chefs. As the most publicized member of the Hawaii Regional Cuisine Group, he has made numerous public relations appearances for Hawaii food on TV and in person, both in Hawaii and all over the world. Formerly at the Kona Hilton, he opened this large, airy room in an industrial area setting in 1992 and it has been consistently filled with discerning patrons with hearty appetites. As a place which features both Hawaii regional cuisine and local dishes like saimin or kau kau, you can't do better.

Serious eaters (one look at Sam Choy tells you he is one of *the most* serious) will especially appreciate the automatic serving of soup and salad upon being seated. Choy's reputation as a master preparer of Hawaiian fish is unsurpassed, so the fresh fish is always an excellent choice. The lamb with somen noodles is one of the rare meat dishes we can recommend in Kona. There are burgers and chicken for children, and a fairly wide menu selection. There is no liquor license (and no liquor store in the

Kona & The Big Island 112

area), so bring your own chilled wine and they will provide the opener and glasses. Our only cullinary disappointment here is the standard Kona blend coffee brewed in a conventional brewer, and the lack of an espresso machine.

Sam's sister, Claire W.S. Choy, operates *Sam Choy's Diner* at the Kona Bowl in Lanihau Center (329-0101) which features good food a notch above standard diner fare along with local specials.

One Star Restaurants

* *Aloha Cafe,* Aloha Theatre Complex, Mamalahoa Highway, Kainaliu, 10 miles south of Kailua-Kona (322-3383). Dinner 5:00 to 8:00 except Sundays. Moderate $. Master Card or Visa, no Amex. Easy parking. Non-smoking only.

More than just a place to eat, the Aloha Theatre Complex is the nerve center of mauka Kona – a meeting place for the neighborhood which includes a cafe, a performing arts center, a dance school and a gift store. The 1930s style theatre building has lots of character, although it makes the logistics of the restaurant a bit difficult. There are about ten tables inside, a few out front, and another fifteen on the long lanai on the south side of the theatre. The best seats are at the end of the lanai, where you have a view of serene pastureland with the ocean in the distance. There is table service for dinner (5:00 to 8:00 p.m.), but customers order at the counter for breakfast (8:00 a.m. to 11:30 a.m.) and lunch. There's also a Sunday Brunch from 9 to 2. The staff is friendly, and the art exhibit on the walls (always a local artist) changes monthly.

Owners Alan and Susan Grodzinsky have strong cullinary backgrounds, and the cafe features consistently good food. Blackboard specials always include at least one kind of fresh fish, pasta, chicken, and soup of the day. Although the menu is short and specials don't change much, what you get is always fresh, homemade and tasty. Prices for the fresh fish and steak dinner entrees have crept up to $14-$16. A soup and salad special is $6.50, special burgers or fresh fish sandwiches are $8, and the chicken or pasta is usually $10-$12. Pastries and desserts are baked upstairs, and you can get fresh squeezed orange or carrot juice for breakfast. Coffee service is pure Kona coffee either regular or espresso. There is a wide assortment of beer and a few decent wines, but no mixed drinks.

There is usually a lunch rush between noon and 12:30, and the cafe can be very crowded before theatre performances on Friday or Saturday evenings. Otherwise, it's a leisurely, friendly place where you can usually find some interesting conversation and find out what's happening in theatre, dance, art, music and metaphysics. No stay in coffee country is complete without at least one stop here.

* *Bangkok Houses Thai Restaurant*, Kamehameha Square, Kailua-Kona (329-7764). Open for dinner 5 to 9 p.m. every day and lunch 11 to 3 Monday thru Friday. MC/Visa, Amex, Discover, local checks. Moderate $$. Smoking allowed. Easy parking in Kam Square lot. No view.

Small, clean, warm and nicely appointed, this fairly new restaurant has consistently been very good and sometimes excellent. The fresh catch-of-the-day ($9.95) comes with ginger, sweet and sour, hot and spicy or Thai red curry sauce. Other entrees are mostly in the $10 to $13 price range.

* *Bianelli's Pizza*, Pines Plaza (Hualalai Road between Kuakini and Queen K Highways), Kailua-Kona (326-4800). Monday through Friday 11 a.m. to 10 p.m., Saturday and Sunday 5 p.m. to 10 p.m. Moderate $. Visa, MC, no Amex. Non-smoking only. Easy parking.

This is probably the most versatile restaurant in Kona – a good place to take a family with five kids that also has a hip bar with sports TV; where singles can eat at the bar or couples can find a secluded table in the back. Probably the predominant crowd here is sports enthusiasts – triathletes, tennis players, bicyclists, etc., although generally the customers are a very diverse group (Wednesday is triathlete's night). Located in the Pines Plaza (the original store opened in 1989 in the Kona Coast Shopping Center), it may be a bit hard to find for tourists. From the center of Kailua, drive up Hulalalai Road (the road that intersects

Ali'i Drive at the Kona Inn Shopping Center) past the theatre complex and take a left turn into the Pines development. Or, take Queen K Highway to the stoplight at Nani Kailua Drive and turn towards the ocean and you can't miss it.

The cullinary strength of Bianelli's comes from the owners' (George and Shawne Goldstine and Bill and Theresa Barto) constant presence in the kitchen, and devotion to all things Italian—especially food, movies, and bicycles as you can see by the posters on the walls. We generally stay with the Caesar salad ($4.95), the all-you-can-eat pasta specials on the blackboard ($8.20 with salad), or the thin crusted pizza which you can also order by the slice ($1.50 and up). We like the house salad (organic local lettuce and sliced olives) with garlic vinagrette dressing, the homemade minestrone soup, and the Peroni beer ($3.50). Fresh ingredients predominate, and all the pasta is made the same day. Large 16-inch pizzas run from $14 to $21; entrees like lasagna, chicken parmagiana, eggplant parmagaiana and manicotti are $9 to $10, including salad. There are some very good wines by the glass from $3.50 to $10 and the desserts from *Jill's Country Kitchen* are some of the best in Kona. Coffee service is pure Kona dark roast with a single group espresso machine. Service can be spotty on busy nights or when new waitpersons are on the job (constant turnover of wait help is a problem with all Kona restaurants). Bianelli's does a large take out business, and they will deliver in the Kailua area, including to hotels. We especially appreciate the no smoking policy throughout the restaurant, the ease with which we can eat at the bar, and the generally friendly and upbeat atmosphere.

Bianelli's has a full bar, but unfortunately no view. We've occasionally seen people wait for 10-15 minutes on a busy Friday or Saturday night, but generally there is no wait and no need for reservations.

* *The Corner Pocket*, Kealakekua below the Post Office, next to UH West Hawaii (322-2994). Monday thru Sunday 11 a.m.-12 p.m., Moderate $, MC, Visa. Against all expectations, the food prepared at this pool hall/biker bar is very good. The makai half of the room has been upgraded to a clean, comfortable dining room with three booths and three tables, quite separate from the pool players and cigarette haze in the other section. The bar section includes two TV's (one giant screen) and a juke box with pretty good selections.

Not everything on this menu is worth trying, but the pastas, shrimp dishes, and hamburgers have been excellent. Service is what you would expect in a greasy spoon diner–the regulars get better than the newcomers. Although the atmosphere at the bar looks raunchy, we've never seen any real disturbances here.

* *Sibu Cafe,* Banyan Tree Court, Alii Drive, Kailua-Kona (329-1112). Simple but good Indonesian food with a few original twists. Our favorite is the garlic shrimp pasta which comes as an appetizer for $4 or as an entree for $12. Try to get one of the outdoor tables and taste the great fresh lilikoi (passion fruit) juice. Large portions, vegetarian selections, good vibes. No credit cards or mainland checks are accepted, so bring cash.

* *Su's Thai Kitchen*, Pawai Place, Old Industrial Area, Kailua-Kona (326-7808). Moderate $.

The Old Industrial Area was supposed to be zoned only for businesses like lumber companies and wholesalers, but now contains a mixture of wholesale, retail, and service businesses, with a few restaurants thrown in. Su's is housed in a building that used to be a hot tub spa but went out of business ten years ago. Consequently, it has an indoor/outdoor feeling to it that is somehow very in keeping with a Thai restaurant. Of the three Thai restaurants in town, this has the most authentic feel to it. In the dark, you won't notice you are in the Industrial Area. To get to Su's, turn north at the intersection of Palani Road and Ali'i Drive, towards the ocean. The turnoff to the Old Industrial Area is Kiawe Street, right across from West Hawaii Motors. Turn right, and then make another right on the first street, Pawai Place. Go about halfway up and Su's is on your right.

We've never had a bad meal or a bad experience at Su's. The service is courteous to the point of being deferential, and the owner/operators do all of the cooking. Have fun. Su's has another location in the Parker Ranch Center in Waimea.

* *Thai Rin Restaurant,* Alii Sunset Plaza, Ali'i Drive, Kailua-Kona (329-2929). Open for lunch 11 to 2:30 and dinner from 4:30 to 9:30 every day. MC/Visa, no Amex. Moderate $$. Smoking allowed. There is ample parking in the plaza lot – turn makai off Kuakini Highway just north of Hualalai Road or enter from Ali'i Drive.

A simple, family run place with quick service and good food which has gotten much better since it moved to the front of the Alii Sunset Plaza complex. The steamed catch-of-the-day special ranges from very good to superb ($18). Most entrees are in the $7 to $10 range. Thai Rin offers a larger beer and wine selection than the other Kona Thai restaurants, and is the only one with a bit of an ocean view. However, its ambiance is less intimate than Su's because of bright lighting. After dinner, it's an easy walk for dessert and coffee at Lava Java or Under the Palm. For music and dancing (Wednesday – Saturday) try Huggo's across the street.

Your Basic Kona Ocean View Restaurant

There are a number of similar restaurants on Ali'i Drive in Kailua-Kona that feature gorgeous oceanfront locations, great sunset views, a usually good catch-of-the-day, and otherwise have nothing special to recommend about the rest of the menu. You will have pretty much the same experience at any of them, but for what it's worth, here are some slight differences.

Kona Inn (Kona Inn Shopping Village, 329-4455). Our favorite Kailua oceanview restaurant, but we hardly ever eat in the main dining area at the south end. Instead, we prefer the outside tables and the short menu next to the bar. Fresh sashimi, fish sandwiches, pasta salad, hamburgers and the like can be quickly ordered ($6 to $10). The mai tais, Long Island iced teas, and other mixed drinks are excellent, and the ceiling fans connected by pulleys are unique. Over on the dining side, you can get a complete menu with prices in the $16 to $23 range for most entrees. Prices are similar at all the restaurants in this section – beer is usually $2.50 domestic, $3.50 imported, mai tais, pina coladas, margaritas and other mixed drinks are $4.50 to $5.50, house wine is $3.50 a glass, and bottles are usually lower- end California wines at $15 to $30.

Huggo's (Ali'i Drive next to the Royal Kona Resort, 329-1493). Built right over the water with a spectacular view and nightly visits from manta rays, Huggo's has long been a favorite of local fishermen. We think the cuisine and wine list are slightly superior to the other restaurants in this category; one of our favorite menu items is the barbequed ribs for lunch on Thursdays. The bar area features nightly entertainment and dancing on the weekends, and is usually one of the more happening night scenes in Kailua.

The Chart House (Waterfront Row, 329-2451). A national chain featuring an all-you-can-eat salad bar ($11). While the downstairs is usually bustling, the bar upstairs is a great place for a quiet, intimate drink. Only a few tables have unobstructed ocean views, but the deck that surrounds the restaurant and bar is a wonderful place to watch the sunset.

Jameson's By the Sea (next to Magic Sands Beach, 329-3195). For a slightly different setting, Jameson's is two miles south of town next to one of Kona's most popular beaches. The best approach here is to have a drink for sunset on the lanai, then perhaps move inside for dinner.

Fisherman's Landing (Kona Inn Shopping Village, 326-2555). Owned and operated by Uncle Billy Kimi, the owner of the mall, this is probably the most tourist-oriented of these restaurants, with buses of dinner guests from the Kohala hotels. It's just a 50-yard walk south from the Kona Inn, and we've often gone bar hopping between the two places. The entrance has an interesting display of the various Hawaiian fishes packed in ice.

The restaurants on the other side of Ali'i Drive have less spectacular views than those just mentioned, and prices are a bit lower. These include the *Kona Galley* (across from the pier, 329-5550), *Marty's Steak & Seafoods* (just a few steps south across from the sea wall, 329-1571), and the Mexican restaurants

Kona Amigos and *Pancho & Lefty's* (see the Mexican food section).

All of these restaurants are usually very satisfactory in their selection and preparation of fresh fish, and are great places to drink and hang out. Although their prices are high, the locations are usually worth it. All of them except the Kona Inn are closed for food service between lunch and dinner (usually 2 to 5 p.m.), and unfortunately none except the *Captain's Table* at Fisherman's Landing serve breakfast.

Mexican Restaurants

Poquito Mas, Kona Coast Shopping Center, Kailua-Kona (329-3528). A new, small, take-out Mexican restaurant with a healthy, tasty menu for those on a budget. There are tables outside in the courtyard of the entrance of the mall, but it is a busy location with bathrooms nearby and a lot of people hanging out, so you might want to take your food elsewhere to eat it. You can order a wide variety of Mexican food from $2 to $5 per item, and drink better than standard beverages like Arizona Iced Tea, Kohala Sodas, non-alcohol beer, or mineral water in addition to the usual, but no alcohol. We liked the stripped grilled beef on the tacos and grilled shrimp soft tacos, and the good variety of salsas on the side.

Reuben's Mexican Restaurant, Ali'i Drive (just south of Kona Marketplace on the mauka side of the street), Kailua-Kona (329-7031). The only Mexican restaurant in Kona owned and operated by Mexicans, and a favorite of Kona Kai's farmworkers. A traditional, medium-priced menu and atmosphere (no view) with occasional mariachi music and dancing on the weekends. The cuisine here is no better than average, but there is no really good alternative to recommend (see the other Mexican restaurants in this section for comparisons).

Rico's Mexican Restaurant, Alii Sunset Plaza, Kailua-Kona (326-7655). Fresh ingredients, moderate prices, no view.

Pancho & Lefty's, 75-5719 Ali'i Drive, across from the Banyan tree, Kailua-Kona (326-2171). A standard chain Mexican restaurant which is especially interesting at sunset when the birds in the Banyan tree across the street go crazy for about twenty minutes. The Mexican menu is standard, with a 2-for-1 deal on Tuesday nights. The lighting is a bit bright for our tastes, and the service uninspired, but if you can get a table by the rail it's fun to watch the people on Ali'i Drive, and you'll have a good view of Kailua Bay and the setting sun.

Kona Amigos, Ali'i Drive, across from the pier, Kailua-Kona (326-2840). Basically the same restaurant as *Pancho and Lefty's*, a half block closer to the pier. This place really rocks on Ironman Saturday as it provides the best view of the start/finish line across the street. There is a slightly more active bar scene here than the competition, but the food and atmosphere are basically identical.

Other Restaurants

Giuseppe's Italian Cafe, Kailua Bay Inn, Kailua-Kona (329-7888). On the mauka side of Ali'i Drive across from the seawall, underneath *Marty's Steak House*. Lunch served from noon to 4 p.m., dinner served until there are no more customers. Affordable $$. A good place for a decent, cheap Italian meal because you can bring your own wine. *Guiseppe's* is too small for bathrooms; hence no liquor license. Pasta dinners from $7 to $10; specials and seafood entrees from $10 to $15. An intimate, informal, open air, almost cramped setting in the traditional Italian style.

Kaminari Japanese Restaurant, Kopiko Plaza, Kailua-Kona (326-7799). Simple and inexpensive Japanese food featuring *yakatori*, *donburi*, *sushi*, and *bento* boxes.

Ocean Seafood Chinese Restaurant, Kamehameha Square, Kailua-Kona (329-3055). Depressing interior belies the good meals we've had there.

Rajun Cajun Grill, Kona Market Place (under the cinema, 334-0615). Didn't have time to eat before the show? No problem, you can get a cheap, tasty bowl of chili or gumbo with rice in a hurry here.

Teshima's Japanese Restaurant, Honalo (322-9140). Local favorite of mauka coffee growers.

Ling Ling's Lean Cuisine, Kealakekua Art Center, Kealakekua (323-3888). A mauka alternative to the Aloha Cafe, this place has about six tables inside and six outside on the lanai where you can see the ocean about two miles out and 1,200 feet below.

Hilo Restaurants

Restaurants in Hilo are finally getting better, thank goodness. The worst thing about a circle island trip was the lack of decent food in East Hawaii, but there are now several places we can recommend:

** *Cafe Pesto* (see review of the Kawaihae restaurant). Their new second location in Hilo is in the newly restored Y. Hata Building on Kamehameha Avenue opposite Hilo Bay (969-6640). Best informal restaurant in Hilo.

** *Pescatore Italian Restarant,* 235 Keawe Street, Hilo, Hawaii 96720 (969-9090). Open every day 11 am to 2 pm and 5:30 to 9 p.m. Fridays and Saturdays until 10 pm. Closed Super Bowl Sunday. Visa, MC, no Amex. Expensive/Moderate $$. Smoking and non-smoking sections.

This intimate little restaurant in downtown Hilo arguably serves the best Italian meals on the Big Island. Though not inexpensive (dinner entrees at $16 to $25), Pescatore is by no means fancy, and is accomodating to all forms of attire, from casual to formal. There are only twelve tables, and although there is no view, the atmosphere is cozy, and accomodating. At our last visit, our waitress was reasonably knowledgable and friendly, and the foods we sampled ranged from good to very good.

** *Roussel's,* Keawe Street, downtown Hilo (935-5111). Lunch Monday thru Friday 11:30 to 1:30, dinner nightly from 5 to 10 p.m.

A fancy New Orleans-style restaurant in a beautifully renovated bank building; definitely the place to go in Hilo. Bert Roussel, one of the owners has a small coffee farm, and has placed twice in the Kona Cupping Competition with his Kaloko Bayou Estate Coffee. Their coffee is served in individual french press coffee brewers at each table.

Lunch specials include grilled chicken and arugula salad ($7.50), shrimp or soft shell crab poor boy sandwhiches ($8), and oyster, shrimp & okra gumbo ($9). Dinner entrees feature several shrimp and crab dishes, fresh and imported fish, and meat dishes from $15 to $22.

* *Lehua's Bay City Bar & Grill* , Waianuene Avenue in downtown (935-8055). Good choice for lunch, varied menu, moderate prices.

Bear's Coffee, Keawe Street in downtown (935-0708). Long time hangout for students and counterculture types, serving a simple lunch (quiche, soups, sandwiches). Until a few years ago, the only decent coffee in East Hawaii.

Jasper's Cafe, Kalakaua Street in downtown Hilo (969-6686). The hippest eatery in Hilo with simple food, good coffee, and an attractive setting.

Picnic Lunches, Grocery Stores, Miscellaneous Food

There are a lot of great places to take a picnic lunch in Kona, but where do you buy the food? If you look hard, you can find a real food store other than a Circle K or 7-Eleven. Try not to gag at the price of food – paradise is expensive.

Kona Wine Market at Kamehameha Square (329-9400). The best wine store in Kona also carries a selection of specialty foods, some of them prepared and packaged to go.

KTA, Keauhou Shopping Village. Full-service supermarket with fish market, bakery, liquor store, and deli. Best parking lot view in the world.

French Bakery, Kaahumanu Plaza (at the end of the Kona industrial section): baked goods, sandwiches, and cold drinks (326-2688).

The Vegetable Stop in Kainaliu: local farmers selling their produce off the back of their trucks at the south end of town next to Sandy's Drive In.

Stan's Fish Market (Kona Seafood, Inc.), Honaunau (328-9777): fresh and dried fish.

Mrs. Barry's Kona Cookies, Kona Inn Shopping Village (329-6055): homemade cookies better than Mrs. Fields.

Kona Healthways, Kona Coast Shopping Center, Palani Road, Kailua-Kona (329-2296). Our choice for organic foods, vitamins, sandwiches and carrot juice to go.

Ohana O Ka Aina Natural Foods Cooperative, Aina Center, Kainaliu (next to Subway, 322-2425). Organic produce, health foods, bulk grains, etc.

Island Lava Java, Alii Sunset Plaza, Kailua-Kona (327-2161): store-baked muffins and other baked goods, *Tropical Dreams* ice cream.

Costco Wholesale, Kaloko Light Industrial Area (between the airport and Kailua-Kona, 334-0770). If you've just arrived for a two-week condo stay and want to stock up on food, this is by far your best deal. Costco was the first of the mainland warehouse stores to arrive in Kona in 1993 and caused a sensation among local shoppers. Temporary one-day entrance cards can be obtained if you don't have one.

Drinking

The best bars are those within walking distance of your hotel, especially if you like mai tais. Our favorite place is outside at the *Kona Inn*, one of the best drinking spots in Hawaii. Another good place is *Fisherman's Landing,* just north of the Kona Inn. Further up Aliʻi Drive are the *Chart House* and *Seafood Pasta Palace* at Waterfront Row, *Huggo's* (next to the Royal Kona Resort), the bar at the *Palm Cafe,* and *Jameson's* at Magic Sands Beach. All of these spots are great locations to watch the ocean and the sunsets. The best sports bars (with satellite TVs) are *Tom Bombadil's* (see pizza section) and *Drysdale's Two* at the Keauhou Shopping Village. For a non-smoking bar, there's *Bianelli's Pizza* at the Pines Plaza, which features TV sporting event nights such as Monday Night Football, which are often seen in Hawaii on a tape delay basis on weekdays). There are occasional DUI checks at checkpoints in Kailua and Kohala, and several fatal car accidents occur each year involving intoxicated drivers, so please drive safely!

ENTERTAINMENT

Kona is not a great place for night life. People tend to get up early and enjoy the day, rather than sleep late and party at night. For those of you with the desire and stamina, we recommend the following:

Luaus: *Captain Bean's* (329-2955, $45) is a tourist-oriented cruise that might scare you off, but even locals pay the $25 kama'aina rate to take the dinner sunset cruise. All you can drink and eat, Hawaiian-style entertainment, and great sunsets make this a fun experience. The audience participation format didn't bother us, and we are usually very uncomfortable in such circumstances. For a land-based luau, the best is the *Island Breeze Luau at the King Kamehameha Hotel* (326-4969), Sundays, Tuesdays, Wednesdays, and Thursdays at 5:30 ($49 adults, children 12 and under, $18, children under five, free). Island Breeze is a Hawaiian and Polynesian dance troupe whose members hail from Hawaii and the South Pacific islands.

Movies, Video Rentals, Theater: The *Kona Marketplace Cinema* on Ali'i Drive in Kailua (329-4488) is the oldest theater in town. It was recently remodeled into a duplex and is part of a multi-island chain. *Hualalai Theaters* on Kuakini Highway (329-6641) is your basic triplex chain operation. A long drive to Honokaa takes you to the newly renovated *Honokaa Theater* (775-0000), an old style Hawaiian theater lovingly restored by a physician/film buff. The best video stores are *Dr. Video* in Kamehameha Square (329-1711) in Kailua, *Video Showplace* (329-4599) in the shopping plaza across the street from Hilo Hattie's, and *Scott's Video* in the Kealakekua Ranch Center in Captain Cook (323-2794). The *Aloha Community Players* (322-9924) produce a season of plays at the *Aloha Theater* and there are often professional productions in dance, music, and theater at the wonderful *Kahilu Theater* in Waimea (885-6017). On Friday's, *West Hawaii Today* newspaper runs a good entertainment guide for weekend special events.

Music and Dancing: Discos go in and out of business in Kona faster than restaurants. Some are open only on the weekends, or only if there are enough patrons, so phone before you go.

Karaoke: A Japanese tradition catching on in America, you sing to prerecorded videos without the lead vocal track, using a heavily amplified and echo-chambered sound system which improves anyone's voice. Of the many karaoke spots in Kona, the most popular are at the *Royal Kona Resort* and at *Kona Bowl*.

Jazz: There is usually a jazz session on Sunday afternoons somewhere. Check the entertainment section of *West Hawaii Today* on Fridays.

Rock 'N Roll: Rock can be heard nightly upstairs at *Marty's Steak House* in Kailua, and weekends at the *Corner Pocket* in Kealakekua (where the crowd tends to get rowdy). You can also usually hear live music at *Huggo's*, the *Ah Dunno Bar & Grille* in the Old Industrial Area, and the *Windjammer Lounge* at the Kona Hilton.

Concerts: Only rarely does a well-known music group come to Kona. When they do, it is usually in conjunction with a concert in Honolulu. Sometimes we get some decent Reggae, and once in a while a good Hawaiian group. Mainland rock/blues/folk artists just don't play this circuit very much; the population base is too small.

Sporting Events: Kona is a sports-conscious place, and there are amateur events every week as well as some professional ones like the *Ironman Triathlon* in October. For example, the Mauna Lani has hosted the *Seniors Skin Game Golf Tournament* and *Davis Cup* tennis matches. Visitors can usually find a tennis or golf tournament they can enter, while other events like canoe races and polo matches are solely for spectators. The *Konawaena Wildcats* are the local high school team, and football games are a real community event.

Radio and TV: The local FM radio stations are KAOY (101.5) and KLUA (93.9). From most places, you can also get the more hip Maui station, KAOI (95.1). AM can be found at 790 (KKON, in Kealakekua). Most hotels have cable TV, since network reception is spotty in most areas. The local access channel is Channel 8, which shows a filmed tour of the Big Island over and over again during the day, and weekly community events at night, as well as local advertisements and real estate shows.

SHOPPING

Shopping in Hawaii, and Kona, is a hit and miss proposition. Many of the stores sell the same tired, tacky, tourist trinkets; the worst examples are the hundreds (literally) of *ABC Stores* that litter Waikiki, and that have begun to appear in Kona. Visitors usually yearn for those one-of-a-kind, owner-operator stores offering locally–crafted products. We hope the stores listed below fill that bill.

Jewelry: *The Pearl Gallery* (326-2667, Banyan Court). Watch out for the "50% Off" sales at many Hawaiian jewelry stores. This is the best place to buy quality pearls. *The Vintage Eye* (Kainaliu, 324-1800) offers an unusual collection of used and Bali-made jewelry and other accessories. *Kona Coast Jewelry Store*, Alapa Street, Industrial Area (329-5005) is a good one, as are *Oscar's* (322-6767) and *Aigner's* (322-9190), both in the Keauhou Shopping Village.

Clothing: *Paradise Found* has three locations: on Ali'i Drive in Kailua-Kona (329-3433), at Lanihau Shopping Center, also in Kailua (329-2221), and at the original store in Kainaliu (322-2111). This is the most popular women's clothing store among people who live here. *Flamingo's*, in the Kona Inn Shopping Village (329-4122) is another place to shop for women's fashions, as is *Noa Noa*, with its two stores in Kailua, one in Kona Inn Shopping Village (329-8187), and the other just down the street, also on Ali'i Drive.

Hobie Sports Kona at the Kona Inn (329-1001) offers surfwear and is a great place to buy clothes for teenagers.

Hilo Hattie's, Palani Road, Kailua-Kona (329-7200), is a muumuu of an experience. Be prepared to be greeted with a shell lei at the door and to be offered free refreshments. This is not one of those owner-operator stores (they have huge operations in Waikiki, Maui, Kauai, etc.) but they are an island tradition, selling everything from clothing to chocolate covered macadamia nuts.

Island Salsa, at the Kona Inn Shopping Village (329-9279) and at the Kona Market Place, both in Kailua, has the best t-shirts. There is also *Crazy Shirts* (329-2176) on Ali'i Drive.

Big Island Hat Company, in the Kona Inn Shopping Village (329-3332) carries a standard assortment of hats, as well as some very nice hand-made Hawaiian feather bands.

Liberty House, King Kamehameha Hotel, Kailua-Kona (329-2901). Kona's best attempt at a department store offers a decent selection of island sportswear. Their discount store, *The Penthouse*, is located at the Keauhou Shopping Village.

Collections by Liberty House, at the Mauna Lani Bay Hotel (885-7494), offers high quality designer sportswear for men and women.

Hyatt Regency Shopping Arcade and *Kings' Shops*, at Waikoloa. These are upscale mini-malls selling a variety of tourist-oriented merchandise. *The Endangered Species* store at Kings Shops is worth seeing.

Kona Historical Society

ARTS, CRAFTS, AND CULTURAL EVENTS

The Big Island's spectacular natural environment, from its snow-capped peaks and rivers of red hot lava, to its misty rainforests and teaming coral reefs, has long inspired the imagination of artists, artisans, dancers, and musicians.

Some of the best preserved artistic efforts of the early Hawaiians can be seen in the stone carvings, or petroglyphs, which are found in many locations around the island, especially on the Kona side. One of the most accessible petroglyph fields is located just off the entrance road to the Royal Waikoloan Hotel, near the King's Shops, where acres of flat lava rocks are covered with countless line drawings, laboriously etched into the rough surface. Another extensive field can be found about four miles south of Kawaihae outside the village of Puako. No one is really sure what the petroglyphs mean, nor when the earliest ones were carved. They might have had religious or supernatural significance, or they might just as easily have been the creative doodlings of a people living in an age of simpler, more spontaneous entertainment. Whatever inspired them, they are something that shouldn't be missed.

Perhaps even more impressive are the massive stone temples or *heiaus* which at one time were the center of the Hawaiian religion. What remains today are only the platforms upon which wood and thatch buildings once stood. To get an idea of what the temples originally looked like you can see authentic replicas next to the Kailua Pier in downtown Kailua-Kona, or at the *City of Refuge (Pu'uhonua o Honaunau)*, about 20 miles south of town.

If you're interested in the Big Island's past, a good collection of Hawaiian artifacts can be found at the *Lyman House Memorial Museum*, 276 Haili Street, in downtown Hilo. Hours are 9-5, Monday through Saturday, and 1-4 on Sunday. The entrance fee is $4.50 for adults, and $2.50 for children 6-17 and for seniors over 60.

Hawaiiana: The Hawaiians have always been a creative people, and are continuing their artistic traditions today, primarily through crafts, music, and dance.

The Big Island offers many opportunities for residents and visitors to either observe or participate in this rich cultural heritage. Special events are announced in the local newspaper, and ongoing programs welcome your participation.

One of our favorites is the *kupuna* demonstration that takes place every Tuesday and Friday in the main lobby of the King Kamehameha's Kona Beach Hotel in downtown Kailua. You don't have to be a guest of the hotel, and there is no charge.

Kupunas are revered elders who are dedicated to sharing their cultural knowledge, and sometimes as many as twenty are on hand at the King Kam to put on a show, then give demonstrations in weaving lauhala hats, making haku leis, or in creating any number of other indigenous crafts. The kupunas overflow with knowledge, patience, and aloha, and are more than happy to answer all your questions.

Cultural demonstrations are also part of the daily program at *Pu'uhonua Honaunau National Historical Park*, and, depending upon what craftsmen are on duty the day you visit, you may observe anything from *ki'i* (wooden image) carving to *lauhala* weaving or feather work. If you're lucky, you may get to see a log being carved into an outrigger canoe, or a woman making traditional *tapa* cloth by beating the inner bark of certain trees until it becomes soft and pliable.

The County of Hawaii Culture and Arts division of the Parks and Recreation Department (935-5068) sponsors a monthly crafts show and puts on a variety of cultural enrichment workshops and classes in such subjects as ukulele, Hawaiian slack key guitar, hula, and palm leaf weaving. Visitors are welcome to join in. Fees vary, and are very reasonable. The Culture and Arts department also sponsors a Hawaiian steel guitar festival, a ukulele festival, and other Hawaiian music festivals.

Probably the most popular and most famous celebration of Hawaiian culture is the *Merrie Monarch Festival*, a week-long event held every spring in Hilo, beginning on Easter Sunday. The focus of the festival is the highly competitive 3-day hula contest that brings together the top hula schools (*halaus*) from Hawaii and the Mainland. In addition to the contest there are also craft shows and demonstrations, non-competitive hula performances, and much more. Because of the festival's immense popularity, airline flights, rental cars, and accommodations are booked up well in advance. For more information on the Merrie Monarch, you may call 935-9168.

Big Island halaus give frequent public performances which are announced in the local newspaper. Hawaiian hula, as well as Tahitian, Samoan, and other South Pacific Island dances can be seen at the *Island Breeze Luau* (326-4969) on the grounds of the King Kamehameha Hotel in downtown Kailua-Kona.

Hawaiian music has evolved into a very distinct genre, and the contemporary sound, though mellow and melodious, is as far removed from the likes of the *"Little Grass Shack"* and *"Tiny Bubbles"* as Michael Jackson is from Frank Sinatra. There are lots of local Hawaiian bands who can be heard at various venues around the island, and you might want to pick up a tape or two by some of the state's top groups.

If you like Hawaiian music, you might want to check out the *Waiki'i Music Fest*, held for the past four years, usually in mid-

June, outside Waimea at the Waiki'i Ranch polo grounds. A crowd of more than 10,000 shows up for two solid days of Hawaiian music played by 30 or more bands. There's also hula dancing, arts and crafts, and lots of good food.

Arts and Crafts: There are plenty of galleries around the island, but whether much of what they contain can actually be considered art is a matter for debate. We tend to think that a great deal of it is nothing more than slick commercial illustration, or as one of our friends put it: "Expensive cartoons." Much of what you see in the galleries is undoubtedly pretty, but does it have any soul? We'll let you be the judge.

There are three galleries we'd like to recommend, not necessarily because they contain the best art, but because they are run by a co-op of 35 Big Island artists and offer a wide range of media. By running the galleries themselves, the *Kailua Village Artists* get to keep 75 percent of sales, rather than having to follow the usual practice of paying a gallery 50 to 60 percent in commissions. You'll find their galleries at The Royal Waikoloan Hotel (885-6789), the King Kamehameha Hotel (329-2911), and the Keauhou Beach Hotel (322-3441).

One of our favorite artistic places is the quiet little village of Holualoa, an old coffee town three miles up the mountain from Kailua that has become one of the most dynamic art centers in Hawaii. There are many different galleries here, and there is always at least one special showing. Our personal favorites are *Hiroki Morinoue's Studio 7 Gallery* (324-1335), *Matt and Mary Lovin's The Holualoa Gallery* (322-8484), and *Shelley Maudsley White's White Garden Gallery* (322-7733).*Wilfred Yamazawa*, a renowned glass blower and winner of the Kona Coffee Picking Contest, takes customers by appointment only (324-1646). Mary Lovein's "Mr. Coffee" is on the front cover of this book, and her poster for the 1994 Coffee Festival won an Ilima Award of Merit, a statewide competition.

The Little Grass Shack, located in Kealakekua (323-2877), is a great Hawaiian arts and crafts store with high quality articles. You'll find a relaxed atmosphere, and no tour buses stopping to shop. Other stores in this category are *Kahanahou Hale Kahu* in Kealakekua (322-3901), *Alapaki's* in the Keauhou Shopping

Village (322-2007), and *Cook's Discoveries*, in Waimea's Waimea Center (885-3633). These stores have some fantastic Hawaiian art, although the best of it is on the expensive side.

Kimura's Lauhala Shop, Holualoa (324-0053). Tatami mats, baskets, and hats, all hand-woven by Mrs. Kimura and her friends. Just south of Holualoa at the intersection of Hualalai road.

H. Kimura Store, Kainaliu (322-3771). Owned by the same family as the lauhala shop–this is the place to buy Japanese or Hawaiian fabric.

Mele Kai Music, located in Kaahumanu Plaza in the Old Industrial Area (329-1454), carries a good selection of authentic Hawaiian music. You might want to start with the Makaha Sons of Ni'ihau, Gabby Pahanui, Eddie Kamai and the Sons of Hawaii, Olomana, the Beamer Brothers, or Cecilio and Kapono.

Middle Earth Book Shoppe, Ali'i Drive, Kailua-Kona (329-2123). Best selection of Hawaiiana reading.

Topstich Fiber Arts, Parker Ranch Center, Waimea (885-4482). Interesting quilts and Hawaiian fabrics, plus espresso.

Cottage Gallery (328-9392) at *SKEA* (South Kona Educational Association) in Honaunau features "mauka" artists for a good cause.

Many of the galleries in Kailua-Kona exhibit art that has nothing to do with Hawaii, or they show only the most commercial "frolicking whales" type of paintings. Besides the galleries run by the Kailua Village Artists, we like the *Showcase Gallery* (322-9711) in the Keauhou Shopping Village.

Dyansen Gallery, in the Hilton Waikoloa Village (885-1204) offers an excellent array of *Erte* statues, *Bill Mack* sculpture, works by *Chagall* and other well known international artists, and some selected local artists. Ask for Maria Echavarri.

The Blue Ginger Gallery in Kainaliu (322-3898) features Indonesian and local arts and crafts in a pleasant place at reasonable prices.

Volcano Arts Center in Hawaii Volcanoes National Park (967-7511) is worth a visit when you're in the area.

The Gallery of Great Things in Parker Square, Waimea (885-7706), is one of the most diverse galleries on the Big Island.

Kona Frame Shop, Old Industrial Area, Kailua-Kona (329-1722), is located in the Gold Coast Center at the north end of Kaiwi Street. Most of our artworks are framed here.

Country Frame Shop, Holualoa (324-1590). Their logo features a coffee branch with ripe cherries.

Brantley Center, Honoka'a (775-9002). A center for Hawaiian woodworking, definitely worth the trip if you are interested in koa, milo, or other exotic wood bowls, boxes, trays, and carvings.

Waipio Valley Artworks, on the rim of the valley (775-0551), carries a great selection of Hawaiian woodworking and other crafts.

Those interested in "space art" might want to see some of the works of local artist Jon Lomberg (328-9692), whose painting of the Kona solar eclipse from an outer space viewpoint is one of the better posters you can buy.

Real Estate

Looking at real estate is one of the most popular visitor pastimes, and it is possible that the next few years may see some of the best bargains of the decade. America's economic slump coupled with the cooling of Japanese demand for expensive houses has pushed prices down since 1990, and they are likely to stay down through at least 1995. A discussion of the ins and outs of Kona real estate is more than we can accomplish here; all we can do is give you a very brief, general overview of the subject.

At the peak of the real estate boom there were over 700 agents in Kona, but lack of business has driven out many of the less committed. All of the large real estate companies are here, and your satisfaction with a broker depends almost entirely on your personal relationship with your agent. There are many good ones, and all are listed in the real estate sections of the local newspaper, *West Hawaii Today* (especially Friday and Sunday), including their photos.

One of the unique aspects about Kona real estate is that a great deal of land is owned by large estates which lease rather than sell property. This is particularly true of agricultural land in Kona, which is largely owned by *Bishop Estate*, the result of Princess Bernice Pauahi marrying missionary Charles Bishop in 1850. Her entire estate of 434,300 acres was left in trust to establish a school for Hawaiian children. Bishop Estate is now a $2-billion company which operates *Kamehameha School* in Honolulu with some of the revenues.

The price of lease land is roughly two thirds that of fee simple land, and the difference is paid out in rent over the term of the lease (20 to 45 years for land). Few leases are left to expire – almost all are renegotiated at higher rents. A typical leased three-acre coffee farm with an old house (often called a "coffee shack") pays about $250 per year (including a portion for the house site) against four-percent of the gross agricultural sales. The lease for such a farm might sell for around $125,000, depending on the condition of the house, the view, and the orchards. Bishop Estate takes 10% of the gross profit on sales of their leases. Court decisions have forced the estate to begin selling the fee to most of their residential properties, and it is possible this practice will be extended to agricultural lands as well.

Another unique term here is "affordable housing," the state of Hawaii's term for housing under $175,000, which they can require developers to build as a condition for developing more upscale properties. This is usually only available to Hawaii residents, who may be required to keep the property for ten years before selling it.

Of the hundreds of real estate agents in Kona, a few are particularly familiar with coffee farms. If you are interested in becoming a farm owner, you might speak with Arnie Rabin (*A Real Estate Concern*, Kainaliu, 322-3677), David Selwyn (*Selwyn Realty Investments*, Kealakekua, 322-6866), or Keith Keffer (*Keffer Properties*, 323-9789).

Agriculture and Horticulture

Next to tourism, agriculture is the Big Island's most important economic mainstay, but Hawaii's largest agricultural industry is virtually invisible. The state's hidden crop, marijuana, grosses over $200 million per year, which just about equals what is earned by all other agricultural products combined. With so much money at stake, you can be sure there are plenty of pot plants hiding amidst the profuse vegetation you see everywhere on the island.

The ongoing military operation to eradicate marijuana, called "*Green Harvest*," consists of spotting and reconnaissance by U.S. Army and Hawaii National Guard helicopters, and actual "harvesting" by state and local law enforcement ground forces. No chemical weed killers are sprayed on Big Island marijuana patches; it is all pulled up by hand, then buried in a secret location.

According to police, a total of 562,000 plants were destroyed in 1993 on the Big Island, while statewide the total was 778,000. Police estimate they eradicate between 60 and 70 percent of what is planted, while wild pigs and thieves also take a big bite out of growers' profits.

The Puna and Hamakua districts, primarily Puna, are the most popular cannabis growing regions because of the abundance of undeveloped lands and forest areas, and because the climate is ideal, with plenty of rainfall. But due to the success of the helicopter raids, more and more pot is being grown indoors under artificial conditions.

Hawaiian *pakalolo* can cost as much as $400 to $800 an ounce, or $5,000 to $8,000 per pound, depending upon seasonal availability, so there are still many growers willing to take the risk.

Sugar: Lush green acres of sugar cane rippling in the trade winds, a sight many visitors associate with Hawaii, will be only a memory after 1996, when the Big Island's last remaining sugar company ends its operations. *Hamakua Sugar*, once the largest employer on the Big Island, harvested its last cane in 1994 and shut down in September of that year. The second largest sugar employer, *Hilo Coast Processing Company*, closed its doors that same month, leaving only *Ka'u Sugar*, which plans to shut down in October 1996. The closings of the three companies will leave more than 1,000 workers unemployed, and will indirectly cost the jobs of at least another 2,000 people – a major economic disaster on an island with a population of only 120,000. Not so long ago, the three plantations, along with 70 independent growers, cultivated 60,000 acres and produced 300,000 tons of sugar annually, worth over $90 million.

Macadamia Nuts: The Big Island is the state's leading producer of macadamia nuts, with more than 96 percent of the total production, or 50 million pounds, worth about $30 million (farm value) annually, two or three times that wholesale, and a great deal more at the retail level. Mac nuts are the largest of the diversified agriculture crops, which include everything but sugar and pineapple.

The macadamia was introduced to Hawaii in the early 1870s, and has been in commercial production since 1948. The nut is grown extensively in the Puna and Ka'u districts. Several companies offer tours of their factories. The biggest company, *Mauna Loa Macadamia Nut Corporation*, gives historical tours at their Kealakekua location on the Kona side (M-F, 9:30 a.m. to 4 p.m., 324-7313), as well as tours of their actual operations, on the Hilo side (966-8618). *Mac Farms*, perhaps the biggest producer on the Kona side (in Honomalino) is not open to the public.

There are many small orchards in Kona, and several processing plants, such as *Kamigaki Orchards* and their *Kona Coast Macadamia Nut and Candy Factory* (328-8141), located at the intersection of the main highway and Ke'ei Road, in Honaunau. They specialize in chocolate-coated nuts.

There is a festival for macadamia nuts held in Hilo during October, that is similar to the Kona Coffee Cultural Festival.

Pineapple: There is no commercial production of pineapple on the Big Island, and it is being phased out on the other islands due to the high cost of land and labor, and high pesticide use. Still, it is a favorite with local gardeners and you can sometimes find the small, sweet, locally grown variety at farmers' markets.

Papaya: Papayas taste best before they get too ripe and mushy, while there is still a hint of green in the skin. A squeeze of fresh lemon or lime enhances the flavor. Although we don't recommend doing this in public, next time you eat a papaya, try rubbing the juicy side of its skin over your face and leave the juice on for about 10 minutes for an invigorating facial. Papaya extract is an ingredient in many natural cosmetic products.

The Big Island is Hawaii's leading grower of papaya, with over 2,000 acres producing 96 percent of the state's crop. Most of the papaya farms are in the Kapoho area of Puna, just this side of Hilo. Papayas like dry weather, and are grown at low elevations, but need irrigation and lots of fertilizer to produce market-quality fruit. The trees are remarkably fast growing, and under proper conditions can begin bearing fruit one year after planting.

Kona Kai Farms started out as a papaya farm before expanding into coffee. Our favorite variety is the "sunrise" (sometimes called "strawberry"), the fruit of which has a distinct ruddy blush and is sweeter and more flavorful than the more common yellow type. Kona Kai Farms is one of the few commercial papaya farms in Kona, but almost everyone seems to have a few trees.

Choose fruit with smooth, unblemished skins. Papayas are ripe when their skin turns yellow, and they should be firm yet slightly soft to the touch. Green or partially green papayas take two to seven days to ripen at room temperature. When fully ripe, they keep in the refrigerator for up to a week. The tart, crunchy flesh of green papayas is an ingredient in various tropical dishes, especially those of Asian origin, while dried papaya enzyme is used as a meat tenderizer, and certain papaya extracts are used in medicines.

Banana: The Big Island is the leading banana producer in the state. The centers of banana production are Kea'au, Kurtistown, and Kapoho in the Puna district. Cavendish and Dwarf Brazilian (apple) are the two main varieties of bananas grown commercially on over 500 acres, by approximately 30 major growers. About 80 percent of the acreage is devoted to the Cavendish variety (your typical, ordinary banana), though many banana aficionados claim that the apple banana, with its more tart, pineapply taste, is a far superior species.

Kea'au Banana Plantation, south of Hilo, produces about half the state banana crop, and thanks to plantation owner Richard Ha, is doing so without relying on pesticides. Ha's efforts to avoid chemicals has won for his farm an "ECO-OK" rating by the environmental group Rainforest Alliance. His is the first banana farm in the world to receive the designation.

Coconut: Coconuts are not raised commercially here, but grow wild everywhere, a reminder of the importance they once had in Hawaiian culture. They are one of the few fruits high in iron and are rich in many other nutrients. Their juice is properly called "coconut water" and makes a refreshing drink. (Coconut milk, an essential ingredient in many tropical dishes, is made from grating the coconut meat, then squeezing out the creamy fluid.) There are many different species of coconut, some of which produce very little meat but an abundance of liquid and are called "drinking nuts" because they were bred for that purpose. The flesh of a young green coconut is called "spoon meat" because it is as soft as jelly and can be easily eaten with a spoon. In the old days, it was fed to babies, invalids, and old people who'd lost their teeth and could no longer chew.

Mango: Late Spring and Summertime is mango season in Hawaii, and one way locals share aloha with their neighbors is to distribute big grocery bags full of this delicious fruit to everybody they know. The different varieties ripen at different times from late spring to early fall, and come in various sizes and colors from the tiny wild yellow mangoes, to the large purple/red Hayden which can weigh more than a pound. The shapely mango tree, with its wide spreading branches laden with dangling fruit, is a front yard favorite in many an older neighborhood. Believe it or not, the mango belongs to the same family as poison ivy and its sap can cause a similar, maddeningly itchy skin rash. Highly sensitive persons cannot even handle the fruit, and for them to eat it is to invite a serious allergic reaction.

Guava: Guavas grow wild throughout the island, and on farms on the east side. There are two distinct types, the strawberry guava, which is a small, sweet, red fruit prized by locals for making jelly, and the common yellow type which is the variety grown commercially. Guavas can be eaten fresh, as is, although they are full of seeds. Products made from guava include puree, nectars, drinks and fruit blends, sherberts, cakes, jams and jellies.

Avocado: There are many different varieties of avocado trees growing in Kona, but the most common commercial variety seems to be the Sharwill, first promoted by Kerry Watson's *Ataraxia Farms* in Honaunau. The Sharwill is consistently medium sized, with a small seed, green rough skin, and a rich, nutty flavor.

There are 60 major avocado growers on the island, whose farms are located mostly on the Kona coast, particularly at Honalo and Honaunau.

Avos are rich in potassium, phosphorous, protein, vitamin A, and niacin. When ripe, they keep well refrigerated.

Exotic Tropical Fruits and Citrus: The cultivation of tropical exotic fruits, most of them native to Southeast Asia and South America, is a new and growing industry for the Big Island.

Among the many varieties to be found here are the cherimoya, atemoya, rambutan, carambola (starfruit), loquat, mangosteen, abiu, durian, longan, and lychee.

One of the nicest farms is *Ka'awaloa Orchards* (323-2933) at the top of Napo'opo'o Road (the road to Kealakekua Bay) a half mile from the *Kona Kai Farms* coffee drop off. You can get a good look from the road, and call about a visit to see the trees.

Many varieties of citrus, such as grapefruits, oranges, tangelos, and kumquats also thrive on the Big Island.

Vegetables: Our island is endowed with a varied climate, from tropical to temperate, thus, a wide variety of vegetables can be successfully grown here. Waimea is the primary vegetable growing area, where about 30 farms are located that produce vegetables on 800 acres of land. The vegetables grown in Waimea include head and leaf lettuce, cabbage, Chinese cabbage, burdock, carrots, broccoli, cauliflower, daikon, sweet corn, cucumber, celery, eggplant, pepper, radish, Italian squash, and onions.

In the Mountain View area, tomatoes and cucumbers are produced, while the adjoining Volcano area produces Italian squash and cauliflower.

In the Kona area, tomatoes, cucumbers, beans, peppers, and watercress are grown.

These vegetables, as well as a wide variety of locally produced fruits, are available at farmers' markets throughout the island, as well as at local supermarkets. *Sam's Organic* lettuce, *Ka'u Gold* oranges, hydroponic strawberries, *Ku'oko'a* Farms goat cheese, *Datta's Adaptions* organic herbs and vegetables, and fresh herbs and spices from *Tip Davis' Hawaiian Herb and Spice Co.* are other popular locally grown products you might want to sample.

Ginger: Hawaiian ginger, produced exclusively in Hawaii, and nowhere else in the United States, is noted for its high quality. Twenty years ago the ginger industry was merely a collection of small backyard operations catering entirely to local markets. Today, it is a multi-million-dollar industry producing millions of pounds annually sold to mainland U.S. and European markets.

Fresh Hawaiian ginger root enhances the flavor of meats, vegetables, chicken, fish, cakes, and candies, and can even be brewed as a tea. Select ginger that is firm with no soft spots. To use fresh ginger, simply peel and prepare as the recipe directs. Ginger is available in the produce section of local supermarkets.

Taro: Taro has been cultivated extensively on the island since the arrival of the Polynesians over a thousand years ago, and was until the modern era the chief staple of the Hawaiian diet. Wetland taro is grown mostly in Waipio Valley, the island's center of *poi* taro production. It is grown in shallow ponds similar to rice paddies, and each new young plant must be set out by hand. The work is wet, muddy, time consuming, and back breaking.

Poi is the sticky, purplish-gray carbohydrate made from mashed taro corms that is found at every authentic luau. Poi lovers can tell the difference between brands produced on different islands and recommend eating it along with fresh fish.

Another type of taro which is steadily gaining significance in acreage is the dry land or *Chinese taro*. The Big Island, primarily the Hilo and Hamakua districts, accounts for about 90 percent of the state's total production.

Chinese taro is used fresh and for making taro chips. The corms can be fried, roasted, baked or boiled, and taste something like potatoes. Taro is widely consumed by Asians, Pacific Islanders, Africans, and Central and South Americans. Taro chips, leaves, poi, and fresh taro are available in supermarkets around the island.

Chocolate: Hawaii has a fledgling chocolate industry, and there are about 14 new farms in the Kona and Kea‘au areas growing cacao (from which chocolate is made) for the specialty market. This is the first time cacao has been grown commercially in the U.S. Despite the youth of the new enterprise, Kona's bittersweet chocolate is already establishing itself as one of the world's premier varieties and is being used by some top restaurants in Honolulu, New York, and elsewhere. The human catalyst behind the new industry is Jim Walsh, a former Chicago advertising man, who has sunk $4 million and years of research into establishing his *Hawaiian Vintage Chocolate Co.* His gourmet product retails for around $16 per pound.

Flowers: Cut tropical flowers are one of the fastest growing of the island's diversified agriculture crops. The largest nurseries grow anthuriums in natural shade or under shadecloth, primarily in the

Puna and South Hilo districts. The anthurium, which means "tail flower" in Greek, was introduced to Hawaii in the late 1800's and grows best in a warm, humid climate.

Orchids flourish to such an extent on the Big Island that it is also sometimes called "The Orchid Isle." Half of the state's commercially produced orchids are grown here, and dedicated hobbyists grow thousands more.

The five most common varieties of orchids grown commercially on the island are dendrobiums, cattleyas, vandas, cymbidiums, and phalaenopsis. The principal growing areas are the Puna, Hilo, Hamakua, and Kona districts. A number of orchid nurseries are open to the public.

Heliconia, varieties of ginger flowers, bird of paradise, and protea are the main types of exotics grown here. There are 40 exotic flower farms primarily in the Puna, Hilo, Hamakua, and Kona districts, with protea production in Waimea, Kona, Ocean View, Glenwood, and Pahoa. Care of exotics includes soaking the flowers in room-temperature water for 30 minutes and re-cutting the stem, then placing them in a warm preservative solution.

Flower farms in the Kona area, as well as in other parts of the island, also raise plumeria, tuberose, jasmine, pikake, pua kenikeni, three kinds of ilima, stephanotis, pakalana, bozus, kika, crown flower, wax flower, and other varieties for the lei market.

Leis are also frequently made from carnations, which are primarily grown in Waimea. They are raised on a smaller scale in Kona, Ka'u, and North Kohala as well. More than 15 different varieties are cultivated on the island for both cut flowers and leis.

The commercial production of roses on the island began ten years ago and is centered in Waimea, where the largest producer of roses in the state is located. About 20 varieties of roses are produced commercially for the cut flower and lei markets.

The Big Island's $11-million foliage industry is one of the fastest growing of the island's major agricultural crops, providing plants for residents' homes and commercial buildings. Palms, bamboo, and a variety of dracaenas are also shipped to the mainland.

The island is the state's center for the production of potted plants for landscape use. The burgeoning hotel and golf course industries have added to the demand for large plants. The island is also the leader in *bonsai* planted on lava rock for indoor use locally as well as for international export.

If you like plants and flowers, there are several botanical gardens around the island that are worth a visit. On the Kona side, the *Amy Greenwell Ethnobotanical Garden* is located in Captain Cook (323-3318) about two miles south of Kona Kai Farms. Hours are 8 a.m. to 3 p.m. on weekdays, with a guided-tour every other Saturday. There is no admission charge.

The *Sadie Seymour Botanical Gardens* is located just outside Kailua on the grounds of the *Kona Outdoor Circle* (where Kuakini Highway merges with Queen Ka'ahumanu Highway). This garden is small, but contains a fairly representative collection. The plantings are arranged in geographically-related sections which exhibit species commonly grown here that are native to other regions of the world. It is interesting to see that most of the plants we associate with Hawaii are really natives of Africa or South America, Asia or Malaysia, the West Indies, Australia, or the Mediterranean. Open daily, 9-5; admission is free (329-7286).

A very special place is the *Kaloko Mauka Cloud Forest Sanctuary*, a twelve-year labor of love in forest preservation by Norman Bezona, an agricultural extension agent with the University of Hawaii. Located only a few miles up the mountain above Kailua, the 40-acre sanctuary is a world apart, a tranquil rainforest sheltering endangered Hawaiian birds and exotic plants. Norman enjoys sharing his special place with the public, but only in groups of twelve or more, by appointment. He may be contacted at 325-6440.

There are three botanical gardens in the Hilo area, *Hawaii Tropical Botanical Gardens* (964-5233), *Hilo Tropical Gardens* (935-4957), and *Nani Mau Gardens* (959-3541). In Honaunau, just before the City of Refuge, you'll find *Wakefield Gardens Restaurant* (328-9930).

Farmers' Markets: Fresh locally produced fruit and vegetables, as well as island-grown coffee, tropical flowers, and other products are available at farmers' markets in Hilo, Kona, and Waimea. In Hilo, the market is located downtown in a vacant lot across from the bus terminal on the bayfront drive, at the corner of Kamehameha and Mamo. Hours are 6 a.m. to 2 p.m. on Wednesday and Saturday, and 9 a.m. to noon on Sunday. In Kona, the farmers' market operates Wednesdays in the parking lot behind the library downtown, across from *Waterfront Row*, on Ali'i Drive and in the Old Industrial Area on weekends. The Waimea farmers' market is held every other Saturday morning during most of the year, and every Saturday morning during the summer, at the Parker School, across from the playground in Kamuela (Waimea).

Aquaculture: Commercial aquafarms in Hawaii County have lately increased in number and acreage, although the industry is still in its infancy and experimentation is more the order of the day than profitability.

A majority of the farms utilize coastal spring and stream water to grow Chinese catfish, apple snails, tilapia, grass carp, common carp, rainbow trout, and mullet, while a few others use surface and deep ocean water to grow microalgae, American lobster, oysters, Japanese flounder, and edible seaweed varieties such as nori and ogo.

High energy costs, pricey real estate, costly maintenance, expensive labor, and the resistance of a public that prefers ocean-caught fish to pond-bred varieties conspire against the aquaculturists' best efforts and have already bankrupted several companies. But those involved in the industry say it's a coming thing for Hawaii, and they point to Asian fish farming as an established success with a thousand-year track record.

Livestock: Hawaiian cowboys, or paniolos, still ride the ranges of the Big Island, fixing fences, roping calves, and rounding up strays, and, because of the rugged terrain, their preferred vehicle will continue to be of the four-legged variety. Horses play an essential role in island ranching. Parker Ranch has more than 300 working horses, as well as another 400 brood mares, foals, and studs. Expert riders keep their edges sharp at regularly scheduled rodeos in Waimea, Ka'u, Honaunau, and elsewhere.

Much of the island's 700,000 acres of grazing land can be

found on the Parker Ranch, located in Kamuela (Waimea) which, at three-fourths the size of the island of Oahu, is the largest privately-owned cattle ranch in the world. Other cattle ranches are scattered throughout the island, primarily in the North Kohala, Kona, and Ka'u districts.

There are some 300 cattle operations on the island, as well as 80 hog farms, 40 dairy farms, 10 egg producers, and somewhere around five honey farms.

The Big Island is the state's leading producer of honey with annual production of about one million pounds. The major producing area is on the west side. *Captain Cook Honey/Powers Apiaries* (328-2279), and *Kona Queen Company* (328-9339) are both located in Napo'opo'o, about a mile down the road from Kona Kai Farms. *Sinclair Honey Farms* (328-2656) is located about 15 miles south of Captain Cook, and features Kona coffee honey.

Kona On-Line

In Kona, you can fulfill the dream of attending to business back home while remaining in paradise, via a computer link up. All the major on-line services have access numbers in Hawaii.

Sending e-mail and using on-line services like *CompuServe* through a telephone line in Kona usually requires a long distance call to an Oahu phone number. We sometimes are cut off due to poor local connections, but it is not an everyday problem. *America Online*, *Prodigy* and *GEnie* offer local access from numbers in Hilo. Connection to CompuServe and other services are surprisingly good, and will be fantastic when a network of fiber-optic cables now being laid between islands is completed.

Checking out on-line Hawaii is very inexpensive and easy. *Hawaii FYI*, a state-run network with local access, is considered one of the best local government networks in the U.S., and is accessible by dialing 935-7388 with N-8-1 modem settings. You will find free access to the Hawaii library system plus a number of local government agencies. There's also a new InterNet linkup service right in Kona called *Inter Link*.

If you need to have equipment mail-ordered to Kona during your stay, add an extra day or two to the normal shipping time. PC Connection and MacConnection usually don't tag on any extra charge for Hawaii shipments, though some of the smaller mail order outlets do.

Napo'opo'o. Kona Historical Society

Big Island History
What You Can See Today

The people of Hawaii look to historic and archaeological sites on the Big Island as the keepers of the past, and to the island's wide open spaces as the hope of the future. Many of the events that have decided Hawaii's fate have occurred on this island, and the key to the preservation of Hawaiian ways, as well as of the race itself, may be here.

Kona alone is a rich nexus of Hawaiian history rivaled only by Honolulu in importance. It is where heroes of ancient Hawaii battled, paid homage to gods brought from the heart of Polynesia, and established a capitol from which to rule all Hawaii.

At first glance this is improbable to the western eye for, as the missionaries who arrived in 1820 recorded in their journals, Kona seems to be a desolate land of bleak lava fields. To the early Hawaiians, though, the abundant fishing grounds and calm waters found offshore, plentiful springs of fresh water along the coast, and rich *mauka* (mountainside) fields perfect for dry land taro and sweet potatoes created ideal living conditions.

The first Hawaiians (descendants of migrant Polynesians) arrived from the South Pacific, probably from islands near Tahiti, aboard large double-hulled voyaging canoes more than 1,500 years ago. A canoe landing site at South Point, still in existence today, points the way south to their ancestral homelands 2,000 miles away.

After several waves of settlers arrived to establish homes and fields, Hawaii experienced an idyllic golden era, according to some historians. This era of settlement and peace lasted until about 1300 A.D., when the arrival from Tahiti or Samoa of the high priest Pa'ao forcibly introduced a sect of the Polynesian religion that focused on the *ali'i* (nobility) and a priesthood who practiced human sacrifice to satisfy their gods.

Genealogies of Hawaii's rulers passed down from generation to generation by trained orators tell of a royalty with legends comparable to those of the European monarchies, with court intrigue and power struggles.

Archaeological ruins of the ali'i of pre-contact Hawaii in Kona remain mostly unrestored and overgrown. Next to the Ranch House Restaurant in Kailua is the supposed site of the compound of Umi, a powerful ali'i of the 1500s. It is believed Kona's place of refuge once stood in the same area, to shield *kapu* breakers from death. Today, only crumbling ruins remain, hidden by weeds.

Attempting to envision how the Hawaiians of old lived in Kona takes an educated stretch of the imagination. Until the mid-1800s most Hawaiians here dwelled in coastal villages near fishing grounds with farming taking place *mauka* (on the mountainside).

A royal compound on the ocean at Kamakahonu, where King Kamehameha's Kona Beach Hotel is today, was for the ali'i alone, and the common people provided fish, taro, the *pua'a* (pig) and any other needs or luxuries their rulers desired. For transportation, the people hiked miles along the coast on a well-marked path through the lava fields to a string of fishing villages near the sea, and on upland trails to their mauka plantations of taro and sweet potatoes.

Just a short walk from the Royal Waikoloan Hotel on the

Kohala Coast lies a field of petroglyphs, the rock etchings that were the only written communication the Hawaiians of old used. In this area are over 12,000 of the carvings, some ancient, some using English words learned after contact had been established with the West.

At the time Captain James Cook of the British Navy set sail from England in 1777 on his way to the Pacific, Hawaii's islands were ruled by separate ali'i and the complex kapu system dictated the lifestyle of the people.

On Cook's second visit to Hawaii his crews sighted Maui and the Big Island, then anchored at Kealakekua Bay, just offshore from where the road ends today, on the north side of the bay. The arrival of the foreign ships was given a friendly greeting by thousands of Hawaiians who swarmed around them in myriads of outrigger canoes.

By entering Kealakekua Bay during the Makahiki season, Cook had unwittingly fulfilled a Hawaiian prophecy about the return of the god Lono. Legend has it that Cook was mistaken for Lono because his square sails on their masts resembled Lono's sacred symbol – a rectangle of white *tapa* cloth fastened by a cross piece to a pole. The resourceful Cook is said to have gone along with the Hawaiians' mistake, and played the part of a visiting god to the hilt, enjoying the feasts and gifts lavished upon him. When fair winds began to blow, Cook's ships sailed away in search of new adventures, but were forced to return by a broken mast.

This time, the Englishman was not so well received, for Lono's festival was over, and it was the season of fierce Ku, the war god. There are many versions of what happened next; the only certainty is that Cook did indeed meet his death at Kealakekua Bay. The place where he went down is marked by a square brass plaque on the lava; usually covered by water. Nearby is a vertical white marble monument easily visible on the opposite side of the bay from where the road ends. It can be reached only by a steep foot path down the cliff, by paddling a kayak across the bay, or by boat.

Standing over Cook's body at Kealakekua was Kamehameha I, a young Hawaiian warrior of noble blood. Known as the "Lonely One," he would within three decades conquer and unite for the first time all the Hawaiian Islands except Kauai, which eventually came to him under a political agreement.

Kamehameha's birthplace at North Kohala's Upolu Point is a well-visited restored archaeological site. However, Kona is most closely linked with the life and times of the "Napoleon of the Pacific," who was born around 1753. The restored Ahu'ena Heiau on the grounds of King Kamehameha's Kona Beach Hotel (call 329-2111 for information about a free daily tour of the grounds) was where he drew on spiritual and political power in ruling all Hawaii from 1812 until his death in 1819.

From his deathbed at Kamakahonu, Kamehameha influenced the course of Hawaiian history when he ordered his retainers not to offer themselves as sacrifices upon his death, nor to deface themselves. His sacred bones were hidden somewhere on the island, perhaps in an inaccessible cave high up a sheer cliff.

Upon the king's death, his young son Liholiho (Kamehameha II) and his favorite wife, Ka'ahumanu, assumed dual control of Hawaii. Perhaps seeing that the ancient gods and kapu system had no real power or effect over the lives of the growing number of westerners in Hawaii, the queen and young king, along with Keopuolani, Kamehameha's most sacred wife and the bearer of his heirs, publicly shared a meal together at Kamakahonu, thus symbolically overthrowing the kapu system that had strictly prohibited men and women from eating together, as well as forbidding women from eating certain choice foods.

Following Liholiho's meal with the women, the old gods were declared dead, and the kapu system officially collapsed, though Hawaiians continued to worship their gods. All wooden idols (*ki'i*) and heiaus on every island were ordered destroyed by Hewahewa, Kamehameha's high priest and direct descendent of Pa'ao. Weeks later, Hawaiians opposing the ending of the kapu system rallied in Hamakua and circled the island, gaining supporters. A pitched battle at Kuamo'o, a coastal plain south of the golf course at Keauhou, was lost by the supporters of the old gods, dooming once and for all the ways of old.

As the kapu system was being overthrown, the brig Thaddeus was rounding the Horn heading for Hawaii with the first party of New England missionaries to Hawaii.

Interestingly, a Hawaiian youth raised in Ka'u and Napo'opo'o was influential in bringing the missionaries to Hawaii. The teenage Opukaha'ia swam out to a Yankee merchant ship to escape his apprenticeship under his *kahuna* (priest) uncle at the Hikiau Heiau on Kealakekua Bay, the same heiau where Captain Cook willingly played out his role as the Hawaiian god Lono.

Opukaha'ia (whose name later was anglicized to Henry Obookiah) spoke eloquently in New England churches after arriving there as a youth in the early 1800s, asking that missionaries be sent to Hawaii. Though he died in his early 20s of typhus fever (in 1818), a slim leather-bound book, "The Memoirs of Henry Obookiah" sold an amazing 50,000 copies following his death, gaining financial support for the mission to Hawaii, as well as attracting the the Thurstons, a missionary family who arrived abord the Thaddeus, the first missionary ship and settled in Kona. Later generations of the family owned the *Honolulu Advertiser* newspaper. In the summer of 1993, Opukaha'ia's family brought his bones back from a grave in rural Connecticut, and he was reburied at the historic Kahikolu Church. A large headstone and lava rock vault now mark the grave which has a sweeping view of Kealakekua Bay.

The missionary party first set foot on the Big Island at a rock that is now buried under Kailua Pier. For decades the rock was known as the Plymouth Rock of Hawaii, in reference to the Pilgrim ancestors of the New England missionaries.

After the death of Kamehameha, Hawaii entered a new era that lasted until the overthrow of the Hawaiian Kingdom in 1893. Imitating the rulers of England and Europe, Hawaii's royalty evolved a grand court life centered in Honolulu. The Hulihe'e Palace (329-1877) in Kailua is the Big Island's most significant site surviving from this period. The unimposing, earthtone, two-story palace, across the street from Mokuaikaua Church near the sea wall, is a poignant reminder of the grand Victorian era in Hawaii and was built first as a lava-rock-walled estate for Governor Kuakini in the 1830s.

Tours through the palace, which is decorated with artifacts, furniture, and finery from the Kalakaua era, are given daily by

Loading cattle at Napoʻopoʻo, circa 1930. Kona Historical Society

members of the Daughters of Hawaii.

Workers for Hawaii's sugar cane plantations began arriving in small numbers in the 1850s. By the turn-of-the-century the majority of Hawaii's population was non-Hawaiian and non-western. Immigrant groups included the Chinese, Japanese, Filipinos, Germans, Scots, Portuguese, Koreans, Puerto Ricans, South Pacific Islanders, and others. The polyglot "Golden Race" of today's Hawaii is the result of this in-migration. Most local people you meet in Kona number plantation workers on at least one side of their family tree.

The first horses came to Hawaii in 1828 from San Diego, and Hawaiians quickly discovered they were as adept at riding horses as at sailing canoes or surfing. Young Hawaiian women took to riding in a long flowing tapa cloth wrap, or *paʻu*, and today at major parades in Hawaii you will see modern paʻu riders wearing colorful, trailing gowns. To teach the Hawaiians how to handle cattle, *vaqueros* from South America and other Latino nations began arriving about 1832. The Hawaiians called them *Paniolos*, pidgin for *Espanolos*, and soon the Spanish-speaking cowboys became welcome members of the community. Corrals, ranches and stables sprouted across the Waimea plain and many Hawaiians became paniolos, skilled with a mount and a lasso.

Shipping cattle without docks was a problem for Big Island ranchers whose main market was two hundred miles away in Ho-

Liliuokalani re-enactmen at Hulihe'e Palace.
Kona Historical Society

nolulu. The paniolos improvised by swimming the cattle out to inter-island steamers. Cranes on the steamers lifted the cows and steers aboard, and they were off to Oahu. Old-time photos of the paniolos can be seen at the Parker Ranch Visitor Center (885-7655), the Kona Historical Society (323-3222) and at the Lyman Mission Houses Museum in Hilo (935-5021).

In 1893, events in Honolulu changed forever the face of Hawaii. Armed U.S. Marines aided American businessmen in overthrowing Queen Lili'uokalani, Hawaii's last reigning monarch. Hawaii became a Republic, and then in 1898, a Territory of the United States. Though Honolulu boomed when the tariffs on Hawaiian sugar were lifted, Kona remained a sleepy, faraway fishing village with dirt roads and as many "Kona nightingales" – the donkeys of the coffee farms – as automobiles.

World War II opened the outside world to the sons and daughters of Kona, and the rest of Hawaii. Visiting soldiers and sailors liked what they saw, too, and a number returned after the war to settle down and marry into the local community.

The 20th Century saw the rise of tourism in Kona, an industry that has changed this land for both good and bad. Inter-island sea planes were replaced eventually by DC-3 prop planes that landed at the Old Airport, now a public park along the coast just north of Kailua town. The center of pre-jet age tourism was the old Kona Inn Hotel along the waterfront at Kailua. The Kona Inn was a sprawling, Key West-like establishment where celebrities and knowledgeable travelers joined tourists for game fishing, sun, and the simple, quiet life of Kona. A watershed event of this era was the arrival of mainland jets in the late 1950s and early 1960s which launched mass tourism. Gradually Kona grew up. The dirt path along the coast south of Kona became Ali'i Drive, roads were paved, traffic lights installed, and shopping centers built to service the waves of tourists.

In 1993, the Hawaiian Sovereignty Movement marked the 100th anniversary of the overthrow of the Hawaiian Kingdom with a procession of Hawaiians dressed in *malo*, pa'u, and feathered cloaks, marching down Ali'i drive for a rally at Hulihe'e Palace. There a declaration of independence by the Hawaiian people was announced, and an ultimatum issued regarding return of Hawaiian lands now overseen by state and federal governments. How this will work out is still uncertain, and sovereignty remains a major issue of the 90s.

Hawaiian Language

The melodious Hawaiian language reflects the harmony and beauty encompassed in aloha, a word and spirit that draws visitors to the islands from across the globe. Though most everyone knows the words aloha and hula, Hawaiian is spoken as a first language only by a few elderly people here and there, by the 200 or so residents of the tiny, isolated island of Ni'ihau and by a handful of residents of rural Hawaiian communities. However, a rebirth of the language is underway at various public schools where children are taught all subjects in the Hawaiian language. Today, there are currently more than 20,000 Hawaiian words in use, and the number is growing.

You will find it challenging to pronounce the Hawaiian names of streets and towns but this simple exercise will give you a good first step in understanding the Hawaiians and their past. Especially unusual to English speakers is the okina, or silent glottal stop indicated by an inverted comma, (') that begins or breaks up many Hawaiian words. Think of it as the silent pause in the phrase "oh-oh!"

The written Hawaiian language was created in the 1820s by missionaries from New England and Tahiti. To put the Hawaiian language on paper the translators used just twelve letters; the vowels a-e-i-o-u, plus the consonants h-k-l-m-n-p-w (w is sometimes pronounced v, especially in the middle of a word after a vowel).

Rarely do you hear the term "white person" used in Hawaii, rather, those of European stock are "haoles," a Hawaiian term that once applied to any foreigner. Generally, the term isn't a slur.

Pidgin is the lingua franca of Hawaii. This simple, makeshift dialect varies from island to island, and even town to town.

Some common pidgin phrases:
 Bimeby.................by-and-by
 Humbug................trouble
 Mo betta...............better
 Da kine.................whatsyamacallit

Hawaiian phrases and words you might read or hear in everyday conversation, and at resorts.

Aloha nui loa	much love
Hana hou	repeat, play it again
Komo mai	welcome
Mele Kalikimaka	Merry Christmas
Mahalo nui	thank you very much

a'a	rough lava
akamai	smart
Akua	God
ali'i	chief, noble
auwe	oh no!
hale	house, building
hana	work
hapa	half
hele	to go
ho'olaule'a	celebration
hui	group, club, partnership
imu	earth oven
kahuna	priest, sorcerer, doctor, skilled person
kama'aina	native born
kane	man, husband
kapu	taboo, keep out, sacred, forbidden
keiki	baby, child
kokua	help, assistance
lanai	veranda, porch
mahalo	thanks
makai	toward the sea
mauna	mountain
mauka	toward the mountains
moana	ocean
ohana	family, extended family
ono	delicious
pahoehoe	smooth lava
pali	a cliff or precipice
pau	finished, done

puka..................... hole of any size
tapa (kapa)............ paper bark cloth
tutu...................... grandparent, elder
wahine.................. woman

Hawaiian Language Coffee Terms:
Coffee................... kope
Sun dried beans..... kope la
Coffee grinder....... wili kope
Coffee grounds...... oka kope
Coffee huller......... la'au kui kope
Coffee mill............ wili kope

Fresh Hawaiian game fish is the top local entree in Kona restaurants. Don't let the Hawaiian names dissuade you from ordering.
Ahi....................... Yellowfin Tuna
Aku...................... Skipjack Tuna
Akule.................... Mackerel
'Ama'Ama.............. Gray Mullet
A'u....................... Pacific or Striped Marlin (best smoked)
Awa...................... Milkfish
Kahala.................. Yellowtail, Amberjack
Kawakawa............. Bonito (a small tuna)
Lomi Lomi Salmon. Chopped salmon, tomatoes, and onions
Mahimahi.............. Dolphin fish, or dorado
Opihi.................... Hawaiian Winkle or Limpet
Onaga................... Red Snapper
Ono...................... Wahoo (a local favorite)
Opakapaka............ Pink Snapper
Poke..................... Chunked raw fish, usually Ahi
Sashimi................. Sliced raw fish, usually Ahi
Tako..................... Octopus (quite good)
Uhu...................... Parrot Fish
Ulua/Papio............ Crevalle, Jack, or Pompano

Hawaiian Politics

Politics in Hawaii is rooted in land control; owning or controlling land equals power. Today on the Big Island, rezoning land for resort development, protecting endangered rain forests, and deciding what rights native Hawaiians have to their lost lands are some of the major, controversial issues.

Much of Big Island land is controlled by the federal and state government, or large landholders. A very small slice of the island is owned by individuals. Whoever controls land, or decides how land is used, gains power. It has been that way here since the days of ancient Hawaii.

Ruling Hawaii through land control dates back hundreds of years before Captain Cook arrived in 1778, to the days when princely Hawaiian rulers battled each other for control of islands and island districts. The *ali'i*, or ruling class, were held as gods and structured their reigns within a *kapu* system. The kapu system created castes among the Hawaiian people with the ali'i at the top, assisted by a class of kahuna (priests) that numbered canoe makers, native healers, taro field overseers, knowledgeable fishermen, and other skilled people, as well as spiritual advisors, among its ranks.

The major break in this land system came in 1848 when the Great Mahele gave title to all Hawaiian lands and allowed common people for the first time to own their own *kuleana* or small homestead. At this time Americans and other foreigners were given the right to buy land, and gradually the Hawaiian monarchs began to lose control of the islands as westerners bought land and intermarried with the ali'i.

During the nineteenth century, governors were appointed by the Hawaiian kings for each island. In the mid-1800s, a legislature comprised of a house and senate was formed in Honolulu and western-type constitutions and laws were enacted, many based directly on the Ten Commandments, through the influence upon the monarchs by American missionaries who first arrived in 1820. Legislative members were Hawaiians and transplanted Americans.

The Republic of Hawaii lasted from 1893 until 1898, when

Hawaii became a territory of the United States. During this time the "Big Five" took control through the Republican Party. These American and British-run companies became flush with dollars from sugar cane plantations, trading, and other ventures.

Following World War II, Japanese-Americans made their mark fighting valiantly in Europe and Asia, and returned ready to change things. With labor unions and popular support, they installed Democratic control over Hawaii in 1954.

Statehood for Hawaii was granted by Congress in 1959. That year the floodgates of tourism were opened with the arrival of long-distance jet flights bringing huge increases in tax revenues from sales taxes and resort property taxes, plus social problems.

Today, the action in local politics on the Big Island centers around the Mayor's Office in Hilo, and the County Council, which is made up of representatives at large from each district, plus the local state house and senate representatives who go to the state legislature in Honolulu from late January to about April.

An important issue is a call to divide the Big Island into two political districts. Hilo, on the rainy east side, is an area with very different development and social issues than Kona, and because Kona is the location of a majority of the island's resorts, and thus the earner of much of the outside tax income, frequent calls for a division of the island into east and west are often heard from Kona.

Election time from September to early November is a colorful Hawaiian event. Candidates take to the streets backed by rows of sign waving supporters and wave to drivers during rush hour. The street theater flavor of this pinky-finger-and-thumb "shaka" shaking roadside campaigning is business-as-usual in the Hawaiian political arena.

The Big Island is somewhat more wide open politically than other Neighbor Islands, possibly due to its size and its larger population, and perhaps because the "old boy" system is not so well entrenched.

Massive spending and state hiring marked the last Democratic governor's term, leaving the state $250 million in debt and the new governor, Ben Cayetano, on the spot to reverse this trend.

Movies Filmed on the Big Island

Since the days of silent films, Hollywood moviemakers have found Hawaii a choice location for film backdrops. In addition to the appeal of the scenery, with its volcanoes, black sand beaches, and aquamarine ocean waters, moviemakers like the politically stable climate, the reasonable proximity to the west coast, and the wide variety of racial types, especially the Polynesians and Asians needed for tropical spectaculars.

Most Big Island films made since the 1960s are available on videotape.

Pre-WWII films include *Hawaiian Buckaroo,* from 20th Century Fox, with Smith Ballew, filmed at the Parker Ranch, and *South of Pago Pago,* from United Artists, with Victor McLagen and Frances Farmer, which includes background shots of the Kona Coast.

The WW II hit *Song of the Islands,* filmed in 1942 by 20th Century Fox Director Walter Lang, starred Betty Grable, Hilo Hattie, Victor Mature, Jack Oakie, Thomas Mitchell, and Billy Gilbert, features historic scenes of loading cattle at Kailua-Kona. The film is set on the make-believe island of Ami-Ami Oni-Oni and is about the blonde daughter (Betty Grable) of an Irish beachcomber and a number of hulas. Some scenes were also filmed at Kalapana's black sand beach, which no longer exists.

The Post-war feature *Bird of Paradise,* was filmed in 1951, from 20th Century Fox. Director Delmar Daves worked with stars Jeff Chandler, Debra Paget, and Louis Jourdan at the City of Refuge in Honaunau, the Shipman Estate in Puna, the black sand beaches at Kalapana and Kaimu, and at Warm Springs near Pahoa. Shots of the 1950 eruption of Mauna Loa provide a backdrop for the classic scene of natives running from a volcano set off by evil gods.

Kealakekua Bay is the backdrop for 1955's *The Sea Chase,* from Warner Bros. Directed by John Farrow, with stars John Wayne and Lana Turner, it tells the story of a German freighter in tropical Australian waters attempting to return to the North Sea.

The Day the World Ended might have ended Paul Newman's career had it been his first film. The film rehashes every disaster movie cliché there is. Shot in 1979 along the Kona Coast, with volcano footage, this highly forgettable feature comes alive for only a brief moment when lava spews forth and covers the Kona Surf. Critics hailed it as the Blubbering Inferno. For TV reruns the film is titled *Earth's Final Fury*.

Debra Winger came to Kona in 1985 for director Bob Rafelson's *Black Widow*, from 20th Century Fox. Winger is a federal investigator who becomes obsessed with a murderer she is investigating, and ends up on the Big Island.

Sliver, from Paramount, filmed in 1992 and released in 1993, starred Sharon Stone and William Baldwin. It's a Manhattan murder mystery with a tie to the Big Island and Hawaii.

Waterworld, starring Kevin Costner, was filmed here in 1994 and 1995 under and on the waters of Kawaihae Harbor. A quarter-mile-wide set depicted a world two hundred years in the future which is covered with water, thanks to the melting of the polar ice caps. A number of local people played as extras and worked in the production crew. The budget on this filmed exploded to over $175 million, making it one of the most expensive movies ever made. Whether it will it be another *Jurrasic Park*, or a flop, is secondary to Big Island residents waiting to see if they appear on-screen.

Kona Kai Farms

Oahu and the
Neighbor Islands

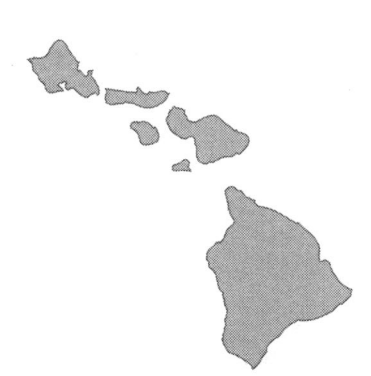

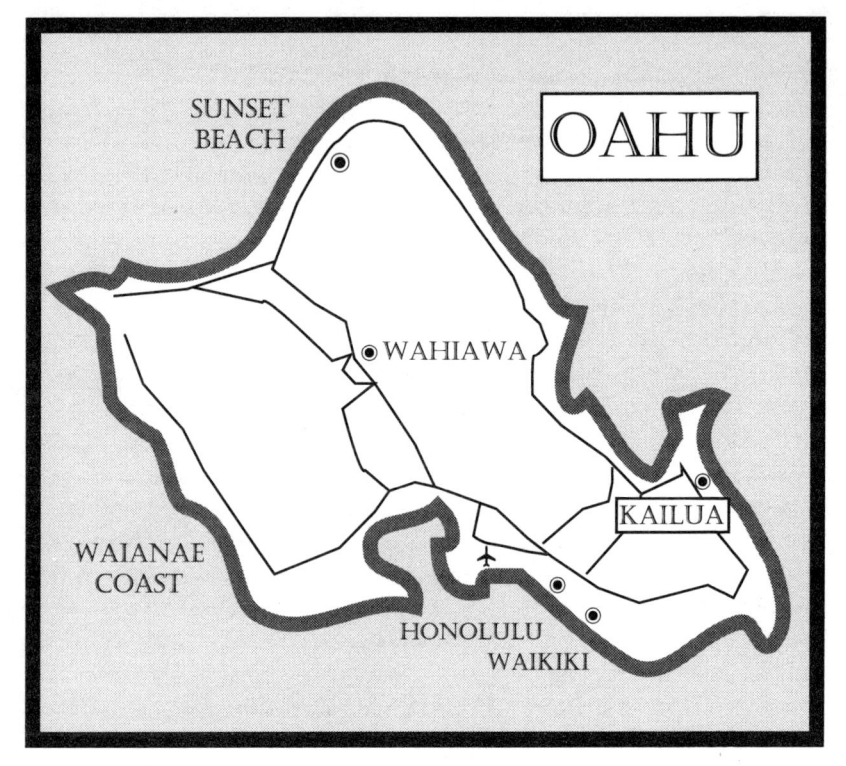

WAIKIKI AND HONOLULU

Even with all its big-city drawbacks, Waikiki is an experience that most visitors to Hawaii want to have. Once a lackadaisical, romantic military outpost, World War II and modern air travel made Waikiki a bustling high rise tourist mecca comparable only to Miami Beach or Las Vegas. You will find cut-rate hustlers next to some of the world's fanciest hotels; sidewalk vendors selling seven t-shirts for $20 in front of an upscale clothing store selling $2,500 Armani suits; prostitutes and presidents. The influx of Japanese and the strength of the yen led to the development of designer stores like *Gucci* and *Louis Vuitton* selling goods at ridiculously inflated prices. However, Asian tourists have become wiser now, and you will find just as many at *Costco* or *Wal-Mart* as in the designer clothing stores.

Waikiki is basically the area between the east end of *Ala*

Moana Shopping Center and Diamond Head, and between the ocean and Ala Wai Canal. Central Waikiki is the strip on Kalakaua and Kuhio Avenues between *Fort DeRussy* and the *Colony Surf Hotel*, about a twelve-by-two-block area. Here are just a few recommendations for your stay in Waikiki, but remember there are hundreds of places we haven't been to or even heard about.

Hotels: The two oldest Waikiki hotels are the most interesting, and we often use our Kama'aina discount to stay at them. *The Royal Hawaiian* (923-7311) is the small (six stories, 526 rooms and suites) pink hotel behind the *Royal Hawaiian Shopping Center* in the center of Waikiki, and the 793-room *Sheraton Moana Surfrider* (922-3111) is a couple of blocks further down Kalakaua Avenue towards Diamond Head. They were the first two hotels on Waikiki Beach, and it is a miracle that either one survives today; the Royal Hawaiian was almost razed to build another skyscraper hotel like the Sheraton Waikiki next door, and the original wing of the Moana Sheraton suvived tacky side additions to be restored to its former glory in the 1980s. Both hotels have wonderful beachfront dining and lounge areas and manage to maintain a relaxed, pampered atmosphere. Don't expect the beach in front, glorious though it is, to be relaxing – sometimes there's no space for a towel.

The Royal Hawaiian has rooms from $260 to $475 and suites from $425 to $1,100 with a 25% discount, or a $160 flat garden view rate for Hawaii residents. If you like pink, this is the hotel for you! The Moana's rooms are $210 to $350, with a great $99 Kama'aina rate (try for the historic wing at $295). If you don't stay at these hotels, be sure to stop in for breakfast, lunch, or a drink.

The 456-room *Halekulani* (923-2311) is newer and really expensive, but if price is no object, this is a wonderful choice, especially for the great hotel restaurants (*La Mer*, *Orchids*). Rooms are $275 to $440 with a 20% Hawaii resident discount. The new 521-room *Hawaii Prince Hotel* (956-1111) is outside of the main Waikiki area (near Ala Moana Shopping Center and next to the Ala Wai yacht harbor), and a bit sterile by our tastes, but it's a very good example of the kind of upscale hotel you find in Japan. It has especially good restaurants (*Prince Court, Takanawa, Hakone*), and an espresso cart in the lobby.

For a smaller hotel, try the 125-room *New Otani Kaimana Beach Hotel* (921-7017) at the calm, quiet Diamond Head end of Kalakaua, right on San Souci beach across from public tennis courts and the Waikiki Shell open-air concert hall. Away from the center of Waikiki, it feels like you are in another city. The rooms are small, but the beach is possibly the best of all the Waikiki hotels. Rates are $109-$220 from December 21 to March 31 and $10 less during off season (20% kama'aina discount).

Some other hotels outside Wakiki are worth mentioning: The former *Kahala Hilton* (734-2211) is ten minutes past Waikiki in the city's most tony neighborhood, and has been a world famous hotel for many years. It was purchased by the group that owns the Mandarin Hotel in Hong Kong, and is now called the *Kahala Mandarin Oriental*. The new owners are making renovations and expect to open in February, 1996. *The Turtle Bay Hilton* (293-8811 or 800-HILTONS) is on the North Shore at the opposite side of the island from Waikiki (a 60 to 90 minute drive) near the prime surfing spots. Rooms are $125 to $220. The newest Oahu mega-resort is the *Ihilani Resort & Spa* (679-0079) at Ko Olina on Oahu's west shore. This resort just opened, with room rates starting at $275, with a 20% discount for locals. Ocean front goes for $395, and suites are $800 to $3,500. The spa at the Ihilani is supposed to be great, but we haven't been there.

Restaurants: A city with the size and international sophistication of Honolulu should have better restaurants. These are our choices.

*** *Keo's Thai Cuisine* (three locations, the original one on Kapahulu is our choice, 737-8240). A modest but beautifully appointed room five minutes outside of Waikiki, famous for Hawaii's best Thai food.

*** *Roy's Restaurant* (Hawaii Kai, 396-7697). A big, open, raucous room featuring the Pacific cuisine of Hawaii's hottest chef, Roy Yamaguchi. Hawaii Kai is about a 30 minute drive from Waikiki.

*** *The Secret* (formerly the Third Floor, Hawaiian Regent Hotel, 922-6611). A very good hotel restaurant, though too formal for our taste (they require men to wear jackets).

*** *Takanawa Sushi Bar & Restaurant* (Hawaii Prince Hotel, 956-1111). Mimi Sheraton's favorite Honolulu sushi bar.

*** *Michel's at Colony Surf Hotel*, Waikiki. For a long time the trendiest restaurant in Waikiki, now taken over by Jean Marie Josselin, chef/owner of Kauai's *A Pacific Cafe*. Set to open in mid-1995 with a more informal, less expensive menu.

** *Restaurant Suntory* (Royal Hawaiian Shopping Center, 922-5511). Owned by Japan's Suntory Beer company, with the personal whiskey bottles of Hawaii's power elite displayed in the waiting area. A great, but expensive, sushi bar.

** *Restaurant Sada* (South King Street, 949-0646). Excellent sushi bar, but no view.

** *Sunset Grill* (Restaurant Row, 521-4409). Our recommendation for Restaurant Row dining. California-style mesquite grilled fish is usually a good choice here. Located between Waikiki and downtown Honolulu.

** *Il Fresco*, Ward Center, Ala Moana Boulevard (523-5841). California cuisine.

** *Castagnola's* (Manoa Market Place, 988-2969). Very good Italian food, usually very crowded with a mixed University/local/tourist crowd.

** *Quintero's Mexican Cuisine* (South King Street, 944-3882). Our choice for Mexican food in Honolulu, but no view.

* *John Dominus* (Ala Moana district, on the ocean, 523-0955). This restaurant should not be missed for one of Hawaii's best views. "Catch of the day, underdone, sauce on the side."

* *Duke's Restaurant and Bar* (next to the Moana Sheraton, Waikiki, 922-2268). The Kona Inn of Waikiki. Noisy, crowded, hot bar, on the beach. Beautiful koa wood interior.

* *Auntie Pasto's* (South Beretania Street, 523-8855). Decent, moderately-priced Italian food with no view.

* *California Pizza Kitchen* (Ala Moana Boulevard, Waikiki, 955-5161, and Kahala Mall). A convenient location in Waikiki with a large bar where you can eat and watch sports TV.

* *Tahitian Lanai* (Oceanside at Waikikian Hotel, Ala Moana

Boulevard, 946-6541). A good place for breakfast, lunch or brunch in a relaxed Hawaiiana atmosphere by the pool.

* *The Food Court at Ala Moana Shopping Center.* Filled with dozens of small, ethnic take-out restaurants with tables in the center. More choices than you can count at reasonable prices.

Coffee: There is one espresso bar and retail outlet in Honolulu which features Kona coffee: *Konacopia*, 1982 Kalakaua near the Kuhio/Kahala intersection (951-KONA), open from 7 a.m. until 11 p.m. every day. Other good Waikiki coffee spots are *Kimo Beans* in the *Hawaiian Regent Hotel* (534-0055) and *Cafe Pronto* at the *King's Shops* (949-0844) just a half block up the street from the Hawaiian Regent. In mid-town Honolulu, there's *Lion Coffee* at 831 Queen Street (521-3479). Other places where you can get a decent cafe latte are *Espresso Bravissimo* at the Kahala Mall (735-1329), *Coffee Manoa* at the Manoa Marketplace near the University of Hawaii (988-5113), and the *Coffee Gallery* in Haleiwa on the north shore (637-5571) and in Hawaii Kai (396-9393).

Night Life: A free, widely available alternative newspaper, *The Honolulu Weekly*, has very good listings of what's happening in the Honolulu entertainment world. The most popular dancing places are *The Wave* (1877 Kalakaua Avenue), *Maharajah* (Waikiki Trade Center, 2255 Kuhio Avenue) and *The Pink Cadillac* (478 Ena Road – hard to find, but it's there). *Restaurant Row* (Ala Moana Boulevard just east of downtown) is a good place to wander through at night. You'll find dance clubs like *Studebaker's* and *The Blue Zebra*, and a late-night crowd at the many restaurant/bar establishments located at The Row.

Places to Go: There are a myriad of historic places in Honolulu, the most famous of which is 'Iolani Palace near downtown. *Chinatown*, a ten-square-block, often overlooked, area just west of the heart of downtown. *The Bishop Museum* (1529 Bernice Street) is on the outskirts of town, but it's by far the best museum in the state for Hawaiiana. The Honolulu Academy of Arts (900 South Beretania Street) is the state's premier art gallery.

Oahu (Beyond Waikiki and Honolulu)

Venturing beyond fast-paced Honolulu and Waikiki to explore Oahu's towns and rural countryside is highly recommended if you have a few free days, or even an open afternoon, during your stay.

In traveling around Oahu don't forget that Honolulu is one of the largest cities in the United States. There are rush hours morning and afternoon when traffic crawls on freeways, and the number of other visitors and locals shopping and lining up for movies and other activities will be much greater than in Kona.

The most logical, and popular, tour outside of Honolulu is to circle the island. This can take the better part of a day, or, if you drive straight through with maybe a lunch stop, at least four hours.

Oahu's outlying districts range from suburban bedroom communities like Kailua and Aiea, to the sugar cane plantation enclaves of Waialua and Waipahu, to the Hawaiian and Samoan strongholds at leeward Waianae. Perhaps the most unique district is the North Shore, which is a world-renowned surfing area complete with a thriving subculture of surfers gathered from across the globe to surf large Hawaiian waves. Oahu is also the Pacific hub of operations for the U.S. military and, unlike the Neighbor Islands, the presence of the Army, Navy, Air Force, Marine Corps, and Coast Guard is visible in every corner of the island.

Pearl Harbor: Located just a few miles west of the Honolulu Airport on Kamehameha Highway (HI-99), Pearl Harbor is one of the most popular stops on Oahu. The federal government-run *Arizona Memorial and Visitor Center* (422-0561) is located just off Kamehameha Highway, west of the main entrance to the naval base

Hawaii Kai, Haunama Bay and Beyond: Driving out of Oahu to the east along Kalaniana'ole Highway, you will pass a string of suburbancommunities that ends at Hawaii Kai. Beyond lies an arid area with some of Oahu's most spectacular snorkeling and body surfing. A well-marked side road and trail at Koko

Head run down to *Hanauma Bay*, an enclosed bay where marine life is protected. Unfortunately, Hanauma is generally overrun with beachgoers and snorkelers. Around the southeast tip of the island are *Sandy Beach* and *Makapuʻu Beach*, both world-class body surfing sites.

Windward Oahu: The east flank of the majestic Koʻolau Mountains borders the windward side of Oahu, which runs from Makapuʻu Point in the south to the former sugar cane plantation town of Kahuku about 30 miles to the north. Miles of open white sand beach, lush foliage, balmy weather, and a quiet, Neighbor-Island pace of life mark this side of the island.

The quickest and most scenic drive to windward Oahu is over the Pali. Take Highway 61 (The Nuʻuanu Pali Highway) from downtown Honolulu for the ten-mile drive to Kailua and Kaneohe, two large suburbs of Honolulu. Kailua is the more sophisticated of the two towns, with bookstores, the affluent neighborhood of Lanikai, and a wide variety of dining. Accommodations are available here in low-key, mostly guest houses and bed & breakfasts.

North of Kailua is *Kualoa Beach Park* fronts the famous landmark *Chinaman's Hat*, a volcanic cone sitting just offshore. You can see Hawaiian sea birds here; the beach is a little rocky, but great for kids. *The Kualoa Ranch* (237-8515) sends horseback riders back into lush Kaʻaʻawa Valley; the 4.5-hour trip goes to a hidden beach near an ancient Hawaiian fishpond.

The windward side ends at Kahuku, a sleepy former plantation town. The fields and ponds west of town produce excellent watermelons and aquaculture-produced seafood, which are sold alongside the highway. *The Last Show In Town,* just west of Kahuku, offers a variety of interesting collectibles. The shop was transplanted from Kauai after Hurricane ʻIniki, and has an engrossing selection of Hawaiian bottles.

Accommodations: Kailua Beachside Cottages (262-4128) is a cluster of woodframe cottages overlooking Kailua Beach Park.

Pat's Hotel at Punaluʻu (293-8111) is a 136-unit highrise condo right on the beach at Punaluʼu. Pat's is a comfortable little hotel not too far out of town.

Dining: There are a number of restaurants ranging from fast foods to French and Swiss in Kailua, Kaneohe, and beyond. Try a Hawaiian food restaurant to sample real local food.

Perhaps the one restaurant that stands out on the windward side as something unique is the *Paniolo Café* (53-567 Kamehameha Highway, Punalu'u, 237-8521). This "cowboy" cafe serves good ribs and beef brisket, plus some exotic dishes.

North Shore: Geographically, the north shore of Oahu runs 20 miles from Kahuku, the northern most point of the island, to Kaena Point, a nature preserve located beyond the end of the road at the northwest tip of Oahu. Culturally, the North Shore today represents a subculture and way of life somewhat set apart from the rest of the island. Honolulu city dwellers call the North Shore "country" and many haven't made the drive out in years. At its heart is a way of life more like the South Pacific than Honolulu. World-class surfing, a sport Hawaii gave to the rest of the world, is its lifeblood.

North Shore surf spots span a twelve-mile stretch from Haleiwa to Velzyland that arguably encompasses more excellent surfing along one coast than anywhere else on the planet. Watching surfers drop into 20-foot waves at Pipeline that are tubular enough to drive a Mac Truck through, breaking over a pin cushion of jagged coral, is entertainment akin to cheering on the gladiators in the Roman Coliseum.

North Shore waves are best from October to March. In the summertime, most surfers clear out as the surf goes flat. For everyone else, the calm ocean waters make for excellent swimming, snorkeling, and scuba diving.

Haleiwa is a quaint plantation town with a fresh infusion of trendy shops with a California beach-town flavor. Avant garde clothing and art, the *Coffee Gallery*, good health food stores, hardcore surf eateries like the Cafe Haleiwa, and endless surf shops line Kamehameha Highway in Haleiwa.

Off the main surf route, to the west, Mokuleia offers Sunday afternoon international polo matches at the Hawaii Polo Club.

Accommodations: The *Turtle Bay Hilton* is a resort hotel with a windswept golf course and a short drive to all surf spots and about one hour from Honolulu. *Turtle Bay Condos* are condominium rooms at the Turtle Bay Hilton Complex.

Plantation Village (638-8663), and *Vacation Inn* (638-7838) are moderately priced accommodations especially popular with scuba divers for their location near Shark's Cove, a popular dive site.

Dining: The quickest way to get to know North Shore surfers is to eat where they eat. Try any of the hamburger shops, Mexican restaurants, and health food stores along the coast.

The *Chart House at Haleiwa* is located where the Sea View Inn once did business overlooking Haleiwa Harbor. Standard Chart House steak and seafood dining with a North Shore twist.

Coffee: Oahu's version of the Aloha Cafe is the *Coffee Gallery* on Kamehameha Highway in Haleiwa. Their coffee is roasted on-premesis, and you can enjoy smoothies, sandwiches, bagels, and vegetarian dinners in the garden cafe area.

Central Oahu: Just before Wahiawa is the island's pineapple center. With the shutting down of pineapple plantations on Lanai, central Oahu is one of the last places in the United States you will see acres of pineapple fields. The triangular *Dole Pineapple Pavilion*, at the intersection of HI-99 and HI-80 is located just north of Wahiawa.

The main drag in Wahiawa is a typical military base downtown. On the back road in Wahiawa is *Keamo'o Farms*, a charming restaurant and piano bar near Schofield Barracks, the setting for James Jones' *From Here To Eternity*.

Leeward Coast: Farrington Highway (HI93) runs the length of the dry, arid Waianae Coast. Resort development is limited here to the *Sheraton Makaha* (695-9511), a golf resort, which is tucked away in Makaha Valley away from mainstream life along the coast. Many of the Hawaiians who live in Waianae see it as their last stand on Oahu for the old ways and are very protective of its beaches and culture. The *Buffalo Big Board Surfing Classic* held annually in March at Makaha Beach celebrates this lifestyle. The massive Ko Olina Resort being built at the south end of the Waianae Coast is a major intrusion into the culture of the Leeward side. What long term effect it will have on Waianae remains to be seen.

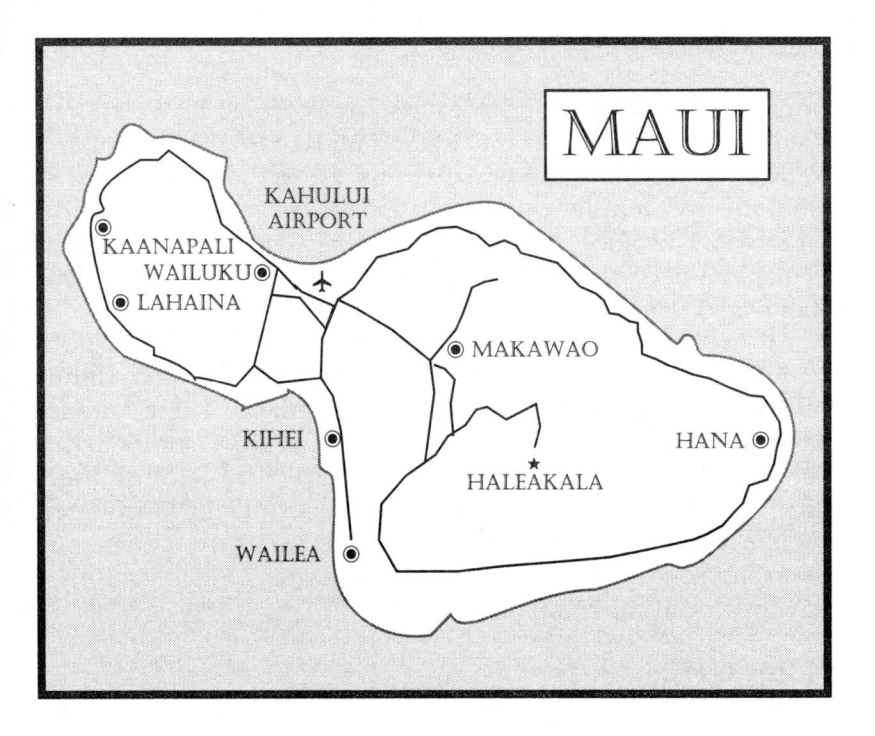

MAUI

Maui is in many ways the most beautiful and certainly the hippest of the Hawaiian Islands. We think anyone with enough time to visit another island should spend time on the Valley Isle. Its only real drawback is its popularity-the explosion of tourists has caused development that dwarfs even Kona's recent mega-expansion, and traffic on the Wailuku-Lahaina road or Lahaina's Front Street can be intense. Yet the island's magical beauty is still intact, and large expanses of sugar cane, pineapple, and open land can be found everywhere. We have been there many times, and offer these recommendations.

There are many complete tour books on Maui, and this does not attempt to systematically cover everything about the island. One good recently published book is Ray Riegert's *Ultimate Maui* (Ulysses Press, 1994).

Maui is very compact compared to the Big Island, and no matter where you stay most other areas of interest are less than an hour away. The three main tourist areas are all in West Maui: Kihei-Wailea, Lahaina, and Kaanapali-Kapalua. Wailuku and Kahului, adjoining commercial towns, are in the center of the island, the upcountry towns of Paia and Makawao, and Hana at the far eastern end of the the island. One of the great things about Maui is that you have wonderful views of four other islands: Molokini, Kahoolawe, Lanai and Molokai.

All the major commercial airlines land at Kahului airport, which is 30 minutes to an hour from the major hotels. United offers several direct flights from the mainland. There are also small airports in Hana and Kapalua. Most visitors opt for rental cars, and you should reserve one ahead of time because there are frequently none available for walk-in customers. Most hotels will be able to get you a rental car package, so we recommend choosing your hotel first and then seeing what kind of deals they have with the car companies.

Accommodations

Kapalua Area: The oldest and most familar visitor destination area runs from the old whaling town of Lahaina twenty miles along the coast north to the Kapalua resort area. In between are the resort areas of Kaanapali (centering around six hotels, two golf courses, and the *Whaler's Village* shopping mall), Kahana, and Napili. Most of the hotels here were built in the 1970s, and are showing their age compared to the newer hotels in the Kihei-Wailea area.

Our first choice for a Maui vacation is the Kapalua area, featuring the *Kapalua Bay Hotel and Bungalows* and *The Ritz-Carlton, Kapalua*. These resorts are in many ways similar to *The Mauna Lani, Ritz-Carlton* complex on the Kohala Coast, and offer a secluded, refined version of the Maui experience which is expensive but hard to beat.

The Kapalua Bay Hotel (669-5656) is relatively small, with 194 rooms. It is the hub of the resort complex which includes several condominiums. Hotel rooms range from $225 to $425, while one bedroom condos at The Villas go for $185 to $385, and two bedroom condos for $235 to $485. There are two excellent golf courses at Kapalua and a serious tennis center. The Ritz-Carlton (669-6200) is newer and larger, with 350 rooms that go for $285 garden/golf course view, $325 partial-ocean view, $400 ocean view, and $495 Ritz-Carlton Club (free food and drink in the lounge on your exclusive floor). Kama'aina rates are $179 to $279. The tennis center at The Ritz Carlton, right by the ocean, is the most beautiful tennis location in the state.

Kapalua can be windy, and is twenty to thirty minutes from the action in Lahaina and Kihei, but these are small drawbacks for what you get. We don't know anyone who has been dissatisfied with a Kapalua vacation.

Kihei-Wailea Area: Except for the Ritz-Carlton, all of the newest Maui hotels have been built in the Wailea area on the southwest side of the island. Our choice, if price is no object, is the 452-room *Four Seasons* (874-8000 or 800/334-MAUI). Room rates here are similar to Kapalua ($295 to $440), with slight discounts for off-season (May 1 through December 21) and golf and rental car packages.

For a more affordable Wailea experience, the *Kea Lani Hotel* (875-4100 or 800/882-4100).has four-person suites for $255 to $425 ($189 to $209 kama'aina). And, the 347-room *Stouffer's Wailea Beach* Resort (879-4900) is an older, less fancy hotel, but offers good value in its kama'aina rates of $99 to $159 per night ($260 to $360 per night at regular rates).

The $600-million, 787-room *Grand Wailea Resort Hotel and Spa* (875-1234) is an ostentatious mega-resort similar to Kona's *Hilton Waikoloa*, only packaged into a much smaller area. It's an interesting place to visit, especially for its art collection, and great for kids with its water slides and child-care facilities.

All four of the above hotels, together with the *Maui Inter-Continental Resort* (879-1922) are right next to each other on the beach at Wailea, and share the golf and tennis facilities across the highway up the mountain. A short drive down the road is the more secluded, 310-room *Maui Prince Hotel* (874-1111) on Makena beach with its own two golf courses and tennis center.

Kaanapali Area: Like Wailea, Kaanapali has a collection of similar hotels on the beach within walking distance of each other. The two nicest are the 812-room *Hyatt Regency Maui* (661-1234) and the 761-room *Westin Maui* (667-2525). The 542-room *Royal Lahaina Resort* (661-3611) has the best tennis center, and the 430-room *Kaanapali Beach Hotel* (661-0011) is the most affordable and old-style Hawaiian. The 720-room *Maui Marriott* (667-8226) and the closed-for-renovations *Sheraton Maui Kaanapali Beach Resort* complete the Kaanapali hotel complex.

Lahaina: There are three unique small hotels to recommend in Lahaina. Right in the middle of town you will find the historic *Pioneer Inn* (661-3636) with its wrap-around lanai. This used to be a pretty cheap hotel, but rates have escalated to $99 a room.

Off Front Street, *The Plantation Inn* (667-9225) has 18 rooms decorated in plantation-era style with four poster beds, antiques and stained glass. There's a suprisingly private pool and spa between the inn and *Gerard's* restaurant. Standard $104, delux $129, superior $145-$157, suites $185-$195. The *Lahaina Hotel* (661-0577) is a similar 12-room inn adjacent to David Paul's *Lahaina Grill*, but has no pool or spa. Rooms have been restored to 1890s style. Suites run $89-$129, with a 10% local discount.

Wailuku and Upcountry Area: Budget-conscious windsurfers stay in Wailuku at the *Banana Bungalow* on North Market Street (244-5090), within walking distance of cheap cafes and markets. Upcountry, there's the *Kula Lodge* chalets (878-1535) complete with fireplaces for $109 to $163, and the *Camp Kula* B& B (878-2528).

Hana Area: *Hotel Hana Maui* (248-8211) has long been one of the world's most exclusive resorts, and approximates the feeling of the *Kona Village* in its relaxed, secluded, Hawaiian atmosphere. The 96 separate cottages have no phones or TVs. Rates range from $325 ($185 kama'aina) for a regular garden view room, to $795 for an ocean view cottage suite ($450 kama'aina). Hana has its own airport, so you can avoid the two to three hour drive from the Kahului airport. A few small lodging places in Hana range from moderate to expensive. Wild coffee trees in Hana are harvested to produce a "Kipahulu Estate Coffee."

Maui Dining

Maui is way ahead of Kona in terms of good restaurants, and you probably won't be able to eat in all of them during your stay. There are some decisions to make about location, because the very top restaurants don't have the best ocean views.

Three Star-Restaurants

We would rate the following as equal or better to *Merriman's* or *The Canoe House*, our three-star restaurants on the Big Island:

*** *David Paul's Lahaina Grill*, Lahaina (667-5117). An intimate restaurant located just off Lahaina's Front Street, featuring Hawaii Regional Cuisine. A favorite of Condé Nast's Mimi Sheraton and winner of the 1994 award for Best Maui Restaurant.

*** *Avalon*, Front Street, Lahaina (667-5559). Owner/chef Marc Ellman's two-story restaurant is bigger, noisier and more casual than the Lahaina Grill, but offers the same high level of Hawaii Regional Cuisine.

*** *A Pacific Cafe*, Azeka Place Shopping Center, Kihei (879-0069). The original Pacific Cafe on Kauai has been recreated on Maui in a big, open-beam dining room in a nondescript mall in Kihei. Chef/owner Jean-Marie Josselin is another one of the founding members of the Hawaii Regional Cuisine group.

*** *Gerard's French Restaurant*, Lahaina (661-8939). Gerard Reversade's intimate restaurant on a Lahaina side street is often called the best French restaurant in Hawaii.

*** *Roy's Kahana Bar & Grill* (669-6999) and *Roy's Nicolina Restaurant* (669-5000), Kahana Mall. Roy Yamaguchi has won a reputation as the hottest chef on Oahu, and has recreated his popular Hawaii Kai eatery in a mall halfway between Kaanapali and Kapalua. Right next door is a companion restaurant, named for his daughter Nicolina, which adds a southwest flavor to the Hawaii Regional Cuisine featured at both places. Both restaurants are big, open, noisy, and fun.

*** *The Prince Court*, Maui Prince Hotel, Kihei (874-1111). This is one of the very best hotel restaurants we have ever experienced, with a menu created by executive chef Roger Dikon, another of the HRC group. Other Maui hotels have well regarded dining rooms like *Raffles* at Stouffer's Wailea Resort, *Seasons* and *Pacific Grill* at the Four Seasons Wailea, and *The Grill* at The Ritz-Carlton, Kapalua. The recently rennovated *Swan Court* at the Hyatt Regency in Kaanapali was mentioned as one of the most romantic restaurants in the world by *Lifestyles of the Rich and Famous*.

Good Restaurants, Great Locations:

**½ *Carelli's On the Beach*, Kihei (875-0001). Excellent Italian and seafood menu, cool bar, sophisticated service, and great sunsets. A table on the water here is about as hip as you can get in Maui – you will probably have to fight a celebrity for one.

**½ *Mama's Fish House*, Hana Highway one mile past Paia (579-8488). A unique family run restaurant right on the beach in a relaxed tropical setting away from the major tourist centers. If you could only go to one restaurant on Maui, this would be a good choice.

**½ *Longhi's*, Front Street, Lahaina (667-2288). Informal bistro style Italian restaurant with a great people-watching bar upstairs, across the street from the ocean in Lahaina. Longhi's has been one of Maui's most frequented places for many years.

**½ *Hailemaile General Store*, Hailemaile (572-2666). An old plantation store recreated into a country restaurant and sushi bar by HRC chef/owner Beverly Gannon. A great spot for Sunday brunch. Located between Paia and Makawao, about fifteen minutes drive from the Kahululi airport.

** *Kimo's*, Front Street, Lahaina (661-4811). Lahaina's equivalent of the Kona Inn, right on the water in the middle of Lahaina since 1979. Known for its dependable steak and seafood, great bar, and waterfront location.

** *Hula Grill*, Whaler's Village, Kaanapali (667-6636). This partnership between Waimea's Peter Merriman and TS Restaurants (Kimo's) is an informal beach grill with a beach bar.

** *Plantation House Restaurant*, Kapalua (669-6299). Located above the Kapalua Plantation Golf Course in a calm, majestic setting with great views of the Kapalua area.

Off the Beaten Path Restaurants
**½ *Chez Paul*, Honoapiilani Highway (661-3843). A very good French restaurant in an unlikely setting – an old, falling-down building five miles before you get to Lahaina from Wailuku, in a place called Olowalu.

*½ *Casanova's Italian Restaurant & Deli*, Makawao (572-8711). One side is an informal deli, the other a more traditional Italian eatery. Best place for espresso in Makawao.

Paia Fishmarket Restaurant (579-8030) on the corner of Baldwin Avenue and Hana Highway, Paia. A good place for fish sandwiches. Right next to the *Peaches and Crumble Cafe & Bakery*.

Vineyard Tavern, Vineyard Street, Wailuku (244-9597). Funky bar with good hamburgers and a juke box.

Siam Thai Cuisine, North Market Street, Wailuku (244-3817). Suprisingly, there aren't too many Thai restaurants on Maui. This one isn't fancy, but not expensive, either.

Hamburger Mary's, Main Street, Wailuku (244-7776). Gay-oriented, with a mixed clientele and decent burgers.

Tokyo Tei, Lower Main Street, Wailuku (242-9630). A popular local Japanese restaurant, similar to Teshima's in Kona.

Fish and Games Sports Grill, Kahana Gateway Center (669-FISH). Brand new state-of-the-art sports bar with seafood market and butcher shop. Excellent beer selection.

Sunrise Cafe, Front Street, Lahaina (661-8558). Just off the main drag in Lahaina, a hole-in-the wall budget cafe with smoothies, bagels, salads, sandwiches and espresso.

Buzz's Wharf, Maalea Bay (244)5426. Nice view of the yacht harbor, menu features local favorites.

Shaka Sandwich & Pizza, Kihei (874-0331) behind *Jack In The Box*. Maui's best pizza.

Coffee
Coffee on Maui is a hot topic of conversation, especially since the *Pioneer Mill* outside Lahaina has begun marketing its new crop of Kaanapali coffee. Most good restaurants have espresso machines, and there is stiff competition between several roasters and retailers for the espresso business. We have

found that (not suprisingly) the quality of the espresso we get on Maui is inconsistent, and some places are always better than others. The best place for coffee in Maui is located on Hana Highway, right across from the Kahului airport road. *Maui Coffee Roasters* (877-CUPS) offers a wide range of coffee roasted in the back room, as well as light breakfast and lunch fare. They also provide coffee to some of the more discriminating hotels, coffee shops, bakeries and Gas Express service stations. Owner Nick Matichyn and roastmaster Dan Kriz have been at this for a number of years, and still provide hands-on supervision of everything sold in the store.

On Lahaina's Front Street, the best place we have found is *Maui Gourmet* (667-2292), at the 505 Front Street mall, where you can get several types of excellent fresh-baked bread along with your *latte*.

In the Kaanapali-Kapalua area, *Sir Wilfred's* (the original store is in the Maui Mall in Kahului) at the *Lahaina Cannery* (667-1941) and the *Kahana Kafe* (669-6699) in the Kahana Gateway Center are recommended. *The Coffee Store* is a Starbucks-like chain which has three outlets: Kaahumanu Center (871-6860), Azeka II Center (875-4244), and Napili Plaza (669-4170). Finally, *Grandma's Maui Coffee*, in upcountry Keokea (878-2140), has an antique coffee roaster than roasts wild coffee harvested from the surrounding upcountry hillsides.

At the turn of the centry, Maui led the state in acres in coffee production (the largest plantation was in the Kapalua area), and there is wild coffee in almost all of the gulchs at higher elevations. Now, besides Pioneer Mill's 500 acre plantation, there are several small farms in the upcountry Kula area. There has been a mixed reaction Pioneer Mill has planted several types of trees trying to come up with one which produces high quality and is also adaptable to mechanical picking. Although there is little rain in Lahaina, all the coffee is irrigated. The coffee sells for about two thirds the price of Kona coffee, and has a mixed reaction from roasters and cuppers. We urge you to try some and judge for yourself!

Maui Nightlife

Probably the biggest difference between Maui and Kona is the much greater number of places to go at night – there are more late night music places on Front Street in Lahaina than probably all of the Big Island. Except for the luaus, you won't be able to tell you are not in southern California, but then a lot of the people in Lahaina used to be from L.A. The best choice for music and an exciting crowd is usually upstairs at *Longhi's* (667-2288) on Front Street. Another popular spot is *Blue Tropix* (667-5309), also on Front Street. Although they don't have live music, *The Hard Rock Cafe* (667-7400) and *Planet Hollywood* (667-7677) are usually jammed late into the evening. In Kihei, the $4 million *Tsunami* disco (875-1234) at the *Grand Hyatt Wailea* is generally the most lively place, while in Kaanapali check out the *Makai Bar* (667-1200) at the *Maui Marriott* or *El Crab Catcher* in *Whaler's Village* (661-4423).

For music in a less formal setting, *Ludwig's* (669-3786) in the Kahana Gateway Center usually has local rock 'n rollers, as does *Stella Blues Cafe & Deli* (874-3779) in *Longs Center* in Kihei. And, Willie Nelson has been known to jam at the *Wunderbar* (579-8808) in Paia.

Maui Shopping

There are places to shop everywhere in Maui, but the most interesting and unique are found in the small towns of Paia and Makawao in East Maui, and also along North Market Street in Wailuku. A stroll through these towns is only a few blocks long and there are dozens of one-of-a-kind stores featuring everything from antique furniture to handmade clothes. You can also find dozens of art galleries featuring Maui artists and a few old time grocery stores and bakeries. Upscale shoppers will find the shopping malls at the fancy hotels to their liking, and Front Street in Lahaina offers everything from very tacky to very high quality merchandise. The two best malls are *Kaahumanu Center* in Kahului and *The Lahaina Cannery* just outside of Lahaina.

Maui Tropical Plantations, Route 30, Waikapu (between Wailuku and Lahaina, 244-7643). A kind of Disneyland of Hawaiian agriculture, has a small patch of coffee and other local crops.

Maui Historical Society Museum Gift Shop (2375-A Main Street, Wailuku, 244-3326). Local history books and art prints.

Maui Crafts Guild (43 Hana Highway, Paia, 579-9697). Good selection of handmade articles by Maui artisans.

Alii Gardens, Hana Highway at the 27-mile marker (248-7217). A 55-acre flower farm which produces just about every variety of cut flower grown in Hawaii.

Hui Noeau Visual Arts Center, outside Makawao (572-6560). Located at the Baldwin mansion, you can see and purchase the work of some of Maui's best artists.

Curtis Wilson Cost Gallery, Hana Highway (878-6544). One of Maui's best oil-landscape artists features his own works and those of others in a picturesque setting.

Protea Gift Shoppe, Haleakala Highway, Kula (878-6464). If you've never seen a protea, it's worth a visit. The upper slopes of Haleakala are home to most of the protea growers in the state.

Hasagawa General Store, Hana (248-8231). One of the most famous stores in all Hawaii, there's even a song about it. A Hana landmark where you can find just about anything you need.

Maui Sights and Activities

Faced with a limited amount of time, we would recommend choosing your activities and places to visit from this list.

Beautiful beaches are what most people think of when they hear the word "Maui." The prettiest is the large beach at Makena, just past the Kihei-Wailea area. Little Makena beach is popular with nude sunbathers. Hookipa Beach Park, two miles past Paia, is one of the world's great windsurfing beaches, and a great place to watch. Beginners should try the waters at Kahana Beach Park outside Kahului. Honolua Bay in northwest Maui (take Route 30 past Kapalua) is Maui's best winter surf spot.

Haleakala Crater: One can see why the ancient Hawaiians thought the 10,000 foot crater was a special place – home to the demi-god Maui who lasooed the sun from the top of the mountain. You can drive up (40 miles, about two hours) and experience breathtaking views, ride a bicycle down the mountain from *Cruiser Bob's* (located at the Chevron station in Paia, 579-8444), or hike the crater trails and stay in the cabins or campgrounds. For a weather report (you don't want to go when it's cloudy) call 572-7749 or 871-5054. National Park Headquarters is in charge of hiking permits and cabin and campsite reservations (572-9306) .

Iao Valley: Just a short five-minute drive outside of Wailuku, the Iao Valley State Monument offers a wonderful view of the jagged, moss-covered West Maui mountains and the 2,250-foot high Iao Needle. Walk out on the trails behind the visitor center for peaceful and nice little hike. Along the road you can see wild coffee trees next to Tropical Gardens of Maui, or visit the Hawaii Nature Center, a botanical garden for kids.

Hana Highway: This is one of the most beautiful roads in the world, winding 51 miles between Kahului and Hana on a twisting road that will take about three hours, not including stops. Many of the curves have been straightened out in the last few years, but there are still plenty left. You can buy tapes that describe all the sights on the Hana Highway as an audio guide while you drive – look for the signs between the airport and Paia. There are too many picnic areas, swimming holes, waterfalls, and vista points along the road to mention, and the old-fashioned town of Hana has many places to explore. If you are really adventuresome and the weather is good, you can keep going past Hana on Route 31 and end up at Ulupalakua Ranch after a five- mile stretch of dirt road. Before the dirt, however, you will find Oheo Gulch, where the famous Seven Sacred Pools provide the opportunity to play in a series of waterfalls pouring into swimming holes, surrounded by tropical beauty.

Whale Watching, Cruising, or Diving: Most visitors will want to spend at least one day on the water, and there are a lot of different options here. West Maui is the best place in the state to see the magnificent Humpback whales that migrate here during the winter from Alaska. You can dive Molokini, the tiny island just off Lahaina, or cruise to Lanai or Molokai. Two boats we can recommend are the *Kapalua Kai* (a catamaran offering day cruises for snorkeling and sunset cruises for watching, 667-5980) and the *Trilogy* (day cruises to Lanai, 661-4743) but there are dozens listed in the guide books. Most of them are docked at the harbor in Lahaina, and you can wander down and look at them before you decide. In Hana, *Hana Hou Charters* (877-7369) is a great way to see the Seven Sacred Pools.

Other attractions: *Alexander & Baldwin Sugar Museum* (Puunene Avenue and Hansen Road, Puunene, 871-8058), the *Maui Sting Rays*, the local winter league baseball team that plays in Wailuku, *Maui Arts & Cultural Center* in Wailuku, the *Holy Rosary Church* (Father Damien Memorial) and the *Makawao Union Church*, *Rainbow Park*, *Tedeschi Vinyards* (878-6058) at Ulupalakua Ranch upcountry, and the *Kapalua Wine Symposium* (July, Kapalua Bay Hotel & Villas). For a good overview of things to do on Maui watch Channel 7's series, *Maui's Hidden Secrets*.

Molokai, Lanai & Kahoolawe

If you want to escape the typical tourist scene and discover something of what Old Hawaii must have been like, Molokai is the place. Sleepy, quiet, and peaceful, the Friendly Isle seems to have been overlooked by the 20th Century. There isn't much to do there but relax, and for that reason, it's one of our favorite places to get away from it all. Of the three hotels on the island, only the Kaluakoi Hotel and Golf Club (800/367-6046, 522-2555) on the west end of the island is a true resort hotel.

Lanai was formerly a Dole pineapple plantation and has only in the past few years begun catering to visitors at a couple of exclusive resorts. The exclusive Manele Bay Hotel (565-7700) and the Lodge at Koele (565-7300) deserve their world class ratings. Contact Lanai Resorts for bookings (800/321-4666, 223-7637.

Kahoolawe is off-limits to visitors because of all the unexploded ordinances still lying around after years of Navy bombing practice. Kahoolawe has been returned to the state government and Hawaiian groups are restoring the island.

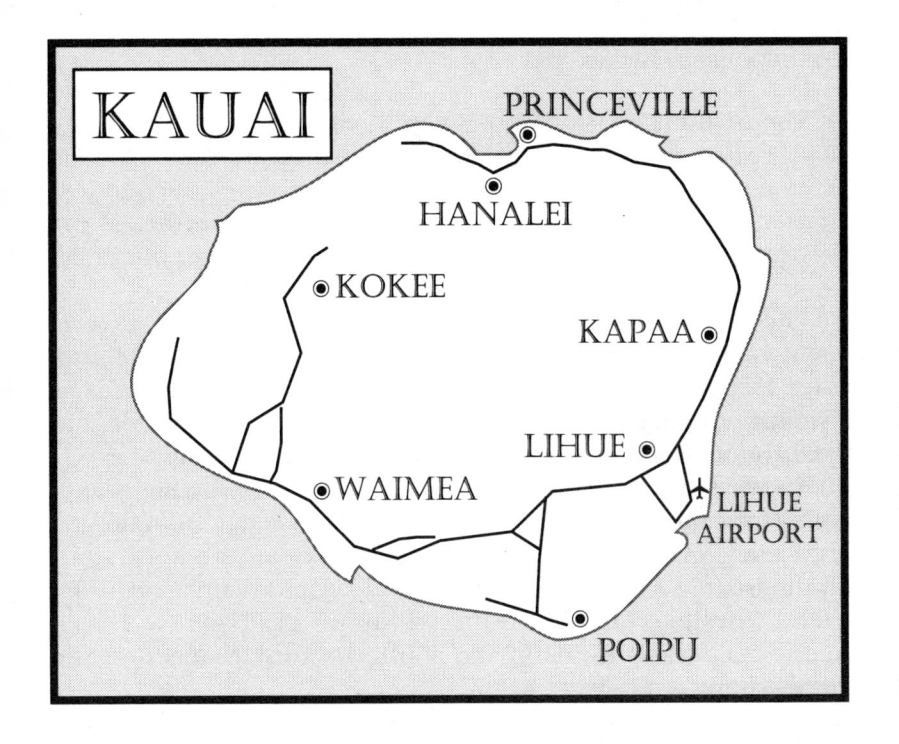

KAUAI

Kauai is well known in Hawaii as "The Garden Island" for its lush landscape, spectacular scenery, cascading waterfalls, miles of white sand beaches, and the natural wonders of its multi-hued Waimea canyon. Set apart both culturally and geographically from Oahu by the 70-mile-wide Kauai Channel, Kauai was considered a separate kingdom in the days of Kamehameha.

As the northernmost main Hawaiian Island, Kauai's climate is noticeably different from Kona's. Kauai seems to catch more of the weather systems that race across the Pacific, and in recent years experienced two devastating hurricanes – Iwa in 1982, and 'Iniki in 1992. And because it is geologically much older than the Big Island, Kauai's scenery is more like that of the South Pacific, with its fantastically eroded volcanic peaks and cliffs. The backdrops draw moviemakers like Steven Speilberg, who filmed scenes here for *Jurrasic Park* and *Raiders of the Lost Ark*.

The island is considerably lower in elevation than the Big Island, rising only to 5,170 feet from the blue waters of the Pacific, due to its older geologic age and the ravages of countless eons of erosion. Its main peak at Wai'ale'ale is nevertheless the wettest spot on earth averaging more than 400 inches of rainfall annually, and as much as 600 inches in some years.

The main port of Nawiliwili sits near the center of government and commerce, at Lihue. The main airport is in Lihue, too, with Honolulu flights coming and going from dawn to early evening. Connections from the Big Island are easily made and take about 90 minutes, counting the stopover in Honolulu.

The districts of Kauai are as varied as those of the Big Island, except for the lack of volcanic activity. They range from the uninhabited Na Pali coastal wilderness valleys on the northwest, to the island's population center at Kapaa and Wailua in the ancient Kawaihau district on the windward east side, and from sunny Poipu and Koloa in the south, to rainy Hanalei on the north shore.

Over a million visitors per year travel to Kauai. Even so, the island retains a low-key ambience with zoning laws that limit buildings to a height no higher than a coconut tree.

A two-lane main highway stretches from the north end of the road at Ke'e Beach in verdant Haena for about 70 miles to dry Kekaha and Barking Sands on the west side, across the great plain of sugar cane fields which blankets the island from Anahola on the east side, to hillside Kalaheo at the beginning of the west side.

The island is still recovering from the effects of Hurricane 'Iniki, though most of the damage has been repaired, or covered over by the island's rapidly growing vegetation. Many resorts and activities are going all-out to attract visitors, offering special packages; call 1-800-AH-KAUAI for a package of Kauai visitor information covering the entire island.

Traveling to Kauai from Kona: Inter-island flights on Hawaiian and Aloha leave from morning to mid-afternoon for Kauai from Keahole Airport and Hilo Airport. The newest inter-island carrier, Mahalo Airlines, has also resumed flying. Commuter planes fly into Princeville Airport on the North Shore throughout the day. A row of rental car companies have kiosks just across from the baggage claim areas at the Lihue Airport. It is highly recommended that you rent a car on Kauai. There is much to see, and the towns of the island are generally miles apart.

Kauai Attractions

The main attraction on Kauai is Kauai itself. A majestically scenic island, it is renowned for its stunning beauty and peopled by an independent, but friendly, population. Hanalei Bay on the North Shore and the Na Pali Coast to the northwest are definitely two of the most spectacular settings in all Hawaii and the Pacific Islands. Visitors repeatedly return here for the quiet, natural beauty and the seemingly endless stretches of beaches. Golfers will find championship courses at the south end of the island at Poipu, near the main airport at Kauai Lagoons in Lihue, and on the North Shore, at Princeville, where Hawaii's number one rated course, the Prince, is located.

Though nightlife exists within the resorts, and to a limited extent in the local towns, the most enjoyable entertainment is relaxing on the beach or in the water, and enjoying life with friends and family amidst the island's beauty.

Day cruises from Hanalei Bay to the isolated valleys of Na Pali are always fun, as well as awe-inspiring, but the boats won't go when the surf is up. Summer months are no problem; call first during large winter surf.

Championship golf courses highlight major resort areas. Princeville offers Hawaii's top-rated, Scottish-links-style Prince (826-5000), as well as woods, lake, and ocean nines at the Makai (826-3580). Kauai Lagoons is a 36 hole course designed by Jack Nicklaus that plays along the ocean (241-6000 or 800-634-6400). Kiahuna, located past Koloa town on the way to Poipu, features 18 holes that are built around ancient Hawaiian archaeological sites (742-9595). The new Poipu Bay Resort Golf Course is across the street from the Hyatt Regency Kauai (742-8711).

Scuba diving on Kauai is best at a handful of dive sites, such as Koloa Landing on the south shore, the caves of Haena Beach on the north shore, and the reefs around Nawiliwili. It is highly advisable to dive with either veteran Kauai locals or with guides from a dive shop. Snorkeling is good just about anywhere, but you'll see the most fish at Poipu Beach Park, off the public golf course in Wailua, or at Tunnels on the north shore.

Kauai lacks Kona's reputation for sport fishing, however there are some big fish to be caught. Charter boats operate year-round out of Nawiliwili Harbor and Port Allen and seasonally out of Hanalei Bay.

The Na Pali Coast, a wilderness area stretching along about 15 miles of rugged coastline on the island's northwest corner, is a world-class destination for hikers from around the world. The hiking is tough here, all uphill and downhill on wet, slippery trails. We've sailed beaches along the Na Pali and had hikers come running over waving money, begging us to sail them out so they wouldn't have to hike back. Don't attempt the entire 11-mile trail unless you're in good shape. Camping permits are necessary. Contact State Parks in Lihue (241-3444).

Accommodations

Kauai resort destinations with hotels are located on the incredibly scenic, but often rainy, north shore at Princeville; along the east side's historic Wailua River area at Kapaa and Wailua; at Kalapaki near Lihue and the airport; on the sunny south shore at Poipu; and, to a limited extent, on the dry west side at Waimea.

Bed & breakfast operations are scattered throughout the island, with a wide range of locales. The highland forest of Kokee has a cool northern California feel and a number of quaint mountain cabins; beachfront homes at Hanalei, Haena, and Poipu are popular. Inland, Wailua Homesteads and Kalaheo are somewhat rural towns with a handful of bed and breakfast rentals.

The resort destinations are somewhat self-contained and feature major oceanfront hotels, championship golf courses, shopping centers, long white sand beaches, and condominiums.

Elegant Princeville is set on a tableland above majestically beautiful Hanalei Valley. Located in a rural, coastal area,

Princeville is a great base from which to explore the isolated Na Pali Coast or to just relax at the beach at Hanalei. Accommodations range from the 5-star, European-like *Princeville Hotel*, to spacious condominiums and vacation homes.

The Coconut Coast is a mid-range visitor area stretching along Kuhio Highway from Kapa'a to Wailua with several hotels, some with budget prices. You might find the boat ride up the Wailua River to the Fern Grotto too touristy, but lots of people love it, and the luau at *Smith's Paradise* is quite spectacular.

At Kalapaki, near Lihue Airport, Marriott is preparing to reopen the *Westin Kauai* as a Marriott resort.

Poipu Beach is a sunny beach resort with an atmosphere similar to what you find along Ali'i Drive in Kona. The *Hyatt Regency Kauai* and several other large hotels dot the coast, with a number of condominiums and B&B's. The beach, golf and sun are the big attractions at Poipu. Nearby Koloa town is an enclave of old Hawaii with a gaudy veneer of tourist shops along its main road.

Our favorite place to stay on Kauai is anywhere on the North Shore, or on the non-touristy Westside at *The Waimea Vacation Cottages* (338-1625). These authentically restored plantation cottages filled with period furnishings are right on the ocean. We like the low-key, '30s ambience, and the soothing peace and quiet.

Dining

It takes a little searching to find a good restaurant on Kauai, but they are there. Located in a nondescript shopping center, *A Pacific Cafe* at the Kauai Village Shopping Center in Kapaa is the best restaurant on the island, and one of the best in the state. Everything is good; the chef imaginatively mixes French and Asian techniques and ingredients to come up with his own original creations that often startle because they are so different, so wonderful to look at, and so delicious. It's expensive, but more than worth it.

Gaylord's Restaurant at Kilohana is located just south of Lihue on Kaumuali'i Highway (245-9593) in the former estate of a Kauai missionary and sugar cane plantation owner. Meals are served indoors, as well as in the pleasant, airy, open court, which we prefer. Try the Alaskan salmon.

Brick Oven Pizza, Kalaheo (332-8561). Tasty Portuguese local-style pizza with excellent service. A good stopover on your way back from the west side.

Pizza Hanalei, Hanalei (826-9494). Another good pizza place. This one serves it California-style.

The Grove at Waimea Plantation Cottages, Waimea, (338-2300) serves good multi-cultural Hawaiian cuisine in a spacious, rebuilt plantation home.

Koloa Broiler, Koloa Town (742-9122). Cook it yourself on the large indoor grill.

Hamura Saimin Stand, Lihue (245-3271). A famous, very local saimin shop serving inexpensive, excellent, homemade noodles and broth. The beef or chicken teriyaki on a stick is cheap and very good. Don't let the looks of the place turn you off.

Bubba Burgers, Kapaa and Hanalei (823-0069). Old-style grilled hamburgers, the real thing, are the specialty here, served with sarcasm and humor.

Ambrose's Kupuna Natural Foods (822-7112), Kapaa. Though not a restaurant, Ambrose Curry's place is the most interesting food store on the island. From a family who owned a small grocery in San Francisco, Ambrose, a surfer and sage, has been in business on Kauai for over 20 years and has a little bit of everything in the health food realm.

Casa Di Amici, Kilauea (828-1388). Adjacent to the Kong Lung Store on the road to Kilauea Lighthouse. Nouvelle Italian cuisine, good wine selection.

Tahiti Nui, Hanalei (826-6277). Run by Louise Marsden, a Tahitian woman, Tahiti Nui is an institution on the north shore. The Hawaiian-Tahitian food is good and tastes homemade. They almost always have fresh fish.

The Bull Shed, Waipouli near Kapaa (822-1655). A steak and seafood restaurant on the ocean. A little hard to find, it's down a long driveway across the highway from the shopping center that houses A Pacific Cafe. Consistently good seafood.

Beaches

White sand beaches are found everywhere on Kauai.

Barking Sands-Polihale: A very long white sand beach on the west side stretching for several miles from Kekaha north to the end of the road at Polihale.

Poipu Beach: A variety of beaches and coves stretching west from Shipwrecks near the Hyatt Regency. Poipu Beach Park is a popular protected children's beach with a lifeguard, and a good snorkeling spot.

Kalapaki Bay: The white sand beach in front of the former Westin Kauai draws visitors and locals. An easily accessible beach a few miles from the airport.

Wailua Beach: Rich in Hawaiian legend, the Wailua Beach area can be a little rough for swimming.

Hanalei Bay/Princeville: The dreamy, crescent bay at Hanalei has a long white sand beach popular for swimming, surfing and sunning, with a fantastic mountainous backdrop.

Coffee

In Hanalei Valley, where Hawaii's largest patches of taro now grow, a coffee plantation was begun in the 1840s by Charles Titcomb. Hanalei is a rainy area and a blight that destroyed his coffee crop forced Titcomb to replant the fields with Tahitian sugar cane. Today, coffee growing is returning to Kauai on McBryde Sugar land below the hillside town of Kalaheo, between the south and west sides of the island. The soil is considerably different than that found in Kona, and the natural afternoon shade of Kona isn't always found here. All McBryde's coffee is picked by mechanical harvesters. You can esaily taste the coffee, as it has started to show up on grocery store shelves all over the state. It remains to be seen whether the Kauai crop (with twice as many acres as Kona) will establish its own market identity, or will adversely affect the Kona coffee market by confusing consumers.

Coffee drinkers will find only a handful of true coffee shops on Kauai. A newer one is the *Old Hanalei Coffee Company*

(826-6717) at Hanalei Center in the beachfront town of Hanalei on the north shore. After being unable to find a decent cup of coffee while on frequent visits to Kauai, the owners returned determined to serve good coffee. According to friends on the north shore, they've succeeded.

Set in an older plantation building, *Papaya's Cafe* (823-0190) on Kuhio Highway in Kapaa also serves a true cup of coffee. A good place to hang out and watch Kauai's visitors and locals cruise by.

Ni'ihau

Though it is a small and arid 73-square-mile island, 17 miles and worlds away from Kauai across the Kaulakahi Channel, the "Forbidden Island" of Ni'ihau is the center of much attention. Off limits to everyone except for its 200 or so native Hawaiian residents and its owner, the Robinson family of Kauai, Ni'ihau has been inaccessible until recently.

Now *Ni'ihau Helicopters*, a touring firm owned by the Robinsons, will fly you over the island.

A very dry island, Ni'ihau lies in the lee of Kauai's mountains which block the trade winds and rains that make the Garden Island so green.

Ni'ihau is best known in Kona for its highly-prized shell necklaces. Jewelry stores carrying the precious shell leis which vary in price according to color and quality.

kona kai farms

Kona and Coffee

Coffee Festival participants.

KONA COFFEE CULTURAL FESTIVAL

The promotional highlight of the year for the Kona coffee industry is the annual *Kona Coffee Cultural Festival*, held in early November. It is an ideal time to see the industry in full production and to take advantage of the numerous special events put on for the local community and visitors. The *Kona Coffee Cupping Competition*, sponsored by Kona Kai Farms, and other events, are of particular interest to coffee roasters and retailers.

Traditionally, each festival has a different theme, symbolized in a button which gives admission to most of the events. The theme for the 24th annual festival in November 1994, for example, was "Perfection in a Cup." A "Miss Kona Coffee" is crowned each year, and a "Pioneer of Kona Coffee" is given the honor of leading the annual parade.

The kick-off event for the festival is the *Big Island Brunch*, which features cuisine prepared by the students of the Culinary Arts Program at the University of Hawaii, West Campus. Portuguese sausage, macadamia nuts, guavas, bananas, taro, and tofu are just a few of the local ingredients used for the multi-ethnic entrees. The festival queen candidates serve as hostesses, and Kona coffee is plentiful. Other regular events that take place during the festival are:

International Kupuna Hula Festival & Craft Fair: Usually held the Saturday before festival week, this hula competition features highly skilled *kupunas* (seniors) invited from all over the world.

Kona Coffee Farm Fair (first Saturday): The *Future Farmers of America* hold this event at Konawaena High School. Live demonstrations, such as chef Sam Choy's cooking exhibition, a variety of farm and garden exhibits, Kona coffee displays, food booths, fresh island produce, orchids, the artistry of *ikebana* (Japanese flower arranging), commercial booths, and door prizes are just a sampling of what you'll find.

Kona Coffee History Day (first Saturday): Old coffee processing methods, photo exhibits, Kona coffee basket weaving, and opportunities to "talk story" with Kona's pioneer farmers are offered at the *Kona Historical Society* in Kealakekua.

Bowling and Golf Tournaments (schedule varies): Usually sponsored by one of the larger coffee roasters, these events feature lots of alcohol and prizes. A lack of seriousness abounds.

Coffee Mill & Farm Tour (mid week): Usually organized by the *Kona Coffee Council*, the tour visits processors of varying sizes and a couple of farms. There is generally just a car caravan, but sometimes there have been buses available, too. Kona Kai Farms has open house all week long for those who miss the tour. We'll even let you pick coffee off our trees to get some hands on experience! Whichever way you go, it's a great chance to observe coffee being processed at the peak of harvest season.

Judges 1991 Cupping Competition: (l. to r.) Ted Lingle, Hitoshi Iwata, Mary Townsend, Martin Elkin, Alfred Peet.

Kona Kai Farms Kona Coffee Cupping Competition & Coffee Theme Art Show: For our money, this is the highlight of the festival, where about fifty growers submit their crop for judging by world-class coffee cup testers. Past judges have included Alfred Peet, the "guru" of the modern specialty coffee industry and founder of *Peet's Coffee* in Berkeley, California; Mary Townsend, green coffee buyer for *Starbucks Coffee* in Seattle, the largest specialty roaster in the United States; Ted Lingle, head of the *Specialty Coffee Association of America*; Takayoshi Kimura, Vice President of *UCC Coffee*, the largest Japanese coffee roaster; and Marty Elkin of *Specialty Coffee Holding Company* in New Hampshire, the largest U.S. consortium of regional specialty roasters.

The names of cupping contest winners are engraved on the *Tom Kerr Memorial Koa Bowl* which is on permanent display at Kona Kai Farms' main office in Kealakekua.

The Kona Coffee Cupping Competition is usually held on Wednesday and Thursday of Festival Week, in conjunction with an exhibition of local artists' works that feature Kona coffee as a subject. The art show now has more entries than the cupping competition and is a great place to pick up coffee-related art.

The only event that is sometimes held outside the Kona district, the cupping competition often takes place at The Ritz Carlton, Mauna Lani Hotel, in Kohala.

Paniolo Steak Fry: An evening for local farmers and visitors from the coffee industry to meet and socialize, and enjoy good food and entertainment. Some of the local entertainers have written their own "coffee" tunes. Usually held Wednesday evenings at the Kona Surf Hotel.

International Lantern Parade and Cultural Event: Thursday evening Ali'i Drive is closed for fifteen minutes for a peaceful and beautiful lantern parade down Kona's main street. Participants include groups from the Portuguese, Filipino, Japanese, and Chinese communities in traditional dress carrying Japanese lanterns led by *taiko* drums. A colorful *Bon Dance* begins as they arrive at their destination at *Hale Halawai*, and the festivities continue for several hours as ethnic groups entertain the audience with traditional music and dance.

Kona Coffee Recipe Contest: Professional and amateur cooks compete in various categories to produce the best recipes featuring Kona coffee. Any recipe can be submitted, the only criterion being that 100% pure Kona coffee be one of the ingredients. The public is invited to taste samples after the judging.

Kona Coffee Grand Parade (Saturday): Colorful floats with the Festival theme highlight this well-attended event which begins around 9 a.m. at *Lanihau Shopping Center* and winds down Ali'i Drive to *Hale Halawai*. Marching units, Kona coffee queen contestants, floats, and *paniolos* are just part of this traditional event.

Heritage Park and International Market: After the parade, there is a day-long food fest outside *Hale Halawai*, the public pavilion next to the ocean between the Kona Inn and Waterfront Row. Hawaiian, Japanese, Filipino, Chinese, English and Portuguese communities set up villages on the grounds that feature their ethnic costumes, food, culture, entertainment, and arts and crafts. Historically, these groups all worked the coffee fields in Kona. Inside the pavilion is a coffee-roasting exhibit, an *ikebana* floral display, historical coffee photos presented by the *Kona Historical Society*, and the entrants and winners of the lei-making competition.

Coffee picking contestants display their baskets.

Coffee Picking Contest (day varies): This is another "must see" event for anyone in the coffee industry, and the most action-packed day of the entire festival. Pickers compete in various divisions for ten minutes of the fastest coffee picking imaginable, offering visitors a great chance to see the real backbone of the industry. Divisions include novice, open men's and women's, keiki, juniors and pioneer. Prizes are awarded to winners of divisions. Bring your own Japanese-style *bento* box lunch (available at many local eateries) for the post-picking picnic.

Pioneer Luncheon: At noon on parade day a special luncheon is held to honor the pioneers of the coffee industry in Kona, mostly Japanese immigrants who came to Kona in the 1920's to work the coffee fields after their sugar contracts expired.

Annual Miss Kona Coffee Scholarship Pageant (Saturday evening, Kona Surf Hotel): Contestants vie for the title in a competition that has traditionally been part of the Miss America pageant system. Carolyn Sapp, Miss Kona Coffee of 1987, became Miss Hawaii, and then Miss America, in 1992. Cash prizes, scholarships and travel are just a few of the incentives for the win-

Coffee Festival parade float passes Oshima Store in Kainaliu.
Kona Historical Society

ner, who will represent Kona coffee at numerous promotional events throughout the year. The pageant is usually sold out, with a large part of the crowd being friends and relatives of the contestants. This is the final event of Coffee Festival Week.

The Festival is run by a non-profit organization headed by a president and a board of directors. You may write them at: Kona Coffee Cultural Festival, P.O. Box 1112, Kailua-Kona, Hawaii 96745.

Konawaena High School and coffee fields, c. 1930. Kona Historical Society

KONA COFFEE HISTORY

The first known planting of coffee in Hawaii was made by the Spaniard, Don Francisco de Paula y Marin at his home in Honolulu in about 1813. Born in Jerez, Spain, Marin came to Hawaii from California in 1791. An interperter and physican for Kamehameha I, Marin introduced coffee growing to Hawaii.

The origin of the first *arabica* coffee beans planted by Marin can be traced back centuries to the fields of distant Ethiopia, where it was first discovered. Coffee was popularly introduced in Yemen in the eighth century A.D., where it eventually spread to the ideal volcanic growing areas of southern Java. In 1714 a coffee tree was given to Louis XIV of France which reportedly was the parent of over one billion coffee trees in South America after the tree was brought to Brazil in 1727. Hawaii's coffee trees would come from South American coffee trees, and from the fields of Java.

The coffee fields of Kona were begun with cuttings from trees planted on Oahu in the mid-1820s. The first noteable planting was made in 1825 by John Wilkinson, a gardener from England brought to Hawaii by the Hawaiian alii Boki to develop and run a plantation. Wilkinson arrived aboard the *Blonde*, which returned the bodies of King Kamehameha II, Liholiho, and his queen Kamamalu, from London following their deaths in England from measles.

Wilkinson started a sugar and coffee plantation in Honolulu's Manoa Valley in 1825. The coffee flourished, but unfortunately Wilkinson died in 1827 just as the coffee trees began to produce.

At about this same time coffee plants were brought to Hawaii from the Philippines by British consul Richard Charlton and from Batavia in the Dutch East Indies.

The first coffee was planted in Kona by missionary Samuel Ruggles. Ruggles, a member of the first American missionary party to Hawaii, planted the first coffee at Naole on property owned by H.N. Greenwell, in 1828 or 1829. Kona's dry sunny slopes proved ideal for them and the trees flourished.

Natural history

Kona produces one of the best tasting coffees available in the world, and the state of Hawaii produces the only commercially grown coffee in the United States. This enviable reputation is the results of perfect growing conditions and generations of painstaking care and ingenuity among local growers.

Coffee growing conditions are ideal along the Kona Coffee Belt, which stretches from Holualoa to Honaunau at an elevation between 700' and 2000' elevation. The fortunate combination of shelter from the tradewinds and sun by Mauna Loa and Hualalai; a rich, porous soil composed of vegetation and ground lava rock; and a weather pattern of morning sun and afternoon overcast make the twelve mile belt one of the best locations on the earth for coffee growing,

The optimal climate morning sun and afternoon cloud cover is created through a natural land-sea breeze system of air circulation that operates like a time clock, except during infrequent storms from the south. Each morning, after the sun raises the temperature of the land, moisture-laden air drifts in from the Pacific Ocean. When this damp air reaches the cool mountain slopes, it rises. By noon cloud cover blankets the slopes at about

2,500 feet. By early afternoon rain begins to fall and the next day the cycle begins anew. Unlike other coffee growing areas in the world, Kona's climate makes it unecessary to plant shade trees to protect the coffee trees.

Robert Louis Stevenson at Hookena, 1889.

From In The South Seas

In the midst of this rough wilderness, I was reminded of the aim of our excursion. The schoolmaster and certain others of Hookena had recently bought a tract of land for some four thousand dollars; set out coffee; and hired a Chinaman to mind it. The thing was notable in itself; natives selling land is a thing of daily custom; of natives buying, I have heard no other instance; and it was civil to show interest. "But when," I asked, "shall we come to your coffee plantation?" "This is it," said he, and pointed down. The bushes grew on the path-side; our horses breasted them as they went by...on every hand enclosed and overarched that thread of cultivation...

Invitation to coffee growers, 1875

Given by Henry M. Whitney, editor of the Hawaiian Gazette, in Hawaii's first guide book, published 1875.

There is no product that promises so well for this group as coffee, provided elevated localities are chosen for it. It is stated that on Hawaii the trees which grow in the woods and at a certain height are not attacked with blight, but are every year found loaded with berries... in Kona, Kau, Hamakua and Hilo, on Hawaii-there are many good localities, possessing sufficient moisture and well protected from the winds, where coffee plantations may be profitably located. These lands, when not purchasable, can generally be leased at a fair annual rental. Though stony, they are said to be all the better on this account for coffee culture. We consider this the most promising business that can be engaged in by foreigners of small means.

A typical "hoshidana" or coffee drying deck. Kona Historical Society

The Kona Coffee Industry 1830-1960

Coffee was initiated as a commercial crop during the 1830s by European and American planters, with some plantings by Native Hawaiians. Following a boom at the beginning of the 1849 California Gold Rush, drought and a variety of infestations, coupled with a shortage of labor, hindered its commercial success and by the 1860s coffee plantations had all but disappeared in the islands, except for the Kona and Hamakua districts of the Big Island. During the 1880s and '90s, a rise in market prices inspired a rush of investment by both Europeans and Americans producing a "boom" in Kona during the 1890s. This boom was followed by one of many "busts" that would plague the industry and by the turn of the century coffee had for the most part been abandoned once again.

In 1885 Japanese immigrants were brought to Hawaii as a cheap labor source to replace the decreasing Chinese workers. They arrived under three year labor contracts for the sugar plantations. As the last ethnic group to be recruited in the late 19th century, the Japanese entered at the very bottom of the plantation system and received the lowest wages.

Many of these Japanese arrived in Kona as laborers to pick coffee during the boom of the 1890s. They either arrived at the completion of their labor contracts or as escapees from the harsh conditions suffered on the plantations. During the boom years, the Japanese population in Kona jumped from 8 in 1890 to 1,718 in 1900; most were males.

The Japanese issei, or first generation, began leasing land to raise coffee as early as the 1890s but played a minor role in the industry until after 1900. It was around this time that the plantation system was replaced by Japanese tenant farmers. The Japanese were leased five acre farms because this was the amount of land a family could successfully manage without hired help. This change, from the large plantation to the small family run farm, revolutionized the coffee industry and helped to keep it alive.

By 1910, Japanese coffee farmers constituted 80% of the total coffee farming population in Kona. With the United States entry into World War I, issei farmers experienced great prosperity. Until 1928, market prices stayed high, and many people enjoyed financial well-being.

During the first half of the 20th century there were two coffee companies that controlled the majority of the Kona crop. Captain Cook Coffee Company, located in south Kona and American Factors, located in Kailua, North Kona.

Near the turn of the century, in an attempt to attain economic autonomy, Japanese coffee growers began forming their own mills. In 1898, a group of the growers organized into the Kona Japanese Coffee Producers Association for the purpose of "processing coffee and marketing it at better prices on their own." In the following year, they established the first Japanese-owned mill, known as the Kona Japanese Coffee Mill, located in Kailua.

In 1929, with the onslaught of the depression, coffee went bust once again. Coffee farmers became ridden with debt. By 1935, their debt grew so big that some farmers ran away and others simply went bankrupt. The majority of the remaining farmers mortgaged their farms and crops for 10 to 30 years.

In 1938, Japanese farmers compiled their total debt and entered into collective negotiation with American Factors to reduce it. The company agreed to reduce the debt to two percent

Kona coffee grower. Kona Historical Society

of the original debt. This so-called "Debt-Adjustment Movement" gave Japanese coffee farmers a chance to make a new start.

Nisei, or second generation, farmers organized the Kona Advancement Club in 1937, in an attempt to break the domination of the Captain Cook Coffee Company and American Factors and to bring Kona farmers more autonomy.

During the 1950s nisei farmers were responsible for establishing the early coffee cooperatives in an attempt to gain more control over marketing of the crop. Between 1955 and 1959 the Sunset Coffee Cooperative and the Pacific Coffee Cooperatives were formed, it was also about this time that Captain Cook Coffee Company lost it's south Kona leases and American Factors dismantled it's Kailua mill.

Both issei and nisei played a significant role in the development of new technology in coffee processing. These technologies helped improve methods of production and are unique to the Kona.

KONA COFFEE PRODUCTION
1946–1995

HARVESTED ACRES ▬
100 LB. GREEN BAGS ▬

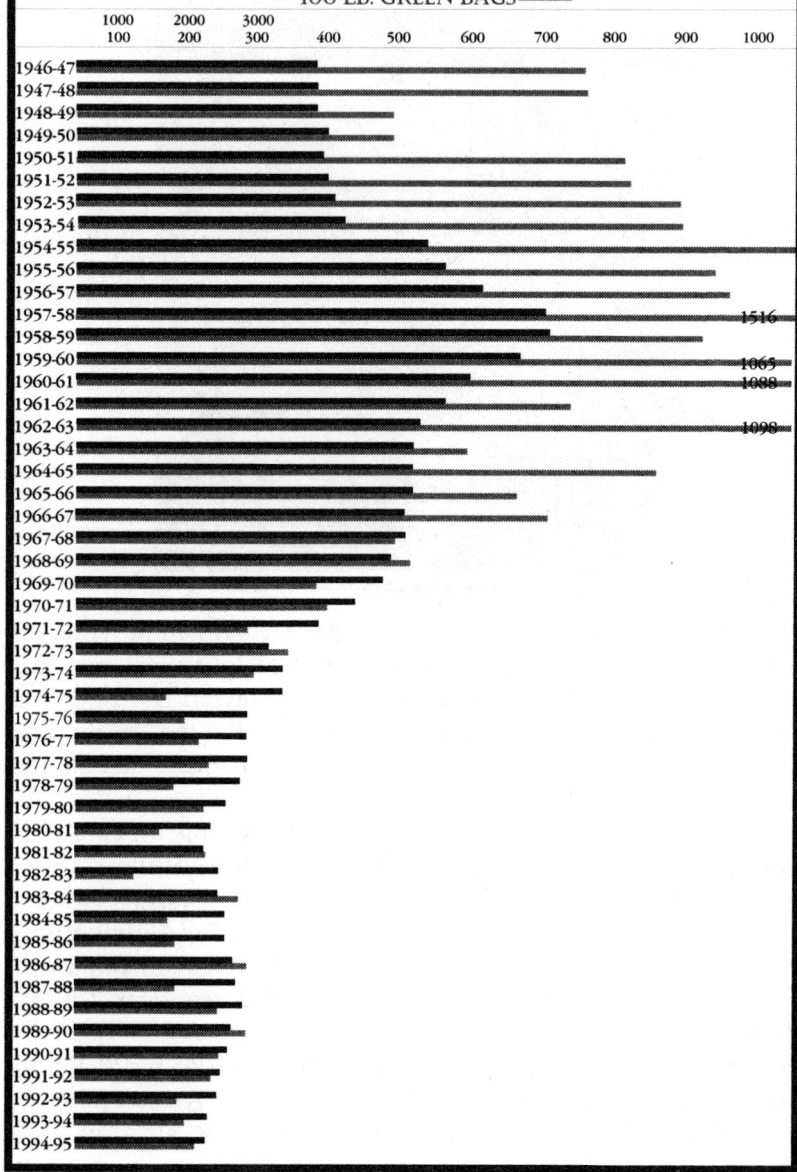

	1000	2000	3000	400	500	600	700	800	900	1000
	100	200	300							

1957-58 — 1516
1959-60 — 1065
1960-61 — 1088
1962-63 — 1098

Parchment mill at Kona Kai Farms

THE KONA COFFEE INDUSTRY 1960-1995

When Hawaii became a state in 1959, the price of land and labor rose so sharply that Kona coffee was no longer competitive with coffee grown in less developed countries. Kona farmers desperately tried to find a separate market for their coffee that was not tied to the world price, and in the mid-60s the two remaining Kona co-operatives (*Kona Farmers Co-operative* and *Pacific Coffee Co-operative*) succeeded in getting *Superior Coffee* of Chicago to agree to purchase the entire crop at a premium. Superior in turn built a roasting plant in Honolulu and began to market its "Royal Kona" coffee blend as an upscale product compared to its regular coffee. Although this agreement probably saved the industry from dying out completely, the premium was not enough to stop the decline in coffee acreage, and by 1980 acreage in production had dipped below 2,000 acres.

Kona coffee history entered its most recent phase about the time *Kona Kai Farms* came into being in 1979. Although a few bags of green coffee were exported to the mainland by fledgling millers between 1979 and 1982, it wasn't until *United Coffee*, a specialty coffee roaster based in San Francisco, opened up the old Donkey Mill in Keauhou Mauka for processing that things really started to change. They immediately attracted a significant number of farmers by paying a few cents per pound more for coffee cherry and parchment than the co-operatives, and opened up the market to sell green coffee to other specialty coffee roasters that had not been able to purchase unroasted coffee because of the exclusive agreement between Superior and the co-ops. United Coffee was soon followed by Kona Kai Farms and *Bong Brothers Coffee Company* in 1983, and *Captain Cook Coffee Company* in 1984. Since 1984 the Kona coffee business has been a turmoil of controversy, with coffee buyers coming and going, prices skyrocketing up and down, numerous attempts to regulate the blending and certification of Kona coffee, and a growing number of estate coffee companies, selling their farm product as roasted coffee.

One constant factor fueling interest in Kona coffee has been the unmitigated rise in the growth of the specialty coffee industry in general during the 1980s and 1990s. The demand for exotic Kona beans by the hundreds of specialty coffee roasters in the United States has pushed prices for green Kona coffee over $7.00 per pound by the spring of 1995, with retail prices pushing $20 per pound.

Kona farmers now receive record prices for coffee cherry and parchment, yet the cost of the land and labor necessary to produce a crop and the uncertain weather make Kona coffee farming a risky business. Kona coffee now competes with large coffee plantings on Kauai, Molokai and Maui run by major agricultural corporations using mechanical harvesting machines. Although there have been some new substantial plantings in Kona, the industry remains very decentralized, with the average family farm size being two to three acres. Of the more than 600 existing farms, almost all are run by part-time farmers.

The Big Island phone book's yellow pages in 1994-95 listed 29 companies under "Coffee & Tea-Wholesale," six under "Coffee Mills" and seven under "Coffee Roasting."

Kona Blend

The issue of "Kona Blend" coffee has been one of the most controversial since we came here in 1979. Specialty coffee is sold both by country of origin (Colombian, Sumatran, Kenya, Costa Rica, etc.) and also by special blends made of a combination of coffees. These blends are usually created to make coffee taste a certain way, and most roasters feel that normally their blends are superior to pure regional varietals because very few coffees are complete in terms of taste, body, mouth feel, and the other qualities roasters look for.

When the coffees in a blend are relatively equal in cost and availability, taste is the prime consideration in creating and naming a blend. However, when one of the coffees in a blend is a high priced exotic like Kona or Jamaican, obvious problems arise concerning how much of the high priced coffee is actually used in the blend. When the price of Kona coffee rose to two and three times the world coffee price, roasters had a big incentive to use as little Kona coffee as possible in their blends, and yet use the name "Kona" as much as possible in marketing the product.

In 1986 the *Kona Coffee Council* proposed a Kona coffee "truth in labeling law" which would have required roasters to list the percentage of Kona blend in their packages, but it was vetoed by the governor. A similar bill was passed in 1992 which required all Kona blends sold in the state to contain at least 10% Kona coffee and say so on the package. No similar law exists on the U.S. mainland, and the issue of labeling of specialty coffees has not been addressed by any U.S. coffee industry organization. Just after the new blending law was passed, a group of estate farmers took over effective control of the Kona Coffee Council and attempted to obtain a federal "certification mark" for the term "Kona Coffee" which they thought would allow them to control the use of the name "Kona" with respect to coffee. Their stated purpose was to eliminate Kona blends from the marketplace. A bitter legal fight ensued among the Council, several processing companies, and Honolulu roasters, and eventually the certification mark application was dropped. Today Kona coffee remains an interesting, diversified, and often disorganized industry with many independent and opinionated participants.

KONA KAI FARMS' GUIDE TO MAKING GOOD COFFEE

Before moving to Kona from Berkeley, California in 1979, I had never consumed a full cup of coffee in my life. I thought coffee was what my father drank (instant) or what you got in a restaurant along the interstate highway. It smelled horrible, tasted worse, and I couldn't understand why anyone drank it. If I wanted caffeine, I drank Coca Cola.

When I became the owner of a coffee farm, I decided I would try drinking what was now the basis of my livelihood. Not only that, I wanted to drink my own coffee. This required considerable effort, but I was determined. Our ancient pulping mill made parchment out of the cherry coffee – that was the easy part. The red coffee "cherry" that is picked from the tree is a fruity pulp surrounding two seeds, covered with a thin "parchment" skin. Many Kona farms have machines which remove the cherry and allow the farmer to sell the "parchment" coffee to mills.

Lacking the proper machines to remove the parchment skin,

I tried to get the local mill to remove the skin for a fee. No deal: I had to resort to a blender. By using the slow speed, the blender took the parchment skin off without damaging the beans too much. I then poured the beans and the chaff over a desktop oscillating fan, which blew the chaff away, leaving the green beans. This was messy, but after a few times it became routine. In 30 minutes I could mill about a pound of coffee.

To roast the beans, I used a frying pan at medium heat, constantly stirring the beans to keep them from burning. Later, I found that a similar technique in the oven would work better (about 450 degrees). Coffee beans pop like popcorn as they expand from the heat. When they start to pop a second time, they are ready, usually after about 20 minutes. I waited for them to cool down, ground them up in a home coffee grinder and brewed the coffee by pouring boiling water over the grounds in a paper filter.

Amazingly, my homemade coffee was wonderful. It had aroma, character, taste and body completely lacking in any other coffee I had ever sniffed before. It was not only drinkable, it was in the same class with chocolate, strawberry papayas, fresh squeezed orange juice, homemade bread, and other delicacies that make food a delight. It became a regular feature of breakfast.

At first I assumed that this difference in quality was wholly due to the fact that I was using Kona coffee, long valued as one of the world's finest. However, as I became more knowledgeable about the coffee business, I realized that there were in fact many great coffees in the world, and that the difference between Kona coffee and these other coffees was extremely subtle and did not account for the difference between my coffee and Taster's Choice.

Now, I believe I understand the factors affecting coffee quality enough to try to explain them in a way that might be helpful to the average person. There are two basic rules that will almost always guarantee a good cup of coffee: (1) Use good quality arabica coffee beans, and (2) make sure the coffee is fresh. There are a lot of other details, but if you follow these two rules, it's hard to go far wrong.

Coffee is divided into two basic types: arabica and robusta. They are very different looking plants, and produce a vastly different kind of bean. Robustas are grown because they are very resistant to disease and produce high yields. However, they have both an inferior, "rubbery" taste, and a much higher caffeine content. Robustas are grown mostly in Africa, Indonesia, and Brazil, and they bring less than half the price of arabicas on the world market.

In contrast, all of the world's prized coffee is arabica. Besides the "elite" very high priced coffees such as Jamaica Blue Mountain, Kona, Celebese Kalossi (Indonesian), and Mocha Harrar (Ethiopian), all of the popular Central American "milds" (Guatamalan, Costa Rican, Honduran, Salvadoran), Kenya AA, and the much-publicized Colombian coffees are arabicas. Other favored arabica coffees come from Sumatra, Papua New Guinea, Zimbabwe, Panama, and Brazil (the world's leading producer).

Robustas have about twice the caffeine content of arabicas. In the past, this has been a desirable characteristic for the marketplace, but times are changing, and too much caffeine can be perceived as a health risk. When you watch a TV ad for a mass consumption coffee that says it has "half the caffeine" as another brand, it just means they switched to arabicas. The only remaining reason to use robusta coffee is cost, but "straight" robusta usually tastes so offensive that it is undrinkable. Therefore, most mass consumption coffees blend robustas with arabicas to develop an acceptable taste at the lowest possible price.

Apart from the robustas, there are much more subtle differences between the various kinds of arabica coffees. Regional differences such as altitude, temperature, rainfall and soil conditions, cultivation and harvesting techniques, and grading during processing produce different products at different prices. For example, Kenya AA coffee is noted for its extreme acidity, or "bite" (a desired characteristic). Coffee from Ethiopia has a perfumey, "winey" characteristic. Kona is noted for its sweetness and intense aroma. Blending of coffees with various characteristics can produce a more "balanced" coffee than coffee from any one geographical location. Part of the fun of drinking coffee is that you can create your own blends.

One of the main differences in coffee preparation at the farm level is the difference between "washed" and "unwashed" coffee. As mentioned before, coffee cherries harvested from the trees are seeds surrounded by a fruity pulp. In the "wet" process, this pulp is removed immediately after harvesting, and the beans are washed and dried either in the sun or by mechanical dryers (often a combination of both). This process removes the cherry fruit before it has a chance to ferment. The rotting fruit produces a strong, disagreeable flavor which would contaminate a bean inside the cherry. This is why farmers try to get their coffee to the mill right after picking, and why mills always try to pulp the cherry immediately. The easiest way to spoil good coffee is to leave it in the picking bag too long, especially in the sun. Then the fermenting beans produce extreme heat, and the bad flavor "burns" into the coffee. After this occurs, the coffee is spoiled forever. Worse, if it is mixed with good coffee it will contaminate the whole batch.

Harvesting for wet processing is extremely time consuming, because the coffee beans ripen three or four times each season, and each "round" must be picked separately. In Kona, the cost of harvesting the beans is more than one-third the farm value of the crop.

In the "dry" process, the beans are allowed to rot on the tree. Although the cherry fruit does rot and dry around the bean, since it is by itself rather than in a bag with lots of other beans, the contamination is very slight. After all the beans have dried on the tree the tree is harvested (only one time) and the dried cherry is removed by milling machines to expose the green beans. This process is much less expensive than the wet process, but produces a slightly inferior quality coffee.

Each country has a different way of grading their coffee and different names for the best and the worst quality. Colombia calls its highest grade "Supremo," while Kenya uses the term "AA" and in Kona we call ours "Extra Fancy." Many other countries use the term "strictly hard bean" (SHB) for their highest quality, high elevation coffee. The standards that govern these terms are very precise, and usually involve size, color, defects, and cup quality (taste). For example, Kona Extra Fancy is green

coffee which has the following characteristics:
(1) It is grown in the Kona district.
(2) At least 90% of the beans will not fall through a hole $19/64$ inches in diameter.
(3) There are less than 10 defects per pound. (A defect could be something like a stick or a rock in the sample, a hollow bean, or a bean with cuts from the hulling process).
(4) It has a good green color.
(5) It has an acceptable and characteristic taste in the cup.

Kona Fancy is $1/64$ inch smaller and can have 16 defects per pound, while Kona No. 1 can be another $1/32$ inch smaller and can have 20 defects per pound. Size and defects are not necessarily related to taste in every case, but on the average the Extra Fancy coffee will cup better than the No. 1. However, appearances are important, and the bigger beans are easier to sell and command higher prices. Roughly 80% of Kona coffee is graded in these three categories. Another 15% is divided into "Prime," "No. 3," and "Unclassified." The Prime grade is noticeably inferior to the higher grades, but most Prime is still good coffee and is used for "Kona blends." The two lowest grades, about five per cent of the crop, are low quality in taste, and are difficult to sell at any price. If you see "pure Kona" coffee at an unusually low price, be sure to check what the grade is.

There is also a small part of the crop which is graded as "Peaberry" coffee, so-called because the beans are round like peas. About five per cent of the cherries produce one round bean instead of two flat beans, and the milling machines can separate this coffee from the rest. Peaberry has slightly different (and we think superior) taste characteristics than the normal beans, perhaps because the flavor characteristics of two beans are compressed into one.

The "shelf life" of roasted coffee is roughly the same as baked bread: no matter how good it was to begin with, in a few days it will be stale unless its shelf life is increased with special packaging or preservatives. Even with the best packaging, nothing will ever match the quality of freshly roasted coffee or freshly baked bread.

There are three basic ways to assure that your coffee is fresh:

(1) Roast it yourself. There are now home coffee roasters on the market which will roast about ¼ pound of green beans at a time: enough for about two pots of coffee. The best electric home roaster we have found is made by Seimens of Germany, and retails for about $250. For less money and more work, you can also roast coffee in a pie pan in the oven, or in a frying pan on the stove.

(2) Purchase freshly roasted coffee from a retail specialty coffee roaster. "Retail-roasters" are the fastest growing segment in the coffee business. These are small stores which roast their own coffee each day, usually in a small (25 lbs. or less) roaster located in the store. In Kona we are fortunate to have a number of these roasters. Once purchased, it is important to keep the coffee away from oxygen. The best way is to put the whole beans in an air-tight, moisture-proof container and keep them in the refrigerator. Grind only as much coffee as you will use at the moment, because grinding exposes more of the coffee to oxygen.

(3) Buy coffee in packaging which best preserves freshness. To understand coffee packaging, you must know that freshly roasted coffee gives off carbon dioxide gas for about two days after roasting. This means that the vacuum-packed cans that were long dominant in the supermarkets contained coffee which had to be "degassed" for two days to allow the carbon dioxide to escape. Otherwise, the gas would explode the can. During these two days, the coffee was exposed to oxygen, and the staling process started.

About 15 years ago, an Italian bag manufacturer developed the one-way valve bag, and it has since become standard for the specialty coffee industry. A special valve in a vacuum sealed bag allows the carbon dioxide to escape from the inside, but does not allow oxygen from the outside into the bag. This allows coffee to be packaged immediately after roasting, before the staling process begins. Roasters without the expensive machinery necessary to package coffee in the valve bags achieve similar results for a short while by poking a small pin hole in a sealed bag.

The valve bags definitely improve the shelf life of roasted coffee – how much is a question of how high your standards are.

Although this coffee is never as good as fresh roasted coffee, it will preserve a good measure of freshness for six months, and is a great improvement over coffee in the standard can.

Types of Roast: There is a big difference in the taste of coffee roasted to different degrees of darkness. Just as some people prefer meat cooked rare, medium, well done, or somewhere in between, everyone likes coffee roasted a certain way. Most mass consumption coffee is roasted as light as possible, because coffee loses weight as it is roasted, so the roaster gets more light roast coffee out of a given amount of green beans than dark roast. Specialty coffee drinkers (who tend to be younger, more educated, and have more money) seem to prefer the darker roasts. There are many different names for the same type of roast, but here are the common ones:

Light Roast (American Roast): coffee roasted to the first expansion "pop," a light brown in color. Since roasting "burns up" some caffeine, the light roast coffee is the most in caffeine content.

Medium Roast (Viennese or City Roast): coffee roasted to a chocolate colored brown, just before the second expansion pop.

Dark Roast (Full City Roast): coffee roasted up to the second expansion pop, just as the oil starts to come out of the beans. Color is similar to dark chocolate.

French Roast: coffee roasted well into the second pop, oil has come fully out of the bean.

Italian Roast (Espresso): One shade darker than the French Roast. The next step is "burned." This coffee is best made in espresso machines (see below).

The correct roast for you is a matter of individual preference. Different coffees "take" certain roasts better than others because of their individual taste characteristics. I find Kona is best about halfway between Medium Roast and Dark Roast. Colombian coffee seems to take a French Roast better than other coffees. There are many other aspects of the roaster's art, which is why the same coffee might taste different from two different roasters. The type of roasting machine, temperature, and method of cooling all play a part, just as one chef can cook scrambled eggs better than another.

Brewing Coffee: Once you have got the right fresh coffee, you must still brew it. The first thing you will need is good cold water. If your water doesn't taste good, neither will your coffee. Many specialty coffee shops now use filtered water (either the charcoal filter process or the reverse osmosis process) for brewing coffee. In Kona, the taste of the county water is not that great, so we recommend filtered or bottled water for brewing the best coffee. Ideal water temperature is 204 degrees (cool about a minute after boiling).

There are many methods of brewing coffee. The difference is how the water comes into contact with the ground coffee. Different methods require different machines and different size grinds for the coffee. A recommended starting point for strength is two level tablespoons of coffee for each six ounce cup, but this is another area where individuals have different tastes.

(1) Filter Drip Method. This is the most popular method of brewing, which involves either pouring (by hand) or spraying (in a Mr. Coffee-type machine) water over the grounds. Special paper allows the infused water to pass through but keeps out the grounds. Some people prefer gold plated filters because some paper filters impart a slight paper taste to the coffee. The drip method requires a medium/fine grind, about a "4" or "5" setting on a commercial coffee grinder.

(2) Immersion or "French Press" Method. This involves putting ground coffee in the bottom of a glass decanter, and adding water, letting the coffee steep as you would tea. A special screen is then pushed down to keep the coffee grounds at the bottom of the decanter, and the brewed coffee is poured out.

(3) Percolation Method. This method used to be used a lot, and is still used in large coffee making machines. Ground coffee is placed in a basket at the top of a tube which carries the boiling water up from the bottom of the pot and over the coffee. The trouble with this method is that after the first pass of water over the coffee it tends to become bitter.

(4) Espresso Method. In a true espresso machine, a boiler produces steaming water which is forced over dark roasted, finely ground, packed coffee to produce a thick, foamy cup. The same steam is then often used to steam milk, which when added to

the espresso coffee produces either cappuccino (a little steamed milk) or caffe latte (a lot of steamed milk). Traditionally, a little chocolate is sprinkled on top of the steamed milk (watch out for restaurants that sprinkle cinnamon instead without asking you). Espresso coffee is very popular among coffee drinkers on the east and west coasts, as well as in Europe where it originated.

Keeping Brewed Coffee Hot: The most grievous sin most people commit with respect to brewing coffee is leaving it on a burner too long. After 10 to 15 minutes, the chemical composition changes and the coffee becomes bitter. This is an especially big problem in restaurants. It is a simple problem to avoid by using a thermos to keep coffee hot rather than an independent heat source. You can purchase filter drip systems, both manual and electric, that brew coffee directly into a thermos.

Coffee in Restaurants: There is a vast difference in quality of brewed coffee in restaurants, and nowhere is this more true than in Kona, where you would expect all of the coffee to be excellent. Coffee is the most abused food at hotels and restaurants, for a number of reasons. Primarily, customers are not demanding enough, and managers are reluctant to spend a lot of money on coffee which is consumed in large part by the restaurant's workers. The situation is changing gradually, and we urge you to take an interest in the quality of the coffee in Kona's restaurants. Here are seven simple steps to improve restaurant coffee:

(1) Buy whole bean, freshly roasted, high quality coffee, hopefully pure Kona. Operating a restaurant in the Kona coffee region is to coffee like having a bistro in the Loire valley is to wine – take advantage of the situation! It is desirable that your roaster be located as close as possible to your restaurant. For Kona restaurants, Kona is better than Honolulu, Honolulu is better than the mainland.

(2) Get deliveries at least once a week, preferably twice. Store coffee sealed away from oxygen at low temperatures, in a refrigerator.

(3) Use a portion-control grinder and grind beans immediately before brewing. If no portion-control grinder is available, take a

measured scoop of whole beans and use a regular grinder.

(4) Make sure your water tastes good. If not, install a charcoal or reverse osmosis filter (this is an absolute necessity in Kona).

(5) Brew coffee into commercial-sized thermal carafes. Do not use "warmers" or reheat the coffee in any way.

(6) Use at least two and one half ounces of coffee per 64 ounces of water (three would be better; most commercial machines work best with three ounces because the water passes over the coffee fairly quickly compared to a home brewer.

(7) Buy an espresso machine, learn how to operate it properly and serve espresso coffee.

Above all, as with all food and beverage, pay attention and understand what you (and hopefully your customers) like. Then try to duplicate it every time. Once a restaurant develops a coffee consciousness, it is surprising how easily the staff adapts to the new procedures, and very quickly it doesn't seem like it takes any extra effort at all.

Decaffeinated and Flavored Coffee: Flavored coffees and decaf are the fastest growing segment of the specialty market, but consumers know very little about what they actually are. A flavored coffee is produced by pouring a concentrated flavoring over roasted coffee beans and mixing the two so that the flavoring is evenly spread over the beans. There are now hundreds of types of flavors–as many for coffee as for ice cream. The most popular flavors in Hawaii are macadamia nut, and chocolate macadamia nut. The ratio of flavoring to coffee is extremely important – sometimes the favoring overpowers the coffee aroma, but properly done it can compliment it.

There has been a lot written about the benefits and dangers of caffeine in coffee, and of the methods used to remove caffeine to create decaffeinated coffee. From a roaster's standpoint, the problem with decaf is that the same process which removes the caffeine also can remove the part of the coffee bean which gives it flavor and aroma. Some of these processes are better than others, but we have yet to taste a decaf which compares with non-decaf coffee.

If you are worried about caffeine, yet love coffee, the first step is to stop drinking robusta. Next, consider some of the "light" coffees which are a blend of decaf and regular coffee. If you want to go all the way to pure decaf, you have two basic products to choose from: the standard chemical process, and the newer and more expensive "Swiss water" process.

In chemical decaffeination, methyl chloride (a chemical used in dry cleaning) is poured over the beans and evaporates, taking the caffeine and other coffee solids with it. The caffeine is then separated out and the solids mixed back into the beans. The residue chemical that is left in the coffee is extremely small, well below government tolerance levels, but it is not zero. In the water process (patented by a Swiss company), steam is used instead of methyl chloride to remove the caffeine, and no chemicals are involved. This coffee usually retails for about $1 per pound more than regular decaf.

The Joy of Pure Kona Coffee: We cannot finish this article without a few words about what we think is the finest coffee in the world, grown here in the state of Hawaii in a twenty-mile "coffee belt" on the Kona coast. Since Mark Twain noticed its remarkable quality in 1861, Kona coffee has enjoyed a worldwide reputation for excellence. Ideal climate is combined with painstaking cultivation techniques to produce a truly unique product. The beans are large, the flavor medium-bodied, fairly acidy, with some subtle winey tones, very richly flavored, and when fresh, overwhelmingly aromatic. If you are serious about coffee, you can do no better than starting out with our own local product.

Kona Kai Farms Administrative Office
Post Office Box C
Kealakekua, Hawaii 96750
Phone (808) 323-2911 FAX (808) 323-2256
Tasting Room Phone 323-2115
Mail Orders (800) 826-5713

Mainland Coffee Sales
2865 Seventh Street
Berkeley, California 94710
Phone (510) 486-8334 FAX (510) 486-8341
(800) 222-KONA

Kona Inn Espresso Bar
329-2262
Kona Inn Kona Kai Retail Outlet
326-4684